Literature and the Political Imagination

This book seeks to show how modern political theory can be enriched through an engagement with works of literature. It uses the resources of literature to explore issues such as nationalism, liberal philosophy, Utopianism, narrative and the role of theory in political thought.

A variety of approaches is adopted and the aim is to show some of the many and diverse ways in which literature may contribute to political theory, as well as to consider some of the problems to which this may give rise. The theorists discussed include Richard Rorty, Alasdair MacIntyre, Charles Taylor and Martha Nussbaum. There are literary references to Greek tragedy, Jonathan Swift, patriotic poetry, Charles Dickens, George Orwell, Samuel Beckett, T. S. Eliot, Brian Moore, Elizabeth Bowen and contemporary feminist Utopian fiction.

All the contributors have a long-standing interest in the relations between literature and moral and political thought and are concerned to resist the restrictions imposed by conventional academic boundaries, but they are not united by any party line or uniformity of intellectual commitments. The result is a diverse and challenging volume that will be of great interest to all engaged in the study of politics and literature

John Horton is Reader in Political Theory at Keele University. **Andrea T. Baumeister** is Lecturer in Politics at the University of Manchester.

Literature and the Political Imagination

Edited by John Horton
and Andrea T. Baumeister

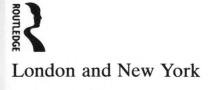

London and New York

First published 1996
by Routledge
11 New Fetter Lane, London EC4P 4EE

Simultaneously published in the USA and Canada
by Routledge
29 West 35th Street, New York, NY 10001

© 1996 The collection, John Horton and Andrea T. Baumeister, individual
chapters, the contributors.

Phototypeset in Times by Intype, London

Printed and bound in Great Britain by
TJ Press (Padstow) Ltd,
Padstow, Cornwall

British Library Cataloguing in Publication Data

A catalogue record for this book is available from the British Library

Library of Congress Cataloguing in Publication Data

ISBN 0–415–12914–1 (hbk)
ISBN 0–415–12915–X (pbk)

Contents

Contributors

Anthony Arblaster is Reader in Politics at the University of Sheffield. Among his principal publications are *The Rise and Decline of Western Liberalism, Democracy* and *Viva La Liberta! Politics in Opera.*

Andrea T. Baumeister is Lecturer in Politics at the University of Manchester, having formerly taught at the University of York. Her research has been primarily on the challenges to liberal theory presented by multiculturalism.

Margaret Canovan is Reader in Politics at Keele University. Her books include *G. K. Chesterton – Radical Populist, Populism* and, most recently, *Hannah Arendt: A Reinterpretation of Her Political Thought.*

Paul Gilbert is Senior Lecturer in Philosophy at the University of Hull. His most recent publications include *Human Relationships, Terrorism, Security and Nationality* and (editor with Paul Gregory), *Nations, Cultures and Markets.*

John Horton is Reader in Politics at Keele University and was formerly Director, Morrell Studies in Toleration at the University of York. His recent books are *Political Obligation*, (editor with Peter Nicholson), *Toleration: Philosophy and Practice*, (editor), *Liberalism, Multiculturalism and Toleration* and (editor with Susan Mendus), *After MacIntyre.*

Stephen Ingle is Professor of Politics at the University of Stirling. He has a long-standing interest in political theory and literature. Among his publications are *Socialist Thought in Imaginative Literature, The British Party System* and *George Orwell.*

Susan Mendus is Senior Lecturer in Politics and Director, Morrell Studies in Toleration at the University of York. Her most recent books are *Toleration and the Limits of Liberalism*, (editor with John

Horton), *John Locke 'A Letter Concerning Toleration' in Focus* and (editor with John Horton), *After MacIntyre*.

Lucy Sargisson is Lecturer in Politics at Keele University. Her principal interests are in the fields of feminism, poststructuralism and utopianism.

Paul Seabright teaches in the Faculty of Economics and Politics, University of Cambridge, and is Director of Studies in Economics at Churchill College. His main research has been in economics but he has also published papers on a number of philosophical topics, including one on Henry James and moral philosophy.

Martin Warner is Senior Lecturer in Philosophy, and was founding Programme Director of the Centre for Research in Philosophy and Literature, at the University of Warwick. His publications include *Philosophical Finesse: Studies in the Art of Rational Persuasion*, (editor with Roger Crisp), *Terrorism, Protest and Power* and (editor with Andrew Barber), *The Language of the Cave.*

Maureen Whitebrook is Honorary Research Fellow in the Department of Politics at the University of Sheffield. She previously taught at Nottingham Trent University. Her publications include *Real Toads in Imaginary Gardens: Narrative Accounts of Liberalism* and (editor), *Reading Political Stories: Representations of Politics in Novels and Pictures.*

Preface

Most of the essays in this book arise from a conference held at the University of York in September 1993. The editors wish to acknowledge their gratitude to the trustees of the C. and J. B. Morrell Trust for their support of the conference and the work involved in preparing this volume for publication. We are also very grateful to all the participants at the conference; to our former colleagues at York, Susan Mendus, who made many helpful comments on our opening chapter, and Peter Nicholson for their advice and encouragement; to Caroline Wintersgill and James Whiting at Routledge for their most efficient and constructive editorial work; to Diane Stafford for seeing the book through production; to Barbara McGuinness and a second, anonymous, referee for Routledge, both of whom made several useful suggestions; and to Jenny Bradford, Caroline Moore, Jackie Morgan, Jane Connor, Paula Barratt and Gill Pulpher for their indispensable assistance in organising the original conference, dealing with correspondence and preparing the manuscript for publication. Inevitably, however, the success of a volume such as this depends crucially on the co-operation of the contributors, all of whom we would like to thank for their patience, efficiency and goodwill.

John Horton
Andrea T. Baumeister

1 Literature, philosophy and political theory

John Horton and Andrea T. Baumeister

The twentieth century has seen a pervasive furtherance of the division of labour, as much in intellectual life as in processes of industrial production. As the world of learning has expanded, both in terms of what there is to know and the number of people directly engaged in the pursuit of knowledge, the tendency towards increased specialisation has been relentless. Typically, scholars and researchers have narrowed their focus, not merely to one discipline or field of enquiry, nor even to one sub-field, but to one specific topic within a closely circumscribed area of enquiry.

It would be foolish to suggest that such developments are entirely negative. This division of labour and specialisation is inseparable from the extraordinary growth of human knowledge which has made such an indispensable contribution to material progress. This is especially obvious in the physical sciences and in those sciences that seek to give practical application to this knowledge. Yet, for all its apparent benefits, such specialisation is a mixed blessing. Even within the physical sciences it has been argued that it promotes a technocratic and inhuman culture in which the human dimensions of scientific activity and the place of science and technology within a wider social context are obscured and lost from sight.[1] However, whether or not this is true of the physical sciences, it is with respect to the humanities and social enquiry that the effects of specialisation may seem to be especially damaging. These forms of enquiry have as their subject our own self-understanding, and it is here that the sense of fragmentation resulting from specialisation is most troubling. While our lives have many diverse aspects and we fulfil many roles, we also understand ourselves as possessing some kind of unity. And it is this sense of unity that is neglected, even undermined, by cognitive specialisation.

Moreover, the tendency towards increased specialisation has been accompanied by another phenomenon also having its origins in the seventeenth century but proceeding apace for much of the twentieth. This is the extraordinary intellectual and cultural prestige of the physical sciences. These have been widely perceived as the model or pinnacle for all forms of knowledge. Hence, any claim to knowledge, any enquiry purporting to objectivity or truth, must seek to be 'scientific'. At its most extreme, this has led to suspicion of all claims that cannot be validated through scientific enquiry. Thus, for example, the logical positivists dismissed moral values and aesthetic judgements as mere expressions of emotion or subjective preference.[2] While logical positivism has largely fallen from favour, it is only one instance of a much more widespread and diffuse process which has led to the epistemological privileging of the physical sciences. The view that science is the exclusive repository of genuine knowledge, that reality is simply whatever science shows to be the case, is commonplace; and to describe a way of proceeding as 'unscientific' is invariably to condemn it. If other fields of intellectual endeavour are legitimately to claim to produce knowledge then they too must be put on a scientific footing. While methods of enquiry to some extent need to be adapted to particular fields, 'scientific method' is the only route to genuine knowledge of the world.[3]

These two developments, the increasing specialisation of intellectual enquiry and the belief that science provides the model for all such enquiries, have for most of this century had a crucial role in shaping the intellectual culture of the West, perhaps especially the English-speaking part of it. In the first part of what follows we shall sketch very briefly how these developments have affected philosophy, political theory and literature and literary criticism. All these forms of intellectual activity have been challenged to develop a distinct and logically defensible identity. We discuss how each has responded to this challenge and how the result has been a marked trend towards reinforcing disciplinary boundaries. Inevitably, these observations will be very general and schematic. In the second part we say a little, also in general terms, about challenges to this trend. More particularly, we look at some of the criticisms that have been made of contemporary political philosophy and how a *rapprochement* between literature and philosophy might help to revivify political theory. Finally, we discuss a number of specific areas, which are explored in greater detail in the chapters that constitute the substance of this book, in which the conjunction of the political, the literary and the philosophical promises to be fruitful and stimulating. These topics are suggestive rather than exhaustive, but they are indicative of at least some of the ways in which political theory and philosophy can be deepened and enriched through an engagement with imaginative literature.[4]

We should make it clear that, along with the contributors, our direction of approach is that of political theorists or philosophers. Hence, our concern is with what and how imaginative literature might contribute to political theorising, and not with whether, for example, greater philosophical or political awareness should inform literature or literary criticism.[5] Nor are we concerned with the philosophy of literature or literary criticism as branches of aesthetics.[6] All of these are of course legitimate areas of interest, but they are not topics we address other than incidentally. Since, however, it is our view that contemporary political philosophy is largely shaped by the contours of the discipline of philosophy more generally, we begin with a brief consideration of the state of modern philosophy.

PHILOSOPHY

Philosophy has been no more immune from the influences described earlier than any other branch of enquiry. Twentieth-century philosophy, especially in the English-speaking world, has become an increasingly professionalised and technical subject. Its central concerns are logic and epistemology, and the associated areas of the philosophies of language and mind. In the process it has become increasingly divorced from the wider humanistic and literary cultures. Of course, there are many exceptions to this claim, but as a generalisation it is true.[7] While the roots of the modern conception of philosophy certainly go back to the Cartesian revolution, which can be seen as a nodal point in the emergence of modernity, still as late as the nineteenth century philosophers typically wrote for and expected to be read by the educated public.[8] They did not understand their subject in the kind of specialised and professionalised way which has become the norm in the twentieth century. What distinguishes twentieth-century philosophy is its technical sophistication, a highly abstract form of argumentative rigour, and the fact that it is entirely the province of academics, rarely even pretending to address a wider audience. A good deal of modern philosophy would be completely unintelligible to even the best educated of lay persons if they had never formally studied philosophy in a university.[9]

One almost inevitable consequence of this changed self-conception of philosophy has been the down-grading of both political philosophy and aesthetics. Branches of philosophy which it is difficult to make conform to such a technical and logically rigorous understanding of the subject have been marginalised and viewed as the 'soft' side of philosophy. Although the fortunes of political philosophy have revived since the publication of John Rawls' *A Theory of Justice* in 1971,[10] a work itself clearly influenced by some of the developments we have described, it remains the case that both political philosophy and aesthetics have been peripheral to the development of Anglo-American philosophy in the twentieth century. Moreover, it is not merely that these sub-fields have been relatively neglected, it is that the whole conception of philosophy, as essentially abstract and ahistorical, makes the inclusion of arguments which are necessarily to some degree contingent and historically specific appear suspect.

In so far as political philosophy has continued to be practised it too has often shown similar aspirations to a conception of rigour associated with abstraction and universality. Although he is perhaps unusual in the explicitness with which he articulates such a view, the work of Alan Gewirth provides a good example of such an approach.[11] Gewirth seeks to provide a logically compelling argument for morality in the form of a structure of moral rights; an argument which can be denied, he claims, only on pain of self-contradiction. While few have been persuaded by Gewirth's arguments,[12] and few have been quite so bold in their claims, the commitment to providing rationally compelling arguments, or arguments which at least no reasonable person could reject, lies at the heart of much recent political philosophy.[13] Yet, somewhat paradoxically, such a commitment has coincided in the contemporary world with extensive disagreement among philosophers about the persuasiveness of any particular principles, arguments or theories. In short, while the aspiration of political philosophy is towards convergence on rational principles of political morality, no such convergence is evident in a world in which fundamental disagreement proliferates. This tension between aspiration and achievement is a matter to which we shall return later.

For the moment, however, we observe how philosophy generally has become an increasingly technical and professionalised activity; and how political philosophy, in so far as it has sought to validate its credentials as philosophy, has tried to adopt a similar form. Unsurprisingly, political philosophy has not been able to match the levels of analytical and formal rigour attained in the 'central' areas of philosophy, yet it is widely accepted that these are the appropriate canons to which it should seek to conform. In consequence, much political philosophy seems to have become increasingly detached from concrete political experience, and often the distinctively political has been submerged within an abstract, universal and ahistorical moralism. Political philosophy is made entirely subservient to moral philosophy; it appears as a series of moral desiderata, perhaps in the form of a theory of justice or some other statement of moral principles or rules, often only dimly connected to the political world we inhabit. In a sense, of course, this drive towards the ideal and the abstract has always been inherent in the philosophical approach to politics, but it has been greatly exacerbated by developments in modern philosophy. Moreover, as we shall see in the next section, the more 'open' or 'relaxed' conceptions of political philosophy which have coexisted with more rigorous conceptions, sometimes referred to as political theory, have struggled to maintain their academic and intellectual respectability.

POLITICAL THEORY

The identity of political theory has always been rather uncertain and shadowy. It has included forms of thinking and writing about politics which are indistinguishable from political philosophy and there has, as a result, been a constant tendency to assimilate political theory in its entirety within political philosophy. Yet political theory has also encompassed ways of thinking about politics which, although conducted at a high level of generality, have a substantial empirical dimension, drawing on what we often now think of as history, sociology and political science. This has made any complete assimilation of political theory and philosophy problematic. Thinkers like Machiavelli, Burke, Paine and Adam Smith have a significant place in political theory which they do not have in the history of philosophy. Certainly, political theory is too 'impure', insufficiently abstract and universal, to be comfortably incorporated within the dominant twentieth-century conception of what philosophy ought to be.[14]

However, if it is the empirical aspects of political theory that have led to doubts about its status as genuine philosophy, it is the persistence of philosophical features which has led to political theory being squeezed, so to speak, from the opposite direction. The aspiration to create a genuinely empirical science of politics during the middle of this century led to dissatisfaction with political theory as *too* philosophical and insufficiently scientific. It was objected that political theory comprised too much *a priori* sociology and armchair empiricism rather than engaging in a disciplined enquiry into the way in which politics works. Thus, the ideal of an exclusively empirical theory of politics emerged as an alternative to the philosophical approach, political theory as traditionally understood being neither fish nor fowl and hence irremediably confused.[15]

Thus, by the second half of the twentieth century, political theory is viewed with some suspicion by both philosophers and social scientists as lacking the rigour for a proper form of intellectual enquiry. When the various components of this hybrid are distinguished and separated out there seems to be no significant role for political theory. Conceptual issues and normative questions, in so far as they are capable of being subject to rational enquiry, are the province of philosophy; though most philosophers in fact view with dismay the messiness of political philosophy. Empirical explanations of political events and processes are properly the province of political science; though in truth the scientific credentials of the activity look forever dubious and are continuously subject to anxious defence. What is left for political theory is mostly the study of a relatively small number of 'great texts' in the history of political thought, without a clear conception of what the purpose of such study is or what its methods should be.[16]

Political theory continues to be practised, and some of its twentieth-century exponents – Hannah Arendt, who also made copious use of literature in developing her ideas, Karl Popper and Leo Strauss, for example – have a significant intellectual profile.[17] However, by and large, political theory has a Cinderella status in the study of politics and philosophy; both philosophers and political scientists viewing it as a rather amateurish affair, lacking precision of argument and methodological rigour, too journalistic and speculative to be a genuine academic discipline.

LITERATURE AND LITERARY CRITICISM

The emergence of a culture of imaginative literature as a significant historical phenomenon in the West begins around the sixteenth century. Of course, drama and poetry go back at least as far as the Greeks in Western civilisation and they played an important role in ancient Greek life. Yet that role was typically bound up with religious beliefs and rituals, and the public life of the community more generally, in ways which importantly distinguish it from the modern literary culture of the West.[18] The plays of Aeschylus,

Euripides and Sophocles may of course still be made to speak to us in ways which are illuminating, as several recent works in moral and political theory have persuasively shown.[19] However, they cannot be performed in a manner that would have been familiar to their contemporary audience as other than a speculative historical exercise, and *how* to perform classical Greek drama is always a pressing and unavoidable problem for any modern production. It is true that, for example, Shakespeare's theatre too was also in many respects different from ours but there is a much closer continuity existing between the Elizabethan and contemporary theatre, linked as they are by a tradition of performance, than between contemporary theatre and Greek drama.

It is probably the development of the novel, particularly in the eighteenth and early nineteenth centuries, and the influence of the Romantic revolt against Enlightenment rationalism that do most to shape a distinctively nineteenth- and twentieth-century sense of imaginative literature.[20] The idea of the 'creative genius' of the individual mind and the emergence of reading as an essentially 'private' experience, both contribute to a distinctive feature of the modern understanding of imaginative literature as something independent and with its own canons of truth and its own standards of value. It is not that literature is generally supposed to be irrelevant or unrelated to life, though some aesthetes have suggested this, but that it is not subservient to any external end. It does not serve a moral, philosophical or religious purpose and it is most appropriately judged by standards intrinsic to the nature of literary work.[21]

The development of this modern sense of imaginative literature coincided with, and was no doubt influenced by, the emergence of literary criticism as a distinctive form of the study of literature. It is often not fully appreciated how recent the phenomenon of literary criticism as an academic discipline is and how controversial its introduction to Oxford and Cambridge was.[22] While aesthetics or poetics has a very long history, Aristotle being an outstanding exponent, modern literary criticism as an organised enquiry forming a distinct discipline does not go back much further than the late nineteenth century. Again, critical and analytical comment on literature was certainly not uncommon before this time but it was not conceived as constituting a distinct intellectual activity. Indeed, with the emergence of literary criticism as a discipline its proponents typically sought to distinguish it from such earlier practices of commentary and criticism. These were often disparagingly referred to as '*belles-lettres*' in contrast to the properly rigorous study of literary criticism.

Inevitably, there have been extensive divisions between different schools of literary critics, one often achieving a brief period of ascendancy before being superseded by another.[23] However, most if not all of these divisions, where they have had an intellectual and not merely personal basis, have been about the nature of literary criticism and the proper role of the literary critic. They have been about how to define the subject and what constitutes its disciplinary identity; and an important part of that process has been asserting the *sui generis* character of literary criticism and denying its dependence on any other intellectual enquiry, including philosophy.[24] Indeed, in the hands of a critic like F. R. Leavis literary criticism was held to be the centre of a proper education and the literary critic was seen as a kind of moral and spiritual mentor.[25] Many subsequent critics have dissented from Leavis' view but frequently they have disagreed not about the distinctiveness of literary criticism, only about how it is to be conceived or practised.[26]

In the last decade or more, however, the situation in literary criticism has changed significantly. With the emergence of deconstructive criticism, associated with Jacques Derrida and his American followers in the 'Yale School' in particular, the lines dividing philosophical and literary critical discourses have been called dramatically into question.[27] In stressing the fact that philosophy and literature are both kinds of writing, and therefore share important features in common, these critics have at least intimated the possibility of more fruitful interaction between them. Indeed, even more subversively, they have called into doubt the very distinction between literature and philosophy. This though is to get ahead of ourselves. For the most part, creative literature has been conceived as a distinct and independent field and literary criticism the proper method for its study. Neither political nor philosophical concerns should have any significant role in the appraisal of literature.

PHILOSOPHY, LITERATURE AND POLITICS

So far we have argued that philosophy, political theory and literature have become, for most of the twentieth century, increasingly separate one from another. The idea of a common human culture has been replaced by a series of discrete and independent disciplines. However, as we have also stressed, this is to talk in terms of broad historical generalisations. It is now time to correct, or rather modify, qualify and elaborate on the rather stark and one-dimensional picture we have so far portrayed.

One respect in which the picture needs to be qualified is to concede the obvious truth that tensions between literature, politics and philosophy are not an entirely modern creation. For example, suspicion on the part of philosophers towards imaginative literature has a long and distinguished pedigree. The very birth of the Western philosophical tradition was marked by Plato's desire to banish the poets from the world of the *Republic* and to censor rigorously all artistic expression. While Plato's argument is more subtle and complex than can be done justice to here, he already voiced what have been the two most recurrent objections of philosophers to imaginative literature.[28] The first, which is essentially epistemological, is that the creations of the great dramatists and poets are in a deep sense false and illusory: they are fictitious and cannot offer any insights into the 'real' world. The second objection is moral, asserting that, unless controlled by a philosophical intelligence, imaginative literature is likely to be harmful and morally confusing.[29] In a suitably rigged fictitious world one can 'prove' just about anything. In Plato's thought there was an especially close connection between these objections because of the relationship which he believed held between knowledge and goodness. However, these objections can be, and often are, distinguished from each other. They are also objections which are worthy of serious consideration.

For our purposes, though, one of the things which interestingly differentiates Plato's attitude to imaginative literature is that, for all his hostility towards it, he was actively engaged with the literary culture of his time and place. He took seriously the claims of the poets and dramatists to provide moral illumination, though of course he thought they were wrong. By contrast, contemporary philosophers simply ignore any such claims, regarding literature as philosophically irrelevant. In our culture, what marks the separation of distinct disciplines and fields of enquiry is an attitude of mutual indifference more than hostility. Many philosophers may, for example, enjoy reading fiction in their spare time (it is rather less common the other way about) but this will be seen as incidental to, and unconnected with, what they do as philosophers.[30] However, as the example of Plato reminds us, it does not follow that an active engagement by philosophers with imaginative literature will necessarily elicit a positive or appreciative response. The results of such an engagement cannot be determined in advance.

This, however, is not the only way in which our earlier story needs to be qualified. For there have always been philosophers and creative writers who have not rigidly separated out the literary, the political and the philosophical; some thinkers who have made significant contributions as both literary artists and political theorists: Milton, Godwin, Shelley, Rousseau, Tolstoy are only a few of the names that come to mind. On the continent, writers such as the existentialists, most notably Jean-Paul Sartre, have to some extent continued this kind of tradition into the twentieth century, but it is hard to think of any comparable figures in the English-speaking world.[31] However, combining the activities of being a creative writer and a philosopher is not in the context of our concerns the only, or even the most important, form of connection.[32] Rather, we are particularly interested in how political theory might be enriched through integrating, or at least relating, philosophical problems and concerns with the distinctive qualities and insights to be found in imaginative literature.

Finally, therefore, we need to qualify our earlier story by mentioning some of the recent developments which have encouraged a more fruitful interchange between political philosophy and imaginative literature.[33] In the next section we shall say a little more about these developments in general terms and offer a couple of suggestions about why they were thought necessary or desirable. Thereafter we will consider more directly some of the specific connections between literature, philosophy and political theory that are discussed in the succeeding chapters of this book.

REFORMING POLITICAL PHILOSOPHY

To recap on what we have been arguing so far, we can summarise our main contentions. First, modern analytical political philosophy is conducted without reference to imaginative literature. The canons of argument and standards of judgement are derived almost exclusively from a particular conception of what counts as philosophy. This conception is highly abstract and ahistorical, and aspires towards, though rarely succeeds in attaining, a structure of argument that is deductive in form. Second, it also has to be said that imaginative writers, and perhaps especially some literary critics, have been highly suspicious of abstraction and of any tendency to utilise novels, plays and poems for political or philosophical purposes or to assess literary works by standards other than those deemed appropriate as categories of literary analysis. Even where, as in the case of Leavisite critics, it has been allowed that literature may have a moral dimension, philosophy has not been thought to be able to contribute anything to it.[34] Finally, we have argued that political theory has been under antithetical pressures to make itself intellectually respectable, either by assimilating itself entirely within the afore-mentioned conception of political philosophy or by aligning itself with the rigorous empirical study of political science.

However, at least so far as theoretical reflection on politics is concerned, some thinkers have come to feel that this situation is unsatisfactory and that something has been lost in this process. Hence, some of the impetus towards reform, towards a reconsideration of the style and substance of much contemporary political philosophy has come from within philosophy itself. There are many aspects of this process, but we want to identify two broad challenges as particularly important. These are the attack on epistemology and the charge of political irrelevance directed at political philosophy. We shall briefly discuss each while merely noting in passing some other developments, including some in literary studies, which have made the ground for cross-fertilisation more fruitful.

By the attack on epistemology we mean those recent movements of thought which have called into question the aspiration of philosophy to discover grounds or criteria of truth, or to act as a guarantor of knowledge. This attack has its roots in a disparate array of philosophers such as Kuhn, Feyerabend, Davidson and Putnam, but perhaps achieves its culmination in Richard Rorty's *Philosophy and the Mirror of Nature.*[35] In this book Rorty offers a powerful internal critique of the basic assumptions and aspirations of analytical philosophy. He concludes that philosophy should be conducted in a more open and relaxed manner and that it should see its role primarily as 'edificatory'. That book does not have a lot to say specifically about political philosophy, though the implications of the overall argument were clear enough. However, during the 1980s Rorty increasingly turned his attention towards politics.[36] In this context he argued for the superiority of imaginative literature to philosophical argument both as a way of gaining a richer understanding of human life and as a more effective means of persuading people to adopt more attractive principles and practices. Rorty advocated what he called 'redescription', the practice of modifying our descriptions to make what we describe look better or worse, as the appropriate form of dialogue about political values; and the masters of redescription, for Rorty, are not philosophers but novelists.

Inevitably Rorty's views have come in for much criticism and they are not widely accepted.[37] They are criticised by Maureen Whitebrook and Susan Mendus in their chapters in this book, for example, and we would not want to deny the persuasiveness of at least some of the criticism to which Rorty has been subject. However, what cannot reasonably be denied is that he has made a major contribution to challenging the prevailing conception of political philosophy and opening up the entire issue for debate. Moreover, Rorty's entry has also taken further some criticisms of the form and substance of the predominantly liberal political philosophy made by its communitarian critics.[38] Writers like Alasdair MacIntyre and especially Charles Taylor have happily drawn on literary sources to support their arguments, and through their employment of concepts such as narrative, discussed in the next section, have forged links between literary and philosophical discourses.[39]

One of the sources of Rorty's attack on the philosophical project of epistemology, the seeking for foundations of knowledge, was his sense of the interminable and irresolvable character of most philosophical disputes. The debates between realism and idealism, free will and determinism, empiricism and rationalism and so on, in different dress but essentially the same, seem to engage every generation of philosophers, but they are never resolved. Indeed, we never get near a resolution and perhaps have little idea about what would count as one. Yet the kinds of problem that confront us politically seem far too urgent to wait on any solution that we might reasonably hope for from political philosophy. In fact, there is a striking incongruity between the way in which political philosophy appears to be grappling with real and important political problems and its more or less complete irrelevance to political life. This then constitutes the second challenge to political philosophy: how can it be made more genuinely relevant to the problems and issues it purports to address?[40]

Here critics have tended to focus on the abstract, decontextualised and ahistorical character of much contemporary political philosophy. Problems are posed in a form which makes them look timeless, and hence implies that the answers will also need to be timeless. Political issues, however, are in some significant part about a particular time and place: how is this group of people to continue living peaceably together given their deep religious differences? How, in a modern multicultural society, are we to reconcile the freedom of people to read and write what they wish with the sense of hurt and pain that this sometimes produces in others? What would be an equitable system of taxation for this society given its history, culture and level of economic prosperity? Political philosophers have frequently seemed to think that these questions can only properly, definitively or finally be answered if we go back to first principles, to a general theory of political morality, utilitarianism or a theory of rights or justice for example, which have universal validity.

Yet these theories never really seem to deliver what they promise, either because we cannot agree on first principles, and there do not appear to be any compelling reasons why we must; or, if we do agree on a particular principle, then because there is ample scope for disagreement about how it is to be applied or how it is to be weighed and balanced against other competing principles. This is not to deny any value to this kind of political philosophy but it does have the consequence of detaching theory from practice. Political philosophy increasingly becomes an area which generates its own problems and in which philosophers respond to other philosophers without too much regard to the political experience or reality to which it is supposed to relate. Theory itself comes to dictate the agenda for political philosophy, and criticising and elaborating arguments becomes an end in itself. Theoretical ingenuity is valued more highly than political perspicacity or what once might have been called, without the embarrassment that now attends it, practical wisdom.

If political philosophy is to engage more effectively with political practice then it will need to be less inward-looking; less concerned, for example, with the problems posed by ingenious but unlikely counter-examples to the universality of a theory, and more concerned to look outward and confront the realities of political life. Additionally, it will almost certainly need to be less ambitious in its scope and aims, less concerned to develop a general theory of political morality and a little more concerned with the contingencies and complexities which are constitutive of practical politics. It is in developing a richer, more nuanced and realistic understanding of political deliberation that imaginative literature may have an especially valuable role to play. Novels and plays, for example, seem much better at exhibiting the complexities of political experience and the open-textured and necessarily incomplete character of real political arguments, as several of the essays in this volume argue, than the linear discourse of philosophy. It is not merely that literature can provide more lifelike examples than the etiolated and simplistic illustrations typically employed by philosophers, but that it should help to shape and inform the very terms in which issues are conceived.[41]

In addition to these pressures for change arising from within political philosophy there have been developments in other fields of enquiry. There has been the emergence of the more consciously 'philosophical' style of literary criticism associated with the influence of deconstruction, mentioned in the preceding section. There has also been the enormous growth in cultural studies involving the deliberate attempt to break down disciplinary boundaries, especially divisions between literary and political analysis, but also embracing philosophical concerns. Here methodological eclecticism is widespread and intellectual specialisation is resisted.[42] As yet, though, it would be fair to say that the impact of cultural studies on political philosophy has been limited, and it has not had the pervasive influence it has had on the study of literature.

Of much greater significance has been the development of feminism and women's studies. Feminist theorists have advanced powerful criticisms of what they argue is the patriarchal character of philosophy in general, and moral and political philosophy in particular.[43] These have often had little direct bearing specifically on the relationship between political philosophy and literature, but by calling into question some of the underlying assumptions of much political philosophy they have contributed to opening up the whole issue of what political philosophy is about and how it should proceed. This is apparent, for example, in feminist critiques of abstract rationalism in moral theory and in the debate about the 'ethics of care'.[44] In this way feminists have helped to create an environment that is more receptive to the concerns which motivate those who want to explore possible relationships between imaginative literature and political philosophy.

So far, however, the discussion has been largely programmatic. It is time now to look at a few specific areas in which the interplay between political theory and imaginative literature might be illuminating and also to consider what obstacles might lie in the way of this interplay.[45] In choosing these areas we have been guided by the topics that are discussed in the chapters that follow. In this way we hope to relate some of the general issues raised in this introduction to the particular points raised in various chapters, since ultimately the justification of this project must lie with the value of its results.

NARRATIVE AND POLITICAL THEORY

One area in which the concerns of literature and political theory have come together in recent years is the role of 'narrative'. Narrative has long been central to the literary imagination and it constitutes a key concept of literary analysis.[46] By contrast, in moral and political theory the concept has rarely figured prominently. In the work of Alasdair MacIntyre and Charles Taylor, however, the idea of narrative emerges as an important component of an adequate understanding of the self and of its relationship to political morality.[47]

In some ways it is surprising that the concept of narrative has not received more attention in the history of political philosophy. Story-telling has played a significant role in the presentation of many political theories. One need only think, for example, of the seventeenth-century philosophers such as Hobbes and Locke whose theories are cast in the form of stories about the transition from a (largely) hypothetical state of nature to political society. Similarly, the conjectural histories so popular in the seventeenth century typi-cally take the form of quasi-historical narratives. So while the con-cept of narrative has not received much attention from political philosophers, this is not because narratives have not played an important role in the history of political theory.[48]

Part of the reason that the narrative form has been so prevalent, if relatively unremarked, is no doubt, as both Taylor and MacIntyre argue, because we understand our own lives in the form of a story. Our understanding of who we are seems inseparable from our sense of the story of our lives, where we have come from and where we are going. This is not because we all have something that corresponds to Rawls' rather demanding idea of a 'rational plan of life',[49] but simply because the most 'natural' way of explaining ourselves, both to others and to ourselves, is through relating what we are now, our present beliefs and intentions, to what we have been and done. Similarly, many of the myths, and what passes as the history, of our political identities are embedded in stories about origins and foundations, heroic deeds, struggles and the like.

The chapters by Maureen Whitebrook and Susan Mendus both take up issues arising from what Whitebrook calls 'the narrative turn' in recent political theory. While both are sympathetic to fea-tures of this move they also express some reservations about it. Whitebrook is critical of philosophers who have simply attempted to apply a concept of narrative from literature to political theory. MacIntyre, for example, is accused of being inattentive to the full implications of the idea of narrative, and Martha Nussbaum is charged with being too preoccupied with a conception of morality as embedded in individual action and understanding. Whitebrook argues that both thinkers are inclined to neglect or elide distinctively political aspects of morality, those to do with the collective and public dimensions of political life. Whitebrook recommends that political theorists be more alert to the complexities of narrative and to its essentially political role in 'ordering' our experience rather than naively embracing too innocent an understanding of narrative which concentrates only on a simplified form of narrative understanding. She urges that political theory learn from narrative theory and narratology to develop a richer understanding of the structure and possibilities of the narrative form in general, and attend more closely to the substantive role of particular narratives as they are employed in specific contexts and arguments.

Susan Mendus' focus on narrative is rather different. She sees at the heart of the debate about literature and philosophy a deeper disagreement about the aims of political philosophy itself. Whereas Charles Taylor, for example, looks for a justification of moral life in terms of Truth, conversationalists like Richard Rorty maintain that such a search is inevitably doomed. For Mendus, however, both these positions are problematic, and indeed ultimately untenable. Philosophers, like Taylor and MacIntyre, who emphasise 'the Good for Man' underestimate the intransigence of the fragmentation and diversity of modern life, while conversationalists neglect the perceived need for justification and guidance if we are to have any hope of negotiating our way through this fragmentation and diversity. Mendus believes that an appeal to narrative may help us to find a *via media* between these two alternatives, an approach which bears some similarity to that adopted by Martin Warner in his related enquiry.

In this appeal to narrative, however, Mendus sees its role as very different from that afforded it by Rorty. Where he emphasises the open-ended and fragmentary character of narrative, Mendus sees narratives as necessarily rule-governed, and on this point she is in agreement with Whitebrook. It is, she argues, by attending to the rules which govern narrative that we can derive a better understanding of the ways in which the self is constructed.[50] We need to appreciate how conceptions of the self may be exclusive and humiliating if we are to increase our capacity to live one with another in a divided and fragmented world. There is a role here for both philosophy and literature, without reducing one to the other; and we do not have to choose between a view in which the self is something to be discovered, as Taylor maintains, or something which is invented, as Rorty claims. Rather, we seek an equilibrium between these positions and between the perception of literature and the reflection of theory.

PARTICULARITY, COMPLEXITY AND THEORY

One of the principal sources of dissatisfaction with much moral and political philosophy, as was noted earlier, relates to its theoretical character, or rather to the highly abstract and formal way in which theory is typically understood. Whether it is the utilitarianism of R. M. Hare or the rights theory of Alan Gewirth, there is present a model of moral and political theory as a systematic structure of largely abstract and general moral principles from which particular judgements can be more or less rigorously derived.[51] Moreover, such theories also tend to employ as small a range of concepts as possible, often using a term such as 'obligation' to characterise almost all moral requirements.[52] While such theories are sometimes very complicated they are not typically complex, and they often seem remote from any phenomenology of moral experience.

This is a point made with some force by Anthony Arblaster in his chapter on 'Literature and Moral Choice'. He supports the arguments of Jean-Paul Sartre in his *Existentialism and Humanism* that the moral rules and maxims formulated by philosophers are too general to be of much help in guiding us when we confront moral dilemmas in our ordinary life.[53] By examining the manner in which works of fiction explore and illuminate dilemmas of choice and responsibility, as advocated by Whitebrook in her chapter, Arblaster seeks to show the extent to which both consequentialist moral theories and the morality of motives are incapable of taking adequate account of the complexities of moral choice. Arblaster draws on a range of literary examples but he pays special attention to Brian Moore's novel *Lies of Silence*, in which the central character, an essentially 'ordinary' and 'non-political' Irishman, has to decide how to respond to the violent threats of the IRA when they invade his life.[54] Arblaster emphasises the complexities of the case as they are brought out by the novelist – complexities of motivation, situation and consequence – and to which moral theory is usually unduly insensitive. There is a richness in such descriptions that captures much better the true dimensions of moral experience than the formal and abstract character of philosophical theory.[55] Moreover, he contends, Moore reminds us of an important moral possibility which philosophical theories of morality may neglect or dismiss, the value of 'taking a stand', of resisting evil because it is evil, even when it may seem hopeless and pointless to do so, and when one may also have other less worthy motives for doing so.

This complaint about the narrowness and abstractness of moral and political theory is one which has been made in distinct ways by contemporary philosophers as different as Bernard Williams, Peter Winch and Martha Nussbaum.[56] Interestingly, all these philosophers, especially Winch and Nussbaum, are very alert to the role that literature can play in helping to remedy these defects of contemporary theorising. John Horton in his chapter looks particularly at the work of Nussbaum. While highly sympathetic to some of her motivations, he explores several difficulties in the execution of her project. He is concerned both with problems inherent in any attempt to appropriate fictional texts for philosophical purposes and with the specific difficulties which confront Nussbaum's attempt to place literary narratives within an Aristotelian conception of ethics.

At a general level Horton raises a number of questions about how fictional narratives function and the kind of responses that are appropriate to the literary techniques and rhetorical strategies which are typical of such texts. He argues that any defence of the value of works of fiction to the enterprise of moral and political philosophy needs to engage with these questions in a way that Nussbaum herself fails to do, especially if there is to be any hope of persuading philosophers sceptical of the value of such a project. This failure also has implications for Nussbaum's attempt to incorporate imaginative literature within a specifically Aristotelian ethical conception. In particular, Horton argues, Nussbaum fails to take sufficiently seriously one of the lessons he believes literature best teaches: the extent and depth of moral disagreement and conflict. One of literature's most significant achievements, and one reason why it has been treated with such suspicion and hostility by many philosophers, is its ability to make plausible and convincing a wide range of conflicting moral conceptions and beliefs. Hence, he is doubtful about the claim that works of fiction or the literary imagination support any *one* ethical conception.

NATIONALITY, NATIONALISM AND LITERATURE

One area in which literature and politics are often closely related concerns the construction of a national identity.[57] Language and literature are frequently invoked as essential components of what makes a nation what it is. This can be seen for example in arguments about literary canons, in the British context in recent debates about the national curriculum or, in the USA, in similar debates about the status of the 'great texts' of Western civilisation.[58] It is commonly the case that countries will take particular writers as their 'national' poets, dramatists or whatever. One need only think, for example, of the role of the classical French drama of Molière and Racine, Goethe in Germany, Shakespeare in England, Pushkin in Russia to see how even the most 'universal' of imaginative writers may come to be seen as embodiments of, or spokespersons for, an alleged national identity.

Paul Gilbert in his chapter in this volume argues that exploring the notion of a national literature can give us a clearer understanding of what is involved in nationhood. For, if nations are at least partly to be identified in terms of their culture, then literature, as an important part of culture, will have a significant role to play. Gilbert identifies two interpretations of nationhood, which he calls 'realism' and 'voluntarism'. Realism interprets national identity as based upon a 'common property of people independent of their will to associate together politically'. Voluntarism, by contrast, sees national identity as dependent upon the voluntary choices of agents to constitute a nation. Gilbert is especially concerned to establish whether realism can be regarded as a plausible theory of nationhood.

As a test case, Gilbert takes the work of the Anglo-Irish novelist Elizabeth Bowen, investigating the claims and supporting evidence for and against her literary Irishness. He argues that no such evidence is, in principle, available. Rather, there are features of her work which those concerned with the construction of an Irish national identity can appeal to in deciding whether or not she should be included in a literature which articulates a shared national experience. What should count as the national experience, Gilbert argues, is essentially a matter of choice and not a matter of the independently discernible properties of a literary work. If a national literature is socially constructed then the question which needs to be asked is: who is responsible for its construction? He argues that if it is the members of a nation generally then their common cultural choices can constitute the association which forms them into a nation according to the voluntarist theory. Thus, the attribution of national identity on cultural grounds does not presuppose the truth of the realist theory.

The issue of how nationhood is to be understood is also a principal concern in Margaret Canovan's chapter. For Canovan, patriotic poetry raises interesting questions about political identity and solidarity.[59] Patriotic poetry has among its characteristic themes a transcendence of individual existence within a wider communal identity, and Canovan is particularly interested in the relationship between the limited national solidarities invoked by patriotic poetry and the universal moral commitments associated with liberal theory.[60] She argues, contrary to the views of many liberals, who tend to regard national loyalty as a somewhat primitive and parochial sentiment, that nations are sophisticated and complex phenomena made possible by a considerable imaginative extension of sympathy. None the less, the type of loyalty evoked by patriotic poetry is also inevitably limited and additionally frequently adversarial, features which cannot be avoided, she claims, by distinguishing a benign patriotism from a malign nationalism.

Canovan's conclusion, however, is one that might come as a surprise to some liberals. For while it is true that the demands of patriotic loyalty often conflict with the liberal aspiration towards universal moral principles and obligations, liberal humanism may also find an ally in patriotism in its opposition to communal conflict based on ethnic, religious or racial hatred. If national identity excludes it also includes, and it may include many of those who would be excluded by different criteria of identity or allegiance. As Canovan warns, the alternative to national identity and the language of patriotism, as expressed in part through patriotic poetry, may not be humanism and universal principles of justice but more exclusive and threatening forms of communalism.

However, there are in any case other contexts in which the role of literature in forming national identity might appear more benign. If the patriotic poetry discussed by Canovan seems to by typically associated with an aggressive nationalism, there are other examples of creative writing in which the connection with national identity might plausibly be seen as liberating. This seems to be especially true of literature which asserts a national identity as a way of resisting imperial domination or of sloughing off its heritage, for example, in what has become known as post-colonial literature.[61] Here what is involved is characteristically the attempt to forge new political identities, frequently but not necessarily national, through creating a literature and language purged of the often racist and hostile legacy of colonialism. This also seems to provide some support for Paul Gilbert's argument about the way in which national literatures are created rather than discovered.

LIBERALISM

The consideration of Margaret Canovan's chapter leads naturally into a discussion of liberalism which is a recurrent, if often subsidiary theme, of several chapters in this volume. This is not surprising, because one might expect the culture of liberalism to be especially hospitable to the literary imagination. Whether or not there is a special relationship between literature and liberal *theory*, however, is less obvious, and this question is the prime focus of Paul Seabright's chapter.

Seabright takes as his starting point a distinction which he rightly regards as crucial to any liberal political theory, the distinction between public and private. While there is of course much dispute within liberal theory about where and how the line is to be drawn between them, any genuinely liberal theory will require that individuals be granted some significant private space, free from political interference, in which people may pursue their individual interests and realise their own conceptions of the good. However, if this private space is to be of genuine value to people then it will need to be furnished in some way. Whilst in a liberal society it should not be the role of the political process to arbitrate between the different uses to which individuals choose to put this space, liberal politics will, for just this reason, be more favourable to some ways of furnishing it than to others. For instance, it will be hostile to ways which unjustifiably encroach on other people's liberty.

It is in this context that Seabright explores the possible roles that imaginative literature might play. He poses two questions. First, can the activity of reading or writing imaginative literature be viewed as paradigmatic of the kind of project that would furnish a private space sufficiently well to have made it worthwhile creating the space in the first place? Second, can imaginative literature provide any guidance as to the furnishing of a private space with *other* projects and activities? Seabright pursues these questions in some interesting and varied directions but he concludes that, although imaginative literature can, and at times has, fulfilled both these functions and has offered positive support for the liberal vision, the fact that so much of modern literature has explicitly sought to erode or undermine the distinction between the public and the private suggests that the relationship between imaginative literature and the liberal conception of a private space is at times a more uncomfortable one than might be expected.[62]

Liberalism is also the starting point of Martin Warner's wide-ranging chapter, 'Modes of Political Imagining', which opens with some reflections on the communitarian critique of the individualism of John Rawls's *A Theory of Justice* and concludes with some critical observations on the role of the distinction between public and private in his most recent work, *Political Liberalism*.[63] In between, however, he covers considerable ground. Warner's reflections, like those of Susan Mendus in her chapter, are prompted by the apparent impasse in contemporary political theory created by the tension between the views of theorists, like MacIntyre and Taylor, who emphasise the embeddedness of our values in particular communities and the desire of some philosophers, including the early Rawls, to ascribe to some values, most notably justice, a universal force. For Warner, the underlying problem here is not so much political or ethical as epistemological. This tension is one aspect of the wider question of whether or not it is possible to give an account of truth that is both socially contextualised and independent of judgement. Again, rather like Susan Mendus in her treatment of the dispute between Taylor and Rorty, Warner's strategy is to seek a middle way. In his pursuit of this *via media* he draws on David Wiggins' account of what he calls the 'marks' of truth, such features as its propensity to convergence, its ruling out of something and its independence from judgement.[64]

Warner relates this debate about the nature of moral truth to a wide range of diverse literary modes of political imagining in order to explore models of justice marginalised by contemporary theory. These give weight both to the cultural embeddedness of justice and to its universalistic force, and seek to resolve the consequent tension by integrating our passional and social lives into our conception of reason. It is this requirement that Rawls's latest formulation of his theory of justice in *Political Liberalism* fails to meet. Its inadequate moral psychology is manifested most damagingly in the unsatisfactory conceptualisation of the relationship between the public and the private in the account of 'overlapping consensus'.[65] Warner suggests we need a somewhat different conception of theory, one in which imaginative literature shows us how the relationships between public and private, universality and particularity, and reason and passion can be better accommodated.

LITERATURE AND UTOPIAN POLITICAL THEORY

One tradition of speculation about political possibilities which historically has an especially intimate connection with imaginative literature is Utopian theorising. The book from which the very currency of the word Utopia derives, Thomas More's work of that name, is considered both a work of imaginative literature and political theory, though it fits easily into neither category as they are currently conceived.[66] Not surprisingly, political theorists radically critical of the political world as it is, or ever has been, have tended to see in imaginative literature a form capable of transcending the perceived limitations of more traditional theoretical discourses about political institutions and ideals.[67] This is evident most recently in the attractions that Utopianism has had for some radical feminist writers.[68]

One of the commonest objections to Utopian thinking, apart from the claim that it is inherently unrealistic or unworkable, is that for all its radical ambitions it seems to seek a model of politics that is inevitably timeless and unchanging. This criticism forms the starting point for Lucy Sargisson's chapter. She agrees that standard approaches to Utopia, with their emphasis on providing a universally applicable blueprint for the future, are, despite their critical qualities, ultimately deeply conservative and repressive of difference and change. However, drawing on strands of recent feminist thinking informed by work within postmodern and poststructuralist theory, she argues that there is a style of contemporary feminist Utopianism which successfully seeks to move away from the static universality and monolithic certainty traditionally associated with Utopian writing.[69]

For Sargisson, this new Utopianism is characterised by an emphasis on process rather than perfection, and it aims at a new open-ended and plural approach towards the present and the future. On this understanding, Utopianism is an ongoing process of challenge and critique, making the rhetorical strategies and tactics of deconstructive reading particularly appropriate to this mode of thought. In this way, the subversive and transgressive aspirations of the Utopian imagination can be sustained and the closure associated with the more traditional conception of Utopia avoided. Such a Utopianism must seek new forms of expression in both literature and politics. In particular, Sargisson claims, it will support and sustain the oppositional character that any form of feminist Utopianism must possess if it is to avoid being implicated in patriarchal structures of domination.

One genre of writing closely related to Utopianism and which is also typically oppositional, though not necessarily to the *status quo*, is dystopianism. George Orwell was a writer who explored the dystopian novel to maximum political effect in his *Nineteen Eighty Four*. Orwell is the subject of Stephen Ingle's chapter. Ingle focuses, however, not on *Nineteen Eighty Four* or *Animal Farm*, Orwell's two most famous political novels, but on how the dystopian vision of totalitarianism which informs both these novels has its origins in

Orwell's experiences of British imperialism as revealed in both his fiction and non-fiction writings.

Orwell consciously chose to express his deepest political concerns in the novel form. Ingle argues that Orwell used the novel to express his understanding of imperialism both as a means of incorporating his first-hand personal experience of British colonialism in Burma and as a way of avoiding some potential pitfalls in a more theoretical presentation of it. For what is crucial to Orwell's model of imperialism, on Ingle's account, is its emphasis on the mutually destructive nature of the relationship between exploiter and exploited, the manifestations of which are both public and private. Indeed, this emphasis on the interweaving of public and private, of the reciprocal influence of the political and personal, something which is often much better captured by literature than philosophy, is a recurrent and fundamental feature of Orwell's writings. Moreover, the corrupting nature of the relationship of domination and subservience as shown most starkly by imperialism was contrasted by Orwell with the values of decency and humanity which the oppressed generally showed to each other. Ingle argues that this model of imperialist power relations forms the basis of Orwell's analysis of totalitarianism, his rejection of the Machiavellian case for a sharp distinction between personal and political morality[70] and his continuing attempt to assert the political significance and worth of those values he found expressed most fully within the daily life of the industrial working class.

The kind of socialism that Orwell espoused was that which he believed to be embodied in the systems of mutual support found in the informal organisation of working-class life. This, combined with the anti-hierarchical thrust of his critique of imperialism, made the novel in two respects a particularly appropriate form for giving expression to Orwell's convictions. First, the novel is a much more appropriate vehicle than the political pamphlet or theoretical treatise for communicating and sharing lived experience. It was this lived experience and not abstract principles or ideologies which was so important to Orwell. Second, the novel implies a relationship between the author and the reader of a more egalitarian and less authoritarian cast than most orthodox philosophical or political modes of writing. The kind of relationship implied by the author as the 'wise man', the authority, imparting his superior knowledge to the ignorant was too close to that imperialist relationship that he believed to be so corrosive of the values of decency and human fellow-feeling, the absence of which makes the soil fertile for forms of cruelty and inhumanity which reach their apogee in totalitarianism.[71]

The themes and issues we have discussed in the latter part of this introduction are not the only areas in which there are potentially interesting connections to be explored between political theory and imaginative literature, nor do they exhaust those explored in the chapters that follow. However, we hope they are sufficient to demonstrate that there *are* interesting connections and to indicate some of the diverse ways in which the subsequent chapters contribute to this exploration. There is no 'party line' in these essays, the authors approach their problems in different ways and there is no unanimity of opinion. They are all united only in their commitment to the value of the exploration of relationships between imaginative literature and political theory; to examining both the possibilities and the problems involved in any such undertaking.[72]

NOTES

1 See, for example, Arnold Pacey, *The Culture of Technology*, Oxford, Blackwell, 1983.
2 For a useful discussion of the philosophy of logical positivism see Oswald Hanfling, *Logical Positivism*, Oxford, Blackwell, 1981.
3 An excellent discussion of this phenomenon in philosophy can be found in Tom Sorrell, *Scientism*, London, Routledge, 1991.
4 For some further instances see Maureen Whitebrook (ed.), *Reading Political Stories: Representations of Politics in Novels and Pictures*, Lanham, MD, Rowman & Littlefield, 1992; and for a somewhat different approach see Michael J. Shapiro, *Reading the Postmodern Polity: Political Theory as Textual Practice*, Minneapolis, University of Minnesota Press, 1992.
5 Marxist literary criticism is one school which has in general been receptive to both a theoretical and political dimension to the understanding and evaluation of literature. See, for example, Terry Eagleton, *Marxism and Literary Criticism*, London, Methuen, 1976; and Cliff Slaughter, *Marxism, Ideology and Literature*, London, Macmillan, 1980.
6 The philosophy of literary criticism is discussed in Colin Radford and Sally Minogue, *The Nature of Criticism*, Brighton, Harvester Press, 1981; and John Ellis, *The Theory of Literary Criticism: A Logical Analysis*, Berkeley and Los Angeles, University of California Press, 1974. For a consideration of the literary qualities of philosophy see Berel Lang, *The Anatomy of Philosophical Style*, Oxford, Basil Blackwell, 1990, Part II. For a helpful introduction to aesthetics with particular reference to literature see Anne Sheppard, *Aesthetics*, Oxford, Oxford University Press, 1987.
7 One particularly important American philosopher whose work has

always had a significant literary and artistic dimension is Stanley Cavell. See, for example, his *Must We Mean What We Say?*, Cambridge, Cambridge University Press, 1976; *Themes out of School: Effects and Causes*, San Francisco, North Point Press, 1984; *Disowning Knowledge in Six Plays of Shakespeare*, Cambridge, Cambridge University Press, 1987; and *In Quest of the Ordinary: Lines of Scepticism and Romanticism*, Chicago and London, University of Chicago Press, 1988.

8 For an interesting discussion of the idea of an educated public which also addresses the issue of specialisation see Alasdair MacIntyre, 'The Idea of an Educated Public' in Graham Haydon (ed.), *Education and Values*, London, Institute of Education, 1987.

9 See Michael Tanner, 'The Language of Philosophy' in L. Michaels and C. Ricks (eds), *The State of the Language*, California and London, California University Press, 1980.

10 John Rawls, *A Theory of Justice*, Oxford, Oxford University Press, 1971.

11 Alan Gewirth, *Reason and Morality*, Chicago and London, University of Chicago Press, 1978; and *Human Rights: Essays on Justification and Applications*, Chicago and London, University of Chicago Press, 1982.

12 For some criticisms and Gewirth's replies see Edward Regis Jr. (ed.), *Gewirth's Ethical Rationalism: Critical Essays with a Reply by Alan Gewirth*, Chicago and London, University of Chicago Press, 1984. For a remarkably comprehensive, if not always convincing, reply to Gewirth's many critics see Deryck Beyleveld, *The Dialectical Necessity of Morality*, Chicago and London, University of Chicago Press, 1991.

13 For instance, the idea of arguments that cannot be reasonably rejected has played an increasingly important role in liberal accounts of impartiality. See Brian Barry, *Theories of Justice*, London, Harvester-Wheatsheaf, 1989, Sect. 35; and *Justice as Impartiality*, Oxford, Oxford University Press, 1995, *passim*.

14 For one discussion of the possibility of political theory in the modern world see John Dunn, *Rethinking Modern Political Theory*, Cambridge, Cambridge University Press, 1985, Ch. 10.

15 For an account of the vicissitudes of political theory for the last century or more, with particular reference to the USA, see John G. Gunnell, *The Descent of Political Theory: The Genealogy of an American Vocation*, Chicago, University of Chicago Press, 1993.

16 Even this residual conception of political theory has been subject to powerful criticism for engaging in amateurish history by historians of ideas such as Quentin Skinner, John Dunn and others associated with the 'Cambridge School'. For a good review of the 'revisionist' debate generally see David Boucher, *Texts in Context: Revisionist Methods for Studying the History of Ideas*, Dordrecht, D. Reidel, 1985, and for an excellent collection of articles by and about the work of Skinner see James Tully (ed.), *Meaning and Context: Quentin Skinner and his Critics*, Cambridge, Polity Press, 1988.

17 Among the most important of their works in political theory are Hannah Arendt, *The Origins of Totalitarianism*, 3rd Edition, London, George Allen & Unwin, 1966; and *The Human Condition*, Chicago, University of Chicago Press, 1958; Karl Popper, *The Open Society and its Enemies*, Fifth Edition, London, Routledge & Kegan Paul, 1966; Leo Strauss,

What is Political Philosophy? and *Other Studies*, Glencoe, IL, Free Press, 1959; and the very useful collection of pieces put together posthumously by Thomas L. Pangle, *The Rebirth of Classical Rationalism: Essays and Lectures by Leo Strauss*, Chicago, University of Chicago Press, 1989.

18 For a brief survey of some of the differences see the entry on ancient Greek theatre in Martin Banham (ed.), *The Cambridge Guide to Theatre*, Cambridge, Cambridge University Press, 1992.

19 We have in mind in particular: Martha Nussbaum, *The Fragility of Goodness: Luck and Ethics in Greek Tragedy and Philosophy*, Cambridge, Cambridge University Press, 1986; Bernard Williams, *Shame and Necessity*, Berkeley and Los Angeles, California University Press, 1993; and J. Peter Euben, *Greek Tragedy and Political Theory*, Berkeley and Los Angeles, California University Press, 1986.

20 On the development of the novel see Ian Watt, *The Rise of the Novel*, London, Chatto & Windus, 1957. For a wide-ranging account of the Romantic sensibility see H. G. Schenk, *The Mind of the European Romantics*, Oxford, Oxford University Press, 1979; and for a good account of the influence of Romanticism, especially the English Romantics, on the development of literary criticism see M. H. Abrams, *The Mirror and the Lamp*, Oxford, Oxford University Press, 1953.

21 For a useful historical survey of literary critical discussions of some of these issues see K. K. Ruthven, *Critical Assumptions*, Cambridge, Cambridge University Press, 1979.

22 See D. J. Palmer, *The Rise of English Studies*, Oxford, Oxford University Press, 1965.

23 See Rene Wellek, *A History of Modern Criticism*, Vols 5 and 6, London, Jonathan Cape, 1986.

24 One tradition of thought in which both literary and philosophical concerns intertwine is hermeneutics. The seminal work here is Hans-Georg Gadamer, *Truth and Method* (ed. and trans.) G. Barden and J. Cumming, London, Sheed & Ward, 1975. For a useful introduction to recent hermeneutic theory see Josef Bleicher, *Contemporary Hermeneutics*, London, Routledge, 1980.

25 See, for example, F. R. Leavis, *Nor Shall My Sword: Discourses on Pluralism, Compassion and Social Hope*, London, Chatto & Windus, 1972; *The Living Principle: 'English' as a Discipline of Thought*, London, Chatto & Windus, 1975; and *The Critic as Anti-Philosophy*, (ed.) G. Singh, London, Chatto & Windus, 1982.

26 See, for example, Northrop Frye, *Anatomy of Criticism*, Princeton, NJ, Princeton University Press, 1957.

27 On Derrida, deconstruction and its influence on literary criticism, see Christopher Norris, *Deconstruction: Theory and Practice*, London, Methuen, 1982; Jonathan Culler, *On Deconstruction*, London, Routledge & Kegan Paul, 1983; and Vincent B. Leitch, *Deconstructive Criticism: An Advanced Introduction*, London, Hutchinson, 1983.

28 For an interesting discussion of Plato's treatment of the arts by someone who is both a philosopher and a novelist see Iris Murdoch, *The Fire and the Sun: Why Plato Banished the Artists*, Oxford, Oxford University Press, 1977.

29 An opinion held in our own time by the moral philosopher Richard

Hare. See R. M. Hare, *Essays in Ethical Theory*, Oxford, Oxford University Press, 1989, p. 57.

30 Of course, there are many exceptions to this generalisation. In addition to the work of Stanley Cavell, cited earlier, one might mention Peter Jones, *Philosophy and the Novel*, Oxford, Oxford University Press, 1975 and D. Z. Phillips, *Belief, Changes and Forms of Life*, London, Macmillan, 1988 as examples of philosophers working through literature on philosophical problems.

31 For an introductory review of existentialism focusing on both its literary and philosophical aspects see Wesley Barnes, *The Philosophy and Literature of Existentialism*, New York, Barron's Educational Series, 1968. Iris Murdoch might be thought a comparable philosophical novelist writing in English, but she has always rigorously distinguished her fiction from her philosophy.

32 Interestingly, a recent best-seller has tried to tell the history of philosophy in novel form: see Jostein Gaarder, *Sophie's World*, (trans.) P. Moller, London, Phoenix House, 1994.

33 A useful brief survey of some of the connections between politics, including political philosophy, and literature can be found in Maureen Whitebrook, 'Politics and Literature', *Politics*, 15, 1995.

34 Leavis, *The Critic as Anti-Philosopher* and *The Living Principle*. On the other hand, Ian Robinson has sought to relate Leavisite criticism to the philosophy of Ludwig Wittgenstein. See Ian Robinson, *The Survival of English: Essays in Criticism of Language*, London, Cambridge University Press, 1973.

35 Richard Rorty, *Philosophy and the Mirror of Nature*, Oxford, Blackwell, 1980.

36 See particularly 'The Priority of Democracy to Philosophy' and 'Postmodernist Bourgeois Liberalism' in Richard Rorty, *Objectivity, Relativism and Truth: Philosophical Papers Vol. 1*, Cambridge, Cambridge University Press, 1991; and Richard Rorty, *Contingency, Irony and Solidarity*, Cambridge, Cambridge University Press, 1989.

37 For some criticisms see many of the essays in A. Malachowski (ed.), *Reading Rorty*, Oxford, Basil Blackwell, 1990; and also Section 1 in Roy Bhaskar, *Philosophy and the Idea of Freedom*, Oxford, Blackwell, 1991.

38 On the liberal/communitarian debate see Shlomo Avineri and Avner de-Shalit (eds), *Communitarianism and Individualism*, Oxford, Oxford University Press, 1992; and Stephen Mulhall and Adam Swift, *Liberals and Communitarians*, Oxford, Blackwell, 1992.

39 See particularly Alasdair MacIntyre, *After Virtue: A Study in Moral Theory*, London, Duckworth, 1981; and Charles Taylor, *Sources of the Self: The Making of Modern Identity*, Cambridge, Cambridge University Press, 1989.

40 See John G. Gunnell, 'Relativism: The Return of the Repressed', *Political Theory*, 21, 1993.

41 This is a point made most emphatically in Martha Nussbaum, *Love's Knowledge: Essays on Philosophy and Literature*, New York, Oxford University Press, 1990.

42 For useful introductory surveys of the field of cultural studies see Lawrence Grossberg, Cary Nelson and Paula Treichler (eds), *Cultural Stud-*

ies, London, Routledge, 1992; and *The Polity Reader in Cultural Studies*, Cambridge, Polity Press, 1993.

43 For a critique of the conception of reason in Western philosophy see Genevieve Lloyd, *The Man of Reason: 'Male' and 'Female' in Western Philosophy*, London, Methuen, 1984. Useful feminist critiques of political philosophy include Diana Coole, *Women in Political Theory*, Brighton, Wheatsheaf, 1988; and Susan Moller Okin, *Women in Western Political Thought*, Princeton, NJ, Princeton University Press, 1979.

44 On the 'ethics of care' see Carol Gilligan, *In a Different Voice*, Cambridge, Harvard University Press, 1982; Joan Tronto, *Moral Boundaries: A Political Argument for an Ethic of Care*, London, Routledge, 1993; and M. J. Larrabee (ed.), *An Ethic of Care: Feminist and Interdisciplinary Perspectives*, London, Routledge, 1993.

45 See also Whitebrook, 'Politics and Literature'.

46 See, for example, Gérard Genette, *Narrative Discourse*, (trans.) Jane E. Lewin, Oxford, Basil Blackwell, 1980; Philip J. M. Sturgess, *Narrativity: Theory and Practice*, Oxford, Clarendon Press, 1993; and, with a specifically 'political' emphasis, Jeremy Tambling, *Narrative and Ideology*, Buckingham, Open University Press, 1991.

47 See MacIntyre, *After Virtue*, and Taylor, *Sources of the Self*.

48 For an interesting and imaginative attempt to engage with the role of narrative in philosophy generally see Jonathan Rée, *Philosophical Tales*, London, Methuen, 1987.

49 Rawls, *Theory of Justice*, pp. 407–16.

50 On the relations between the self and narrative see also Genevieve Lloyd, *Being in Time: Selves and Narrators in Philosophy and Literature*, London, Routledge, 1993. Milan Kundera boldly claims that 'All novels, of every age, are concerned with the enigma of the self', *The Art of the Novel*, London, Faber & Faber, 1988, p. 23.

51 R. M. Hare, *Freedom and Reason*, Oxford, Oxford University Press, 1963; and *Moral Thinking*; Alan Gewirth, *Reason and Morality*; and *Human Rights*.

52 Bernard Williams, *Ethics and the Limits of Philosophy*, London, Fontana, 1985, Ch. 10.

53 Jean-Paul Sartre, *Existentialism and Humanism*, (trans.) Philip Mairet, London, Methuen, 1948.

54 Brian Moore, *Lies of Silence*, London, Bloomsbury, 1990.

55 For a more critical attitude to the use of literary examples see Onora O'Neill, 'The Power of Example', *Philosophy*, 61, 1986; and also the trenchant defence in reply in D. Z. Phillips, 'The Presumption of Theory' in R. Gaita (ed.), *Value and Understanding: Essays for Peter Winch*, London, Routledge, 1990.

56 See Williams, *Ethics and Limits of Philosophy*; Nussbaum, *Love's Knowledge*; and Peter Winch, *Ethics and Action*, London, Routledge & Kegan Paul, 1972.

57 For some interesting examples see the discussions in Homi K. Bhabha (ed.), *Nation and Narration*, London, Routledge, 1990.

58 For contrasting views on the US controversy see Allan Bloom, *The Closing of the American Mind*, Harmondsworth, Penguin Books, 1988;

and Gerald Graff, *Beyond the Culture Wars*, New York, W. W. Norton, 1992.

59 For a wide-ranging exploration of the relationship between nationality, poetry and politics by a practising poet see the essays in Tom Paulin, *Minotaur: Poetry and the Nation State*, London, Faber & Faber, 1992.

60 This issue is also discussed with considerable incisiveness in Alasdair MacIntyre, *Is Patriotism a Virtue?*, The E. H. Lindley Memorial Lecture, Lawrence, University of Kansas Department of Philosophy, 1984.

61 See Eugene Benson and L. W. Connolly (eds), *Encyclopedia of Post-Colonial Literatures in English*, London, Routledge, 1994.

62 Although Seabright himself does not suggest it, it might be interesting to read his paper in the context of Lionel Trilling's famous collection of essays *The Liberal Imagination*, London, Secker & Warburg, 1951.

63 Rawls, *Theory of Justice*; and John Rawls, *Political Liberalism*, Columbia, Columbia University Press, 1993.

64 See David Wiggins, *Needs, Values, Truth: Essays in the Philosophy of Value*, Oxford, Blackwell, 1987.

65 Rawls, *Political Liberalism*, Lecture IV.

66 Thomas More, *Utopia*, (ed.) George M. Logan and Robert M. Adams, Cambridge, Cambridge University Press, 1989.

67 This probably accounts for the vigorous tradition of socialist literature. See, for example, Stephen Ingle, *Socialist Thought in Imaginative Literature*, London, Macmillan, 1979; David Smith, *Socialist Propaganda in the Twentieth-Century British Novel*, London, Macmillan, 1978; and H. Gustav Klaus (ed.), *The Socialist Novel in Britain*, Sussex, Harvester Press, 1982.

68 See, for example, F. Bartkowski, *Feminist Utopias*, Lincoln, NB, University of Nebraska Press, 1989.

69 For useful discussions of Utopianism see Krishan Kumar, *Utopianism*, Buckingham, Open University Press, 1991; Ruth Levitas, *The Concept of Utopia*, Hemel Hempstead, Philip Allen, 1990; and Barbara Goodwin and Keith Taylor, *The Politics of Utopia*, London, Hutchinson, 1982.

70 On the relationship between personal and political morality, and the Machiavellian problem of 'dirty hands' see the essays by Hampshire, Nagel and Williams in Stuart Hampshire (ed.), *Public and Private Morality*, Cambridge, Cambridge University Press, 1978. The issue is also considered in the chapters by Maureen Whitebrook and Anthony Arblaster in this volume.

71 More critical views of both Orwell's politics and writing are expressed by several of the contributors to Christopher Norris (ed.), *Inside the Myth, Orwell: Views from the Left*, London, Lawrence & Wishart, 1984.

72 In addition to Whitebrook, *Reading Political Stories*; Nussbaum, *Love's Knowledge*; and Shapiro, *Reading the Postmodern Polity*, mentioned earlier, other interesting contributions to the project include Peter Johnson, *Politics, Innocence and the Limits of Goodness*, London, Routledge, 1988; Ethan Fishman, *Likely Stories: Essays on Political Philosophy and Contemporary American Literature*, Gainsville, FL, University of Florida Press, 1989; Catherine Zuckert, *Natural Right and the American Imagination: Political Philosophy in Novel Form*, Savage, MD, Rowman and Littlefield, 1990; Benjamin Barber and Michael McGrath, *The Artist*

and Political Vision, New Brunswick, NJ, Transaction, 1981; and Maureen Whitebrook, *Real Toads in Imaginary Gardens; Narrative Accounts of Liberalism*, Savage, MD, Rowman & Littlefield, 1994.

2 Taking the narrative turn

What the novel has to offer political theory

Maureen Whitebrook

There are potential connections between political theory and literature which are more sophisticated than the old practice of trawling
literature for political illustrations and more interesting – pertinent
to theory's interest in process, for instance – than 'political literary
criticism', where that has been the study of themes *per se*. The
question of what literature has to offer politics – a debatable question from Plato onwards, across the tradition of political theory –
has usually come down to some variation on one of two possibilities:
literature as example for or illustration of arguments in political
theory, or, one step on, literary examples as a form of moral education (with which political theory might be concerned). While both
of those possibilities are of continuing interest, neither sufficiently
address the benefits for political theory as such of taking a specific
form of literature – the novel – as source of political understanding;
but neither do more recent developments.

Present understandings within political theory of what literature
might contribute, and how that contribution might be made, draw
on two major sources from outside of political theory: the general
injunction to 'turn to narrative', originating (in those words) with
Richard Rorty and also expressed, rather differently, by Alasdair
MacIntyre and Charles Taylor; and the attention in philosophy and
literature to literary texts as expositions of moral behaviour,
especially in the work of Martha Nussbaum. However, there are
qualifications in respect of 'the narrative turn' in social and moral
theory. How then should political theory take this version of 'politics
and literature'? Is the correct direction some refinement of the work
on 'the narrative self' or 'literature and ethics', or should different
connections be made, for the benefit of a specifically *political* understanding?

Transfers between disciplines often prove problematic, methodologically speaking, but in this case, to draw on these sources as major ways into work in 'politics and literature' which will benefit contemporary political theory may also be substantively misleading. In Part I of this chapter I suggest why this is the case: the limitations include a predominantly individualist focus which fails to address the 'Machiavellian' problem of behaviour in the political realm. I therefore introduce, in Part II, criteria for a distinctive approach which would allow political theory to gain from literature some enriched understanding of the public and collective life of the individual – those aspects which are distinctively political. I suggest that in this respect the novel, as the literary form of narrative, has a particular relevance for (liberal) political theory. In Part III, I indicate in broad terms what that relevance might be. Both the content and form of the novel contribute to political understanding. The novel's capacity for allowing reflection, and thence the refinement of discrimination and judgement, has a potentially political relevance inasmuch as politics is concerned with judging and choosing. Novels present choices, the implications and consequences of choices. I suggest that novels do offer political theory some insight into the Machiavellian problem. Individuals making choices, in so far as they are *political* agents, are faced with particular political dilemmas involved with those choices, problems of responsibility. And novels also contribute, by way of their depiction of character, to consideration of the way in which the individual constructs and maintains identity, including the political implications and outcomes of that process.

These separate but interconnected sections together offer a response both to my particular questions and to the general intention of this volume – to explain how and what literature can contribute to political theory and political philosophy. I argue overall that neither social theory's attention to narrative nor work in philosophy and literature can be relied on entirely to provide political theorists with a sufficient basis for bringing literature into their work. Rather, political theorists ought to develop their own approach(es) – and are capable of so doing, as work in this volume and elsewhere is beginning to suggest.[1]

PART I

Prominent critics, philosophers and social theorists argue for – and to an extent practice – a 'turn to narrative'; these indications of the potential utility of narrative are recognised in political theory, at least to the extent that 'narrative', 'story' and 'story-telling' are terms in regular usage beyond the work on, or deriving directly from, particular theorists – Rorty, MacIntyre, Taylor, Nussbaum. Rorty is the most passionate advocate of 'the narrative turn'. In the course of his discussions of the nature of philosophy he has made suggestions about the usefulness of literature and literary criticism – providing new vocabularies, or as a way of interpreting people to each other, for instance. Then, in *Contingency, Irony and Solidarity*, he argues specifically for a 'turn to narrative', suggesting the possibility of 'a liberal Utopia' in which human solidarity would be achieved through imagination, 'the imaginative ability to see strange people as fellow-sufferers', a process involving description and redescription, 'a task not for theory but for genres such as ethnography, the journalist's report, the comic book, the docudrama, and, especially, the novel'.

> Fiction ... gives us the details about kinds of suffering being endured by people to whom we had previously not attended ... gives us the details about what sort of cruelty we ourselves are capable of, and thereby lets us redescribe ourselves. That is why the novel, the movie and the TV program have, gradually but steadily, replaced the sermon and the moral treatise as the principal vehicles of moral change and process. In my liberal utopia, this replacement would receive a kind of recognition which it still lacks. That recognition would be part of a general turn against theory and towards narrative.[2]

His belief that the novel is a better guide for human community than philosophy is reiterated in *Essays on Heidegger*:

> A society which took its moral vocabulary from novels rather than from ontotheological or ontico-moral treatises would not ask itself questions about human nature, the point of human existence, or the meaning of human life. Rather it would ask itself what we can do so as to get along with each other, how we can arrange things so as to be comfortable with one another, how institutions can be changed so that everyone's right to be understood has a better chance of being gratified.[3]

In *After Virtue*, Alasdair MacIntyre suggests that it is possible to understand human action in terms of narrative: 'Narrative history of a certain kind turns out to be the basic and essential genre for the characterization of human actions.' And, 'It is because we all live out narratives in our lives and because we understand our own lives in terms of the narratives that we live out that the form of narrative is appropriate for understanding the action of others.' And he stipulates what type of story is (morally) significant: '[T]he unity of a human life is the unity of a *narrative quest*.'⁴ Charles Taylor, in *Sources of the Self*, explicitly endorses and glosses MacIntyre's utilisation of 'narrative' as a crucial part of his own argument:

> in order to make minimal sense of our lives, in order to have an identity, we need an orientation to the good which means some sense of qualitative discrimination, of the incomparably higher . . . this sense of the good has to be woven into my understanding of my life as an unfolding story. But this is to state another basic condition of making sense of ourselves, that we grasp our lives in a *narrative*. . . . It has often been remarked that making sense of one's life as a story is also, like orientation to the good, not an optional extra; that our lives exist also in this space of questions, which only a coherent narrative can answer. In order to have a sense of who we are, we have to have a notion of how we have become, and of where we are going . . . My life always has this degree of narrative understanding, that I understand my present action in the form of an "and then" . . .

This is not merely a matter of structuring the present. Assessment of our moral condition is only possible through narrative – 'we determine what we are by what we have become, by the story of how we got there'; and, 'we cannot but strive to give our lives meaning or substance, and . . . this means that we understand ourselves inescapably in narrative'.⁵

At first, like MacIntyre, Taylor tends to use 'narrative' as equivalent to a simple story where the sequence beginning–middle–end is used to represent the (possible) unity of a single life. Narrative is an explanatory tool, a way of giving account of ourselves by telling stories. But he then goes further than MacIntyre in specifying types of narrative and the different ways they might order human lives (though for the most part he retains the notions of history and progress as characteristic of narrative). The form of the novel and the way in which modern identity is shaped are inextricable, so that changes in narrative form are associated with, and provide evidence for, the changes in senses of identity which he records.

For Rorty, MacIntyre and Taylor, 'narrative' is not necessarily equated with literary fictions.⁶ MacIntyre uses 'narrative' interchangeably with 'story-telling' and understands both in the limited sense of recounting a series of events to make a whole, getting from beginning to end with everything between fitted in intelligibly, with reference to an end, a goal, an overarching explanation. When he speaks of stories and story-telling, he is referring to something much more like autobiography than fiction, or myths and legends (as proto-history) rather than novels; and in places the 'narrative' referred to is actually narrative history. And although Taylor and Rorty take actual literary texts into their argument, they also frequently use 'narrative' as referring to narrative history.

More significantly, each of these theorists advocate 'the turn to narrative' for specific ends, and each has a persuasive intention in advocating the narrative turn. Thus, Rorty suggests that,

> we distinguish books which help us become autonomous from books which help us become less cruel... The second sort of book is relevant to our relations with others, helping us notice the effects of our actions on other people. These are the books which are relevant to liberal hope, and to the question of how to reconcile private irony with such hope.[7]

Rorty's advocacy is part of his continuing argument against philosophy and/or, particularly as developed in *Contingency, Irony and Solidarity*, in part defence of liberal democracy and as a means to his liberal Utopia. (And he has lately said that in the end, '[P]hilosophy is not *that* important for politics, nor is literature': narrative is superior to philosophy as an intellectual activity, whereas pragmatically, repression and injustice is 'so blatant and obvious that it does not take any great analytical skills or any great philosophical self-consciousness to see what is going on.')[8]

Both MacIntyre and Taylor posit a narrative construction of identity because they *want* life to have a form, order (a telos): at the most basic, to narrate – to tell a story – is to order, to impose a pattern on otherwise inchoate events, taking in coincidence and contingency and giving them meaning. The quest for (narrative) unity is a quest for order. The unity of a human life rests in narrative, story-telling, the recounting of events from beginning to middle to end, entailing coherence and intelligibility. These accounts of a 'turn to narrative' are, then, persuasive claims, made in the context of particular arguments, so that it is likely to be misleading, if not dangerous, to extract parts of these arguments – a central part, in MacIntyre's case – without regard to that context.

Rorty's advocacy of literature, situated in the particular context of the academic discipline of philosophy, puts literature *against* philosophy. Prior to this extreme claim, there has been a good deal of work in 'philosophy and literature' which explores the possibility of interconnections.[9] Iris Murdoch's work is an obvious case (and particularly interesting because she writes as a philosopher *and* as a novelist). In 'Against Dryness', she comments on the relation of literature, specifically the novel, to the politics of welfare state democracies where 'our central conception is still a debilitated form of Mill's equation: happiness equals freedom equals personality', and where '[W]e have suffered a general loss of concepts... a moral and political vocabulary.' Accordingly,

> We need to return from the self-centred concept of sincerity to the other-centred concept of truth... what we require is a renewed sense of the difficulty and complexity of the moral life and the opacity of persons... It is here that literature is so important... Through literature we can re-discover a sense of the density of our lives.[10]

Murdoch's remarks presage much recent work in moral philosophy.

The most obvious – and much-cited – exponent of the turn to narrative in moral philosophy is Martha Nussbaum. Nussbaum argues for the place of emotion and particularity in moral philosophy, as against theoretical abstraction, and for,

> a conception of ethical understanding that... gives a certain type of priority to the perception of particular people and situations rather than to abstract rules... this conception, rather than being imprecise and irrational, is actually superior in rationality and in the relevant sort of precision... [it] finds its most appropriate expression and statement in certain forms usually considered literary rather than philosophical... if we wish to take it seriously we must broaden our conception of moral philosophy in order to include these texts inside it.[11]

Nussbaum is engaged in 'a project of the dialogue between philosophy and literary analysis in pursuit of the human question, 'How should one live?' at the core of which,

> is the claim that literary form and human life are inseparable... that literary forms call forth certain specific sorts of practical activity in the reader that can be evoked in no other way... [and] that we need a story of a certain kind, with characters of a certain type in it, if our own sense of life and of value is to be called forth in the way most appropriate for practical reflection.

This project,

involves supplementing abstract philosophical attempts at self-understanding with concrete narrative fictions, which . . . contain more of what is relevant to our attempts to imagine and assess possibilities for ourselves, to ask how we might choose to live.

Thus, the project is concerned with 'the sense of the deep connections between content and form' in relation to questions of ethics, through 'the detailed study of complex particular cases'.[12]

In *Love's Knowledge*, Nussbaum supports her argument by close readings of novels, mainly those of Henry James. Following James, she believes that 'the work of the moral imagination is in some manner like the work of the creative imagination'; but this is more than analogy: 'this conception of moral attention and moral vision finds in novels its most appropriate articulation . . . the novel is itself a moral achievement, and the well-lived life is a work of literary art'. Hence, the strong claim that 'certain novels are, irreplaceably, works of moral philosophy . . . the novel can be a paradigm of moral activity'; and,

> certain truths about human life can only be fittingly and accurately stated in the language and forms characteristic of the narrative artist . . . form and style are not incidental features . . . [T]he telling itself – the selection of genre, formal structures, sentences, vocabulary, of the whole manner of addressing the reader's sense of life – all of this expresses a sense of life and of value, a sense of what matters and what does not, of what learning and communication are, of life's relations and connections.[13]

However, like the social theorists, Nussbaum has a particular case to make. Her specific focus on love somewhat limits the applicability of her argument, and it is arguable that her project requires a prior knowledge of those emotions that are recognisable (understandable) through literature. (Similarly, Barbara McGuinness suggests, in response to Rorty's supposition that certain books provoke reactions against cruelty, that 'it is not clear why . . . illustrations of cruelty through the medium of the novel will evoke sympathy rather than inciting further cruelty'.[14])

Much work in 'philosophy and literature' is suggestive, at least by analogy, for connections between politics and literature; and there is actual coincidence of focus, where the philosophy is moral philosophy and where that philosophy is equated with political theory (as is somewhat the case, for example, in Horton's essay). Geoffrey Harpham's summary of 'literature's ethical utilities' makes this clear:

Literature, it is said, articulates goals, instructs people on how to picture and understand human situations, moralizes action by showing its ends, provides models of motivations and a set of character types and decisional models, structures an opportunity for the reader to test his or her capacity for discovering and acknowledging the moral law, holds the mirror up to the community so that it can identify and judge itself, represents negotiations between the community and the individual, engenders a relation between author and reader, promotes explanatory models that help make sense of different situations and that shelter the subject from the threat of the inchoate, fixes the past and so makes possible free action in the future, and models the "unity" that might be desirable in a human life.[15]

(Harpham's own work has a distinct political relevance: ethics as 'the privileged form of commitment to justice', attention to 'the other', the complex interrelationships between freedom, necessity, and obligation, for example.)

There is, then, an ostensibly strong case for assuming that the extensive work in ethics which utilises literary texts is directly relevant for political theory. However, that work from philosophy which has influenced political theory to the extent that it is now common to talk of 'the narrative turn', together with that social theory which has made 'the narrative self' a commonplace of theories of identity and of social action, is not unproblematic; and the hints, analogies or direct transfers from these sources carry with them an accompanying baggage of reservations, criticism, counter-argument which needs to be acknowledged and dealt with. There are potential problems if these sources are transferred directly and unthinkingly into political theory.

All these theorists are inattentive to the full implications of 'narrative' or 'literature', and they tend to ignore the problematic aspects of their chosen term – thus, their ready assumption of a simple sequence beginning–middle–end which can be transferred from stories to human lives and vice versa. As I have already pointed out, the social theorists frequently use narrative as synonymous with 'narrative history of a certain kind' – the quest, for instance. Nussbaum does, of course, pay more attention to literature as such but, as John Horton's essay in this volume suggests, her close reading of texts is prone to ignore the problematic aspects of narrative. And that, as he also points out, raises problems for the integration of literature into political theory. This is the case for all of these recent attempts to take the narrative turn. Claims about narrative are not backed up by any extended discussion of the implications of using that term. There is, for instance, no acknowledgement of the extensive work in narrative theory, or narratology, which examines the complexities of terms such as 'authorship', 'closure', 'sequentiality' or 'narrative unity'. But these are significant questions both in themselves and for the transfer of the concept of narrative into political theory. Thus, for example, questions about authorship or voice – who tells the story – are, for political theory, questions related to authority and legitimacy.

Not only are there 'internal' limitations to these versions of 'the turn to narrative' in social and moral philosophy, however, but there are 'external' problems as well, specific limitations in respect of their relevance for political theory. Most significantly in this context, if this work is to be taken as analogy for, or transferred directly into, political terms, then its predominantly 'individualist' aspect has to be recognised. To transfer work from social theory and moral philosophy directly and unquestioningly into political theory (concentrating so much on its advocacy of literature that its distinctive features *as* philosophy are lost sight of) risks reinforcing that (over)emphasis on the individual that has been widely recognised as a shortcoming of modern liberal political theory. That is, these theorists and philosophers are concerned with (explaining) the actions and behaviour, motives and intentions, of the individual self. Individual ethics are, of course, of central importance to the moral philosopher; moral philosophy does overlap with political theory; and the individual who is, as a moral being, of interest to moral philosophy is also, *inter alia*, a political agent. But political theory is primarily interested in 'the political self', the ways in which the individual behaves within a political context. Individuals acting politically do so in public, and in concert with others, and with widespread and often unforeseeable consequences; and these factors make a difference to their ethical behaviour – as distinct, that is, from their individual behaviour in a private setting, which philosophers such as Nussbaum seek to understand, or from social action, the behaviour of individuals in their social setting which is MacIntyre's concern.

Moral philosophy is concerned with how to live; social theory examines how life is lived; both of these contribute to political understanding but do not fully explain how to live a political life, or how political life is lived – how the political impinges on the individual. In particular, attention to social action or individual ethics does not directly address a problem central to politics, and which political theorists must address, the gap between morality and political necessity. This is the classic Machiavellian dilemma (and in effect a rejoinder to Nussbaum):

> the gulf between how one should live and how one does live is so wide that a man who neglects what is actually done for what should be done learns the way to self-destruction rather than self preservation. The fact is that a man who wants to act virtuously in every way necessarily comes to grief among so many who are not virtuous.[16]

There are complex and continuing issues for political theory here. Choice and responsibility – as a modern commentator on Machiavelli has it,

> There are times when it is necessary to do admittedly evil things for the preservation and welfare of the political community – and if one is not so willing, one is simply stepping outside politics and, incidentally, abandoning it to those who have no scruples.[17]

the culpability of innocence – 'moral innocence consists precisely in the belief that moral goodness does not compromise ... moral innocence can lead to political catastrophe'.[18] The extent to which politics is, in practice, necessarily utilitarian – as another commentator on Machiavelli sharply remarks, 'Let us be clear about one thing: ideals and ethics are important in politics as norms, but they are scarcely effective as techniques.'[19] All these issues are depicted and discussed in literature – but none of them is central to 'ethics and literature' or attention to the narrative self.

'Goodness, therefore, as a consistent way of life, is not only impossible within the confines of the public realm, it is even destructive of it.'[20] Hannah Arendt's version of the Machiavellian dilemma is made in the context of her discussion of the public and the private realm; and to raise the question of *political* action and *political* morality necessarily draws attention to what is distinctive about the 'public realm' – the proper context of political theory. The nature of the public, political, realm is, of course, debatable – as several chapters in this volume, notably Paul Seabright's, make clear. Nevertheless, it is just this distinction which concerns those theorists who take the Machiavellian point. Peter Johnson suggests that, 'The political world is a public world involving public aims and purposes which cannot be reduced to the aims and purposes of private individuals'.[21] There is a 'disanalogy' between public and private which makes questions of character, intention and motive problematic, disrupting the assumptions of ethics and moral philosophy, and putting into question generalisations about 'the narrative self'.

PART II

The public nature of politics and the political carries with it an implication of concerted or collective activity which works against the individualist element in social theory and moral philosophy. Furthermore, apart from the respect in which political activity is necessarily always entered into with others, for any individual, 'in political life actions are not just of significance for the agents who perform them', and '[T]he special responsibility of public affairs lies in the fact that its policies have consequences for the lives and well-being of great numbers of persons unknown to those forming the policies.'[22] Then individualist theories of responsibility, intention and effect are less significant (in this context) than, or have to be reconciled with, concepts such as accountability and justification, prudence and *political* responsibility. The contribution of literature to politics would need to address these conjunctions: and the novel, especially as it focuses on individuals for whom private behaviour and public, political activity is interrelated in the single self, is apt to do just that. That attempt to explain behaviour which leads MacIntyre into talk of narrative, and which is shared by the moral and political philosopher in their interest in how people should live, involves consideration of agents' intentions and motives. And that suggests that the narrative turn should be in the direction of narratives – novels. Novels deal explicitly with questions of intentions, motives and consequences, and make the 'inner workings' of human selves available for theoretical attention.

For Nussbaum, there are certain 'plausible views' about human life that can only be stated in 'a literary narrative of a certain sort'.[23] A more recent argument as to the impossibility of full understanding *without* recourse to literature, treating literary texts as indispensable, more than mere examples, is contained in Bernard Harrison's *Inconvenient Fictions: Literature and the Limits of Theory*. Harrison bases his argument on two assumptions: that serious narrative fiction and its study is essential to the intellectual life of civilised society, and that the goal of serious intellectual life is the acquisition of knowledge.

What literature in general, and narrative fiction in particular deals in is not knowledge as an amenity of the Will, but dangerous knowledge: knowledge the price of whose acquisition is the risk the reader runs of being changed in his or her self by what he or she reads.[24]

(Other literary critics have also argued the case for the indispensability of literature for human understanding, but their work has not, on the whole, fed into the current discussion of 'politics and literature'.[25])

There is, then, a general case for attention to the novel as a source for understanding human behaviour. Beyond this, however, there are more specific reasons why political theory should have regard to narrative fiction, the novel.[26] Interest in narrative identity, and in other usages of 'narrative', in political theory directs attention towards the novel as typical narrative genre. The novel's particular focus on the individual would ostensibly work against political significance. However, there is a sense in which, paradoxically, the novel counters excessive individualism. The novel depicts the individual in relationship with others, and in their social setting, and thus extends interest in individual selves to a potentially political context. Modern political theory is interested in aspects of identity formation – 'the politics of self-formation' as it were, including the extent of choice available to the individual self. This in turn has a bearing on questions of political responsibility. Modern novels suggest the connections between the development of identity and the political realm, the link between self-identity and the taking on of responsibilities, including political responsibility.

Ronald Beiner asserts that,

> we require a mental faculty by which to assimilate the phenomena of the public world and make sense of the stories of what men have done. It is the faculty of judgment that fits us into this world of phenomena and appearances, and makes it possible for us to find our proper place in it.[27]

The faculty of discrimination and judgement is improved by the particular kind of reflection which novels allow. Narrative form has a distinctive characteristic of potential benefit to political theory, that of its capacity for enabling reflection and speculation. Simply put, novels offer something to think about, the occasion for the imaginative contemplation of possibilities, 'seeing the story as an episode around which thought might move and imagination play'.[28] 'Imagination' has too often been a suspect term in political theory;

but as the classic liberal reliance on 'reason' and 'rationality' is increasingly put in doubt, so fictional sources can be taken as valid sources for political theory. There is a connection between thinking about politics and the 'real world' of politics which is mediated via the imagination. Imagination can be expressed though and exercised by literature. There is, then, an interrelationship and movement – political thought – imagination assisted by literature – political life.[29] In that sequence, thought – imagination/understanding – action, novels have much to offer the central term. Novels allow a particular kind of reflection:

> Fiction is imaginative creation, projective thought.... The concreteness of literary images seems to obscure the fundamentally thoughtful character of fiction. Yet it is just the combination of the particularistic, concrete character of the novel's presentation of human life with its inventiveness that enables it to make a distinctive contribution to political thought.[30]

This is somewhat akin to Nussbaum's use of the novel; but political theorists who have recognised this quality in novels have wanted to stress reflection and interpretation rather than direct teaching:

> The literary work, in its evocation of exemplary types, does not offer direct practical injunctions of the form, 'Live your life thus.' Rather, it recommends, 'Reflect on life in the light of these truths about our common situation.'[31]

The question remains, though, as to what would make that process – reading and reflecting on a novel – distinctively political? How does such reflection relate to the 'Machiavellian problem', essentially a concern about how to *act*, how to live the *political* life? Beiner's sense of 'finding a place in the public world' is part of the answer; another part lies in attention to the purpose and outcome of reflection and judgement – judgement about what? The novel allows for reflection and judgement about the making of choices and those choices are, in part and potentially, political.[32]

It might still be objected that 'reading for life', engagement with 'fictional friends' hardly constitutes engagement in politics. As Horton comments, on Nussbaum, 'to put the point too bluntly, being "richly responsive" to a situation in a novel does not require us to *do* anything.'[33] Similarly, McGuinness, commenting on Rorty's view of literature as *alternative* to philosophy, asserts that, 'Redescribing, telling a multiplicity of stories from a variety of views will give us alternatives to choose from. But this is where the novel stops, and the point for political theorists is that we do have to choose . . .'. This apparent limitation on the usefulness of narrative is, I suggest, less restrictive than might appear. Alternatives (in a sense the very stuff of politics, the business of politics as negotiation) are useful in helping political theorists consider how to choose. More importantly, McGuinness's objection is (as she continues) that 'Different narrative techniques . . . will expose and highlight relevant factors but alone will not give us adequate information for action.'[34] But politics is not just a matter of action, but of the processes which issue in that action. Novels assist those processes of thought which are necessary to any but the most instinctive or impulsive decisions to act: they allow understanding which then makes possible the decision to act or not to act.[35] This decision is flawed, or just not possible, if the perception of political choices is clouded – novels can clarify.

PART III

Apart from the enrichment of vocabulary to be gained from fiction – and this is not insignificant given that much political activity is, of course, a matter of words – close reading, of the Nussbaum kind, inasmuch as it encourages reflection is a necessary pre-requisite to action; and inasmuch as it assists judgement, it contributes to *prudential* behaviour (a modern form of responsibility).[36] Or, to put the matter somewhat differently, political action can also be construed as the making of choices and the taking on of political responsibility, for which reflection and judgement are also necessary. The connection between the novel and political action is a mediated one: novels assist thinking prior to (or subsequent to) action.

In presenting choices, and in allowing reflection on those choices, novels offer unique assistance to political theory.[37] As John Schaar has it, 'Nor can we refuse to play the game. Human beings . . . must choose what they will do and be . . . we are free; and our freedom puts us under an imperative of decisions and action.' And as he says, some stories are 'concentrated descriptions' of that imperative. And hence their usefulness to political theory:

> the outcomes of action are unpredictable. Hence the question of
> what the actor is responsible for, and what not, can almost never
> be answered in a thoroughly satisfactory way, but must be the
> subject of endless discussion and meditation. That is in large part
> what accounts of action are all about, and the story form is as
> competent a form of discourse for the discussion of this question

as any of the other forms we have devised (such as law, abstract ethical philosophy, the social sciences, ideology).[38]

Political choices are especially difficult because of unknown consequences – particularly as they result from the public, plural and collective nature of politics. And hence the problem of political morality, the 'Machiavellian' dilemma (and the preponderance of discussion of *Billy Budd* in 'politics and literature'?). Choice requires judgement, and

> the task of judgment at its most acute is situated (sometimes tragically) at the intersection of conflicting and nearly incommensurable moral and political claims: for instance the claims of the local and particular versus those of the general and the universal, the perspective of the involved participant versus that of the detached outsider.[39]

Political choices are not purely 'political' for the persons making the choices. Commenting on the connection between literature and politics in respect of the emotional component of choice, Joel Kassiola says,

> Given the undeniable emotional nature of actual political experience where life and death are often at stake (or at least the quality of life with regard to its most important dimensions), why not extend the literary capabilities of expressing and illuminating human emotions and behavior relevant to political life, especially when human value choices need to be made.[40]

Kassiola's examples indicate the possibilities: the perpetration of acts of political violence in Camus' *The Just Assassins*, for example, or the denial of human dignity and freedom in Alice Walker's *The Color Purple*. Similarly, I have shown how Henry James's *The Princess Casmassima* presents a concern for personal identity, anxiety about conflicting loyalties in the personal sphere, as having political outcomes. Or again, Nadine Gordimer's *A Sport of Nature* depicts a character for whom not only is sexuality a primary force but the choices made on that basis can also be construed as political.[41]

Just as Nussbaum maintains that it is not possible to talk about love in the analytical, diagrammatic, mode of formal philosophy,[42] so the discussion of political choices cannot be restricted to the conventional mode of political theory. Nether literary nor political texts can make a choice for the reader – but there is a question as to where the choices are presented most clearly. Novels are particularly good at showing the necessity of making choices, the psychological pressures on the individuals who face them, the moral dilemmas involved and the consequences of choice, the political effects of reactions to those problems. It is that characteristic which allows for movement from excessive concentration on the individual to the socio-political implications of the behaviour of persons. For instance, as Anthony Arblaster demonstrates by reference to Brian Moore's *Lies of Silence*, many modern novels pose basic questions about human existence, including its political aspects, and depict the dilemmas which make moral *and* political demands on human beings, not least because of the effects of individual choices on other human beings. Novels have the capacity to explore motives and consequences, to show how choices are arrived at and the effects of those choices on individual and community. They depict the moral dilemmas that arise from the working-out of political concepts such as order, authority or rights. And, 'At their most searching, they lead the reader to confront the possibility and even the necessity of having to choose between ethical guidelines appropriate to private relationships and those entailed by responsibility to larger, more public constituencies.'[43]

As I have already suggested, the distinction between personal and political morality lies in part in the imperative, for the individual as political agent, of taking responsibility: leaving things to others is culpable, and innocence is no excuse. There is then a connection between reflection, judgement, choice and responsibility. Simply put, there are choices about identity, about whether to act or not. And *those* choices are connected: the capacity for action depends, to some extent, on self-knowledge. As Schaar has it, 'human beings must choose', and that choice includes what they must *be* as well as what they must do.[44] Novels indicate that self-understanding (and self-trust) is necessary to that understanding and trust of others which is in turn necessary to a developed theory of political responsibility. And novels help to mediate between modernist responsibility to action and postmodernist responsibility to other/otherness, showing the injunction to put oneself in the place of others as not only as a question of 'moral compassion' (as in Nussbaum's work) but *politically* necessary.

PART IV

The narrative turn has much to offer political theory, but, paradoxically, it can offer too much where it implies order and coherence as imposed or achievable through narrative telling. The political theorist can endorse all those functions listed by Harpham but still recognise that they are not exclusive to political theory and do not constitute particular reasons why *political* theorists should take the narrative turn. They suggest, in effect, that reading novels will refine their thinking as philosophers, but only indirectly that it will improve their work as *political* philosophers. Literature then remains an optional extra for political theory, whereas I argue that it is, in the form of the novel, essential for a full discussion of central questions in political theory. There may be political understandings which can only be had from sources outside of political theory as such; what is already known in political theory may be extended and enhanced by sources from outside of itself. In either case, the novel is a necessary complement to theory.

I have suggested that the political theorist should not rely on work in social theory or moral philosophy; but in a sense my reservations are only valid where there is an overemphasis on the moral and/or a neglect of the political. What attention to the novel makes clear is, indeed, the inextricability of the moral and the political. Those political theorists who have already acknowledged the benefit to be gained from literature are aware of the moral dimension of political choices – and vice versa. The political theorist is, as it were, concerned with questions of how one should behave *politically* – the ways in which individuals acting publicly, in conflict or consensus with others, make choices, exercise responsibility. Those questions are also in effect the themes of modern novels, which thus offer assistance to that aspect of political theory which is concerned with formulating an 'ethic of action'.

I have outlined here what I take to be a central argument for using the content of novels as source material for political theory. There are, of course, further possibilities, some of which are inherent in my discussion. Attention to the novel entails attention to form as well as content, always content mediated through form and sometimes form itself as significant. There is, then, a connection to be made between narrative ordering, personal order – identity, and human behaviour understood, *à la* MacIntyre, in narrative terms – and 'order' as a political concept. The suggestions in recent social theory that the construction of identity is a matter of story-telling, implying that a stable, integrated identity depends on telling a coherent story, and that the human capacity for story-telling, specifically related to the construction of identity, also relates to the concept of order, the ordering of one's self and one's place in the world, a political matter, in part at least. Such versions of 'the narrative turn' point strongly towards attention to the *mode* of narrative discourse, to narrative theory and narratology. That, in turn, might cause political theorists to consider how literary devices such as irony or metaphor work in political theory, making overt, and then examining, the rhetorical, 'literary' qualities of political theory texts. Such analysis would complete 'the narrative turn'.

NOTES

1 For example, Peter Johnson, *Politics, Innocence and the Limits of Goodness*, London, Routledge, 1988; Catherine Zuckert, *Natural Right and the American Imagination: Political Philosophy in Novel Form*, Savage, MD, Rowman & Littlefield, 1990; *Reading Political Stories: Representations of Politics in Novels and Pictures*, ed. and with an Introduction by Maureen Whitebrook, Lanham, MD, Rowman & Littlefield, 1992; Maureen Whitebrook, *Real Toads in Imaginary Gardens: Narrative Accounts of Liberalism*, Savage, MD, Rowman & Littlefield, 1995.

2 Richard Rorty, *Contingency, Irony, and Solidarity*, Cambridge, Cambridge University Press, 1989, pp. xv, xvi.

3 Richard Rorty, *Essays on Heidegger and Others: Philosophical Papers 2*, Cambridge, Cambridge University Press, 1991, pp. 73, 78.

4 Alasdair MacIntyre, *After Virtue: a Study in Moral Theory*, second edition, London, Duckworth, 1985, pp. 208, 212, 219 (my emphasis added).

5 Charles Taylor, *Sources of the Self: the Making of the Modern Identity*, Cambridge, Cambridge University Press, 1989, pp. 47, 48, 51–2.

6 Cf. '[T]he word "literature" now covers just about every sort of book which might conceivably have moral relevance . . . The application of the term has nothing to do with the presence of "literary qualities" in a book.' Rorty, *Contingency, Irony and Solidarity*, p. 82.

7 Ibid., p. 141.

8 Richard Rorty, *Objectivity, Relativism and Truth, Philosophical Papers 1*, Cambridge, Cambridge University Press, 1991, p. 135.

9 See *Philosophy and Literature*, Royal Institute of Philosophy Lecture Series 16: Supplement to *Philosophy*, 1983, ed. by A. Phillips Griffiths, Cambridge, Cambridge University Press, 1984, as representative: *Philosophy and Literature* includes the use of literary examples and discussion of their status and literature as a source of philosophical ideas; see also Peter J McCormick, *Fictions, Philosophies and the Problems of Poetics*, Ithaca, NY, Cornell University Press, 1988.

10 Iris Murdoch, 'Against Dryness, a Polemical Sketch', *Encounter*, 16,

1961, pp. 16–21; see also *The Sovereignty of the Good*, London, 1970; *Metaphysics as a Guide to Morals*, London, Chatto & Windus, 1992.

11 Martha C. Nussbaum, *Love's Knowledge: Essays on Philosophy and Literature*, New York, Oxford University Press, 1990, p. ix.

12 Ibid., pp. 288–9.

13 Ibid., p. 5.

14 Barbara McGuinness, 'Narrative and Political Theory' (unpublished paper), presented at the Political Studies Association Annual Conference, Belfast, April 1992; cf. Bernard Harrison's comment that Nussbaum's conception of the cognitive gains to be derived from literature may not 'involve much more than the claim – certainly an entirely sound and reasonable one as far as it goes – that there are some things that we can only come to know about (where "know about" includes access to knowledge of one's own part in and relationship to the things in question) by living through them. To affirm that much is at best to equip literature with a special subject-matter which can only be explored by its means', and 'Even granting the existence of such a subject-matter it still remains unexplained how any cognitive gain can result from the exploration of that subject-matter in a fiction'. Bernard Harrison, *Inconvenient Fictions: Literature and the Limits of Theory*, New Haven, CT, Yale University Press, 1991, p. 15.

15 Geoffrey Galt Harpham, *Getting it Right: Language, Literature and Ethics*, Chicago, The University of Chicago Press, 1992, p. 158.

16 Niccolo Machiavelli, *The Prince*, trans. with an Introduction by George Bull, Harmondsworth, Penguin, 1961, Section XV: 'The things for which men, and especially princes, are praised or blamed' (p. 91).

17 Niccolo Machiavelli, *The Discourses*, ed. and with an Introduction by Bernard Crick, Harmondsworth: Penguin, 1970, Introduction, p. 66.

18 Johnson, *Politics, Innocence and the Limits of Goodness*, p. 3.

19 Niccolo Machiavelli, *The Prince and The Discourses*, with an Introduction by Max Lerner, New York, Random House, 1950, Introduction, p. xliv.

20 Hannah Arendt, *The Human Condition*, Chicago, The University of Chicago Press, 1958, p. 77: though note that 'in the modern world, the distinction has been eroded and the two realms indeed constantly flow into each other' (p. 33); cf. Wolin's notion of 'political space' in Sheldon S. Wolin, *Politics and Vision: Continuity and Innovation in Western Political Thought*, Boston, Little Brown & Company, 1960, pp. 7, 16–17.

21 Johnson, *Politics, Innocence and the Limits of Goodness*, p. 76, and Chapter 3, 'Political Autonomy', *passim*.

22 Ibid., pp. 6, 78.

23 Nussbaum, *Love's Knowledge*, p. 7.

24 Harrison, *Inconvenient Fictions*, p. 4.

25 But see, Wayne Booth, *The Company We Keep: an Ethics of Fiction*, Berkeley, CA, University of California Press, 1988; Milan Kundera, *The Art of the Novel*, New York, Harper & Row, 1988 [1986]; some of the work on the genre of political fiction is also relevant: see especially Michael Wilding, *Political Fictions*, London, Routledge and Kegan Paul, 1980; Robert Boyers, *Atrocity and Amnesia: the Political Novel Since 1945*, Oxford, Oxford University Press, 1985.

26 See Whitebrook, *Real Toads in Imaginary Gardens*, Chapter 2.
27 Ronald Beiner, *Political Judgment*, London, Methuen, 1983, p. 14.
28 John Schaar, *Legitimacy in the Modern State*, New Brunswick, NJ, Transaction Books, 1981, 'The Uses of Literature for the Study of Politics:
   the Case of Melville's *Benito Cereno*', p. 57: Schaar's essay is a good
   example of this in practice; cf. Catherine Zuckert, 'On Reading Classic
   American Novelists as Political Thinkers', *The Journal of Politics*, 43,
   1981, pp. 683–706.
29 Cf. Conor Cruise O'Brien, 'Imagination and Politics' in Conor Cruise
   O'Brien and W. D. Vanech (eds), *Power and Consciousness*, London,
   University of London Press, 1969.
30 Catherine Zuckert, 'The Novel as a Form of American Political
   Thought', in *Reading Political Stories*, p. 139.
31 Ronald Beiner, *What's the Matter with Liberalism?*, Berkeley, CA, University of California Press, 1992, p. 6.
32 These issues are further discussed in Anthony Arblaster's chapter in this
   volume (p. 129).
33 See the essay by John Horton in this volume (p. 70).
34 McGuinness, 'Narrative and Political Theory', p. 20; note that her objection overall is to Rorty's *replacement* of theory by literature; she is of
   course correct in any sense of literature impelling action: there is no
   evidence for the 'Uncle Tom's Cabin' syndrome.
35 Cf. Zuckert's qualification: 'There is an important distinction to be drawn
   between revealing the truth about something and that truth's having an
   effect. The people to whom a novelist shows the truth may not understand; or, the truth may not require any visible change in their action.
   They may simply come to a better, deeper understanding of what they
   do and why.' Zuckert, 'The Novel as a Form of American Political
   Thought', p. 138.
36 Beiner treats judgement as 'a *cognitive* faculty, or a distinct sphere of
   mental activity' *and* 'a *practical* faculty, or what might otherwise be
   called prudence.' Beiner, *Political Judgment*, p. 168, note 5; and cf. John
   Dunn, *Interpreting Political Responsibility: Essays 1981–1989*, Cambridge, Polity Press, 1990, pp. 3–4, and *passim*.
37 'Unique' in respect of their characteristic form: other arts or media can
   also convey political understanding but only the novel – or properly,
   reading a novel – allows for the speculative contemplation of possibilities
   that I am discussing here. For instance, the effects of *seeing* a play are
   different from the individual experience of reading a story; and poetry
   makes a more specific appeal to the emotions and/or uses language in
   a particularly heightened – and hence moving – way.
38 Schaar, *Legitimacy in the Modern State*, p. 79.
39 Beiner, *What's the Matter With Liberalism?*, p. 177.
40 Joel Kassiola, 'Political Values and Literature: The Contribution of Vir-
   tual Experience' in *Reading Political Stories*, p. 59.
41 See Whitebrook, *Real Toads in Imaginary Gardens*, Chapter 5; Maureen
   Whitebrook, 'Choosing Identity: Negotiating Race, Gender and Ethnicity – Nadine Gordimer's Depiction of the Possibilities', (unpublished
   paper), presented at the American Political Science Association Annual
   Meeting, Washington DC, September 1993.

42 Cf. Nussbaum, *Love's Knowledge*, p. 20, no. 33.

43 George Von der Muhll, 'The Political Element in Literature' in *Reading Political Stories*, pp. 31–2.

44 See also, S. L. Goldberg, *Agents and Lives: Moral Thinking in Literature*, Cambridge, Cambridge University Press, 1993, Chapter 2; and cf. 'For a subject to play a role in shaping the contours of its identity requires a certain faculty of reflection. Will alone is not enough. What is required is a certain capacity for self-knowledge, a capacity for . . . agency in the cognitive sense.' Michael Sandel, *Liberalism and the Limits of Justice*, Cambridge, Cambridge University Press, 1982, p. 153.

3 'What of soul was left, I wonder?'

The narrative self in political philosophy

Susan Mendus

There is an 'ancient quarrel' between poetry and philosophy, which began in the fourth century BC when Plato banished (some) artists from his Republic. Artists, on Plato's account, are dealers in lies and half truths. They turn our minds away from the good and towards the corrupt. They appeal to the lowest part of the soul by feeding base emotions which ought properly to be left to wither. Like sophists, they glory in image-making without knowledge and, living in a world of fiction, they blur the distinction between true and false. They are, in brief, subjectivists, relativists, and cynics.

Tout ça change... and modern philosophers also have their doubts about the ability of art to illuminate philosophical problems. R. M. Hare writes:

> It is very easy for a novelist (D. H. Lawrence for example) to depict with great verisimilitude, as if they were everyday occurrences, cases in which the acceptance by society of the traditional principle of, say, fidelity in marriage leads to unhappy results. The public is thus persuaded that the principle ought to be rejected. But in order for such a rejection to be rational, it would have to be the case, not merely that situations *can* occur or be conceived in which the results of the acceptance of the principle are not for the best, but that these situations are common enough to outweigh those others in which they are for the best.[1]

Again, poetry (widely interpreted) deceives by appealing to the emotions aroused in a particular case (to the many rather than the one), whereas philosophy is concerned with the discovery of general principles (the one *in* the many). Moreover, the modern quarrel is not motivated simply by a concern for rationality rather than emotion, but also by the thought that literary examples fail to add anything to the examples which philosophers themselves might advance, or to examples which are available from the real world. A literary example is therefore, and at best, the lazy philosopher's device for drawing attention to a philosophical problem. At worst, it is an instrument of moral seduction.

All this, of course, assumes that philosophy really is a matter of rational evaluation, and that literature really is a matter of emotional seduction. Some philosophers and some literary theorists dissent, claiming that emotion should be a central part of the philosophic enterprise and that rationality is central to the evaluation of literature. Thus, Martha Nussbaum has recently argued that the relationship between style and content is significant, that:

> style itself makes its claims, expresses its own sense of what matters. Literary form is not separable from philosophical content, but is, itself, a part of content – an integral part, then, of the search for and the statement of truth.[2]

By adopting a formal, abstract style, philosophical writing stakes its claim to the priority of the formal and abstract over the emotional and particular. And similarly Michael Fischer denies the contention that literary discourse consists of untrammelled appeal to emotion: literature is not 'imprecise, capricious and methodologically dishevelled'.[3] It too is governed by rules, even if not by scientifically exact rules. These appeals to the need for rationality in literature and sensitivity in philosophy promise an end to the ancient quarrel and the dawn of a new age of harmonious symbiosis between the two old enemies.

Plato and Hare will not, I suspect, be amused – or repentant. They will readily admit that philosophical style stakes its claim to the priority of rationality, but go on to contend that that is precisely because rationality is, or at any rate should be, prior. Lurking beneath the surface of debates about the need for rules in literature and for sensitivity in philosophy lies a deeper disagreement about the aim of philosophy itself. Thus, Richard Rorty tells us that 'the real issue [in the quarrel between poetry and philosophy] is between those who think our culture, or purpose, or intuitions cannot be supported except conversationally, and people who still hope for other sorts of support'.[4] There are those who believe that there is nothing beyond the contingencies of the world, and that therefore the purpose of philosophy is simply to examine those contingencies until finally, and with Wittgenstein, they can say only 'this is where my spade is turned', and there are those who believe that beneath the contingent clutter of the world lies a justification of our moral and political intuitions. They believe that when our spade is turned, it will have 'Truth' or 'Rational Justification' inscribed on it. Ultimately, then, the quarrel is between philosophers who yearn for a justification of moral life in terms of Truth, *Geist* or the Good, and poets who believe that such yearning is in vain.

My starting points in this chapter are two beliefs: first, that the yearning for something beyond ourselves is indeed doomed, and we should renounce it. Second, that the attempt to replace *Geist* or the Good by narrative misconstrues both the nature of political philosophy and the nature of literary discourse. Narrative, I shall argue, does have a role to play in political philosophy, but not the role allocated to it by conversationalists such as Rorty. I shall begin by giving some reasons for thinking that the search for something transcendent is doomed. I shall then go on to voice some reservations about the substitution of narrative for philosophy, and finally I shall present some tentative suggestions as to how we should understand the contribution which narrative can make to political and moral philosophy.[5]

THE SEARCH FOR TRANSCENDENCE

As noted already, Rorty's narrative turn is motivated by scepticism about attempts to find something 'beyond ourselves' which will justify moral and political beliefs. Modern moral and political philosophy are rich in such attempts, and examples of it are to be found in the recent writings of Alasdair MacIntyre and Charles Taylor. In *Sources of the Self*, Taylor has described the modern age as one in which we are driven to look for our values entirely within ourselves, yet also condemned to find those inner meanings inadequate. The 'stripped down' secular outlook cannot, he says, satisfy our longing for the 'incomparably higher', which can be slaked only by appeal to theism. As long as we remain closed to a theistic perspective, we shall find ourselves tied to a narrow subjectivism and, for that reason, the 'potential of a certain theistic perspective is incomparably greater than any purely secularized vision of the moral life'.[6] Similarly, MacIntyre's Thomism answers to a yearning to find something beyond ourselves which can justify our moral and political practices. For MacIntyre, the error of pragmatism lies precisely in its refusal to align the concept of truth with 'something external to one's own particular scheme of concepts and beliefs', specifically in its refusal to subscribe to something like a Thomistic correspondence theory of truth.[7]

These views share a conception of moral and political philosophy which is quite at odds with Rorty's narrative turn: Taylor traces the inadequacy of modern moral and political philosophy to an attempt to investigate what it is right to do without first considering what it is good to be, i.e., without invoking any background assumptions about the character of the Good Life. His 'basic and very interesting criticism of contemporary moral philosophy is that it suffers from a lack of articulacy about these higher goods, and a consequent narrowing of focus which is not merely impoverishing but delusive'.[8] There is, of course, a great deal of dispute about the interpretation of Taylor and about the role of theism within his account. Skinner interprets him as insisting that the impoverishment of moral philosophy will persist unless and until we turn to theism. Taylor retorts that this is not his argument: he does find value in the values of unbelievers, and claims only that appeal to theism provides a 'bedrock' of explanation which is both satisfying and comprehensive. The unbeliever may still yearn for further justifications of moral belief; the believer, equipped with God, has a full and complete explanation.[9] But either way, the contrast with conversational understandings of philosophy is stark, for both Taylor and MacIntyre are ultimately searching for something which Rorty denies is there to be found – namely, a justification beyond ourselves.

These 'transcendent' understandings of philosophy have, of necessity, the defects of their virtues. They promise to satisfy a yearning for something in virtue of which moral and political practices are right, or true, but the promise can only be fulfilled on the assumption that there really is such a thing as Human Nature or The Good For Man, and that that something can be discovered by reflection or revealed by God. Yet such an understanding threatens to lead in the direction of ethnocentrism and oppression, since the statement of what will satisfy 'our' yearning depends crucially on who 'we' are.

Quentin Skinner makes this point in his discussion of Taylor's *Sources of the Self.* He writes:

> For Taylor, therefore, the problem is how to satisfy our craving to converse with the angels, or at least to see ourselves as part of some larger scheme of things. It is striking that ... Taylor never suggests that the answer may lie in putting ourselves in contact with other cultures less contaminated by western individualism and science. He looks for his solutions entirely within the resources of our own civilisation, describing his work as an

attempt to "retrieve" a number of neglected values and thereby "bring the air back again into the half-collapsed lungs of the spirit".[10]

Moreover, this silence about other cultures is not a mere oversight on Taylor's part; it is a necessary concomitant of his search for something beyond ourselves. In so far as he regrets modern philosophy's neglect of what it is good to be, he implies that there *really is* something which it is good to be, and that that something transcends considerations of time and place. Or if not, then his conception of narrative collapses into Rortyian conversationalism and becomes, not a philosophical claim, but an unsubstantiated generalisation about modern psychology.

One problem, therefore, with the attempt to attain transcendence is that, even when (as in MacIntyre and Taylor) it has a conversational flavour, it nevertheless tends to homogenise by its covert assumption of a single Good for Man. In doing this, it threatens to ignore many of the most pressing problems of modern moral and political life – problems which derive precisely from the conflict of cultures, the fragmentation of individual identity or the difficulties inherent in the construction of female identity – problems which arise precisely because there is no specification of who 'we' are, or what 'we' are yearning for.

Skinner's proposed remedy for the problems encountered by Taylor's theory is that we 'put ourselves in contact with other cultures less contaminated by western individualism and science'. And this is, of course, a remedy most enthusiastically embraced by those, such as Rorty, who favour a rejection of transcendent explanations – for those who believe that 'our culture or purpose or institutions cannot be supported except conversationally'. On Rorty's account, philosophical conversation, like literary discourse, succeeds 'without argument. It succeeds simply by its success.' In the context of political philosophy, this issues in the conclusion that moral communities cannot be judged against 'the moral law itself', but since they must be judged somehow, they are to be judged via the conversation of mankind which (it is held) will enable us to distinguish between better and worse communities. Rorty writes:

> The view I am offering says that there is such a thing as moral progress, and that this progress is indeed in the direction of greater human solidarity. But that solidarity is not thought of as a recognition of a core self, the human essence, in all human beings. Rather, it is thought of as the ability to see more and

more traditional differences (of tribe, religion, race, customs and the like) as unimportant when compared with similarities such as pain and humiliation – the ability to think of people wildly different from ourselves as included in the range of 'us'. Detailed descriptions of particular varieties of pain and humiliation (e.g. in novels or ethnographies), rather than philosophical or religious treatises, [are] the modern intellectual's principal contributions to moral progress.[11]

The differences between Rorty's narrative account and Taylor's transcendent account appear vast: where Rorty sees the search for something beyond ourselves (*Geist* or the Good) as doomed to failure, Taylor sees it as an insatiable longing which must (somehow) be satisfied. Where Rorty takes the facts of cultural and racial disharmony as his starting point, Taylor neglects these issues almost entirely, assuming that 'we' are easily identifiable. And where Rorty insists that success can be understood only conversationally, Taylor insists that success requires the discovery of bedrock or complete explanation 'beyond ourselves'.

Each account trails its own problems in its wake: Taylor's explanation provides direction for our enquiries, but the direction threatens to be one way for everybody. Thus, he fails to address problems which arise from the fact that in the modern world 'we' may lack a single denotation. By contrast, Rorty's account acknowledges, indeed begins with, the problem that 'we' has no single denotation, but fails to provide direction for moral enquiry. In the end, there is simply the bald statement that, like literary discourse, philosophical discourse 'succeeds because it succeeds', and this leaves questions about what counts as success unanswered. To return to the language of the 'ancient quarrel', 'philosophers' (like Taylor) who assume that there is something which it is good to be, end up underestimating the facts of diversity, and the intransigence of modern political problems, such as problems of fragmentation and diversity. By contrast, 'poets' (like Rorty) recognise such diversity, but must strike an attitude of ungrounded optimism if they are to guard against the possibility that conversation will lead in the direction of less, rather than more, solidarity. Ultimately, Rorty is left with only the criterion of stability by which to judge diverse communities, and we do not have to look very far in order to find stable communities which condone slavery, the subordination of ethnic groups and the suppression of dissenters. Indeed, it is no accident that such societies are to be found, since their repressive practices are adopted precisely in order to retain stability and, conversely, the threat to stability is the price an 'open' society pays for its openness.[12]

These two theories therefore pull in different directions and give different priority to the facts of human difference. To revert again to the language of the ancient quarrel, there appears to be no Archimedean point between the claim that philosophy has a privileged position in virtue of its ability to excavate and articulate what, beneath the clutter and confusion of contingent circumstance, we essentially are; and the claim that philosophy is vanquished by literature in virtue of the fact that, beneath the clutter and confusion of contingent circumstance, there is nothing which we essentially are. The former account threatens to provide us all with a male, Western, liberal self; the latter threatens to provide us with no self at all and, most worryingly, with no guidance as to how we might go about constructing such a self.

I want now to suggest some ways in which appeal to narrative may help us to achieve that Archimedean point. This task will involve drawing attention to the precise ways in which literary discourse can be both seductive and instructive. *Pace* Rorty, I shall argue that it is instructive *not* because it is conversational, but because it is rule-governed. *Pace* the 'philosophers', it is seductive and (potentially) misleading, *not* because it is cluttered up and contingent, but because, however rich and detailed it may be, it still has a tendency to oversimplify.

THE NARRATIVE TURN

The claim that narrative is seductive (rather than instructive) because it oversimplifies might be thought to be an implausible one: as we have seen, the standard philosophical charge made against narrative is precisely the reverse – that it confuses principle by its emphasis on contingent clutter and extraneous detail. Nevertheless, there are important ways in which narrative, despite its attention to detail, still oversimplifies. One obvious way is that narratives present the moral and political world 'pre-packaged'; the authority of the text imposes on the reader an understanding of what the moral or political problem is, and a largely shared interpretation of examples which permits only those disagreements for which there is textual warrant. Thus, for example, it is inappropriate to ask whether Raskolnikov was mistaken in thinking that he had murdered Alyona Ivanova, who survived his assault and was finished off by someone else. The text rules out this possibility and renders the thought of it faintly comic.

In life, however, things are not so certain and there may be difficulties both in identifying what the problems are and in deciding what is the appropriate action to take in response to them. Onora O'Neill refers to these differences as ways in which literature imposes a spectator perspective, and she notes that that imposition is not without costs when we attempt to transfer the literary perspective to a moral or political context. She writes:

> Literary examples may be of the greatest importance in moral development and education: but the Wittgensteinian claim that moral thought can be 'reduced to looking at particular examples and seeing what we do want to say about them' excludes elements which are indispensable if moral thought is to be not just a spectator sport but a guide to action.[13]

Chief amongst the elements excluded is the decision as to what kind of moral or political problem we have before us: in literature that question has at least the form of an answer from within the text itself. In life, that is not always so, and much of the difficulty of moral life is consequent upon the struggle to categorise the kind of situation we find ourselves in; we need to know not only what we want to say about the literary case before us, but also whether and to what extent the political dilemma in which we find ourselves in the real world is relevantly similar to the literary example. And obviously, the example itself cannot provide an answer to that question.

Much more could be said about this feature of the case, but I want to concentrate here on a rather different assumption made by supporters of the narrative turn, one which does not emphasise the relationship between specific narratives on the one hand, and moral and political problems on the other, but which emphasises the general aim of the narrative turn. Rorty's claim is that by employing narrative in place of philosophy we may more readily be able to encourage the development of solidarity between apparently different people. Distancing himself from the arguments of 'philosophers', he denies that rationality, appeal to the Good for Man, or to *Geist*, can enable us to discover something which is common to us all. Nevertheless, human difference remains a problem which stands in need of a solution. Solidarity cannot be discovered by reflection, but it can be created by imagination. He therefore concurs with his adversaries at least in this – that lack of unity is the problem in political life, and the creation (if not the discovery) of unity must therefore be the solution. To this extent, Rorty himself is on the side of the philosophers because, like them, he searches for the one in the many. He writes:

> Solidarity is not discovered by reflection, but created. It is created by increasing our sensitivity to the particular details of the pain and humiliation of other, unfamiliar sorts of people. Such increased sensitivity makes it more difficult to marginalize people different from ourselves by thinking 'They do not feel it as *we* would' . . . This process of coming to see other human beings as 'one of us' rather than of 'them' is a matter of detailed description of what other people are like and of redescription of what we ourselves are like. This is a task not for theory, but for genres such as ethnography, the journalist's report, the comic book, the docudrama, and, especially, the novel.[14]

And he goes on to cite cases in which the detail and textual richness of the novel has been a vehicle of moral progress and has enabled the reader to see others as similar rather than as alien creatures. But it may be that even in this, the narrative turn deceives. We may wonder how much, for Rorty, hangs on the moral goodness of the particular novel under consideration and on its ability to deliver exactly the right kind of moral message. If narrative is to be consistent with moral progress and the novelist is to be a kind of moral missionary, then how are we to know when the missionary has 'gone native'? How, even, are we to decide who is the missionary and who the native? Connectedly, it may be that the problems of political life are not to be addressed either by discovering or by creating similarities between different people, but rather by learning to live with the fact that often there are no such similarities.

In his autobiographical account of India, James Cameron writes:

> [In Hinduism] it is the *dharma* of the wind to blow, and that of the rain to fall; it is the *dharma* of a stone to be hard and of a leaf to be soft. It is likewise the *dharma* of a Brahmin to be respected, and that of a sweeper to be despised. There is no getting away from it. The sacred Bhagavadgita, which cannot properly be questioned, says: 'Even should one's *dharma* seem to be mad, its performance brings blessing more than the assumption and pursuit of another's *dharma*'. This age-old and barbaric philosophy maintained the debased Indian victims in the

gutter ... [it is] why India remains basically a country of the
hungry and unhappy.[15]

As Cameron's final commentary implies, this does not mean that
since 'they' are different from 'us', their suffering does not matter.
But it does raise questions about what grounds the belief that, when
we have held the conversation advocated by Rorty, the result will
be an increase in similarity between them and us. Might it not
rather be that we will be yet more acutely aware of differences? Of
course, I do not mean to imply by this that one should be indifferent
to the suffering of others who are not like us, nor that one should
conclude that, since they are different, their suffering does not
matter. Indeed, it is one of the less honest features of Rorty's
account that he tries to force upon us a choice between seeing
others as like ourselves and concluding that their suffering does not
matter. This is not necessarily the choice, and it may be more honest
to concede that the suffering of those who are not like us has a
different significance. Or even that what counts as suffering is different – that pain and humiliation, like everything else in Rorty's
scheme of things, do not hang free of cultural considerations.

In brief, then, the move to narrative may serve to oversimplify in
two ways: by ignoring the difficulties inherent in identifying a moral
or political problem as a problem similar to that provided by the
text and by assuming (without warrant) that the result of literary
discourse will be to increase the similarities between otherwise different people.

The above considerations lead to the suggestion that, far from
being valuable in virtue of enabling us to create or discover similarities, it might be that narrative is important for its ability to enable
us to recognise differences between people. More importantly, it
may be valuable for its ability to enable us to recognise the intract-
ability of problems arising from difference. On this account, difference is not something to be eliminated, but something to be
recognised and (where possible) accommodated.

But this insistence on the ineliminability of difference might suggest that, after all, there is no escape from a cultural relativism
according to which we can do no more than recognise others as
alien. In the language of Wittgenstein, we can acknowledge different
forms of life and different language games, but we have no way of
breaking into those language games. Earlier in the chapter I referred
to the difference between poets and philosophers as a difference
between two conceptions of the task of political philosophy: there

are those (the poets) who hold that political philosophy serves only to interpret and there are those who insist that political philosophy serves to provide foundations for our beliefs. But, it might be said, either there are such foundations, or there are not; either there is something transcendent which justifies political practices or there is simply the recognition that in the end all is contingent and accidental. The Archimedean point between these two conceptions is in fact a chimera. In what remains of the chapter I shall try to explain how the Archimedean point can be attained, and also to say something about the importance of attaining it. My claim here will be that the narrative turn can assist in the enterprise, but that, *pace* Rorty, it is the fact that literary discourse is rule-governed which provides the route to the Archimedean point.

The claim that literary discourse is rule-governed is one which Rorty strenuously denies, and he yokes this claim to his rejection of truth or right answers. Thus, it is the rejection of rules and the concentration on detail and specificity which enables the novelist to persuade us of the essential relativity of things human – of the absence of the Supreme Judge. Quoting Milan Kundera, he says;

> Man desires a world where good and evil can be clearly distinguished, for he has an innate and irrepressible desire to judge before he understands. Religions and ideologies are founded on this desire . . . They require that somebody be right: either Anna Karenina is the victim of a narrow-minded tyrant, or Karenin is the victim of an immoral woman . . . This either-or encapsulates an inability to tolerate the essential relativity of things human.[16]

By contrast, he urges, there is no overarching truth, everything is detail, contingency and accident. It should be noted immediately that this conception of literary discourse is itself highly controversial. The contention that Dickens is 'all fragments, all details' and that he wants nothing more than that people should recognise each others' suffering is both disputable and disputed. Lionel Trilling interprets Dickens' *Bleak House* as 'about society in relation to the individual human will' (not a matter of detail at all, but one of sweeping generality). And more recently, Stein Haugom Olesen has argued that in the evaluation of literary texts there is an important distinction between topical thematic concepts (those which define problems of interest to a group of people), and perennial thematic concepts (those which constitute the 'fingerprints of a culture' and which define 'mortal questions', questions about how to understand mortal life and how to live it). What characterises the great novelist, on Oleson's account, is precisely the ability to move beyond local and parochial concerns to the general question of how to lead one's life.[17] The Supreme Judge, banished by Rorty the philosopher, is soon reinstated by Oleson the literary critic. So the charge against Rorty is that he purchases the victory of poetry over philosophy by robbing the former of its seriousness and cognitive power. For him, literature doesn't become more important than philosophy; philosophy becomes just as trivial and capricious as literature.

However, beyond this somewhat ironic rear-guard action on the part of literary critics in defence of the 'philosophical' status of their own discipline, lies a further point – that, whilst insisting that literary discourse is all fragment and detail, Rorty nevertheless urges that 'what the novelist finds most heroic is not the ability sternly to reject all descriptions save one, but rather the ability to move back and forth between them'.[18] What is involved in this 'moving back and forth' and what help can it be to us in elucidating the role of political philosophy?

First, and as has already been noted, the very categorisation of some action or event under a description itself requires reflection and judgement. It involves not only fragment and detail, but the identification of detail *under* that description. Moreover, descriptions themselves carry their own conceptual and ideological baggage with them. Thus, for example, the conventions which govern the genres of romantic fiction and of detective fiction assume a specific understanding of women's proper place in the world, and this is why it has been so difficult for feminist writers to construct feminist fictions within those genres.[19] More generally, recent attempts to subvert the genres in question have revealed the extent to which novels do not consist simply in the open display of alternative descriptions; rather, there are limits on the alternative descriptions available. *Pace* Rorty, beneath the multiplicity of discourse within the novel lies an assumption about what human beings really are. In the specific cases of romantic and detective fiction, these include assumptions about what women really are (and also, of course, about what 'real men' are), but the point may be generalised to cover other literary forms.

Rorty makes much of the possibility that, by reading novels and entering into conversations, we may come to see others as more like ourselves. And he argues that, in consequence, we will be less likely to behave cruelly towards them or to pretend that their suffering does not matter. But this assertion risks both condescension and a mislocation of the importance of narrative: condescension, because it implies that we can only recognise others' suffering if, via conversation, we can come to see them as 'like us'; mislocation because it takes no account of the assumptions which underpin the very construction of narrative.

Nevertheless, it is the constricting and rule-governed nature of literary discourse which provides a clue to its ability to inform moral and political discourse. I have noted that narrative (unlike life) presents problems under a description, and that literary discourse generally is rule-governed in a way which dictates which descriptions are apposite. The contention that we may use narrative to increase sensitivity towards others is therefore appropriate only in so far as those others can accurately be described within the rules of narrative itself. But they cannot always be so described. For example, the novel's traditional insistence on the importance of individual character makes it ill-suited to describe a culture or ideology in which individuality matters less than it does in Western liberal democracies. And it is significant that novels such as *Germinal* or *The Ragged Trousered Philanthropist*, which attempt to question the supremacy of the individual, are not usually seen as great works of literature.[20] In this respect, the novel is not the obvious vehicle for questioning different ideologies, since it is not itself wholly independent of ideology.

What, then, are the reasons for thinking that the rule-governed nature of narrative may nevertheless enable us to discover an Archimedean point between transcendent Truth and cultural relativism? In *A theory of Justice* John Rawls appeals to the importance of 'moving back and forth' in proposing his device of reflective equilibrium. He says; 'the best account of a person's sense of justice is not the one which fits his judgements prior to his examining any conception of justice, but rather the one which matches his judgements in reflective equilibrium'.[21] Rorty's call for a movement back and forth between descriptions in narrative echoes Rawls's call for a movement back and forth between judgements in philosophy. What I am suggesting is that there may be a similar value in movement back and forth between literary and philosophical theory. There may be an equilibrium which results from the interplay of the descriptions contained within the narrative and the principles or rules which make that description plausible or acceptable. Here, what is significant is precisely the fact that narrative is not all detail and fragment. Like the philosophers, the poets too present a version of what human beings are like: they frequently advance (however covertly) a specific and contestable conception of the self. Thus, it would be the role of narrative to provide descriptions, and the role of philosophical theory to expose the conceptions of human nature which are presupposed by those descriptions, to consider what this set of descriptions includes and what it cannot include.

In the ancient quarrel between poetry and philosophy, the philosopher has been understood as one who searches after Truth, and the poet as one who recognises that beneath the contingency of life there is no Truth. What I am suggesting is that in this quarrel the narrative turn may be both seductive and instructive, but not in the ways traditionally supposed. Narrative is seductive, not because it turns our attention to detail but because it oversimplifies. It is instructive, not because it has no rules but because it is rule governed. By acknowledging the rules under which specific narratives operate, we may see that, far from ridding us of an objectionable essentialism, they in fact threaten to replace one kind of essentialism with another – an essentialism which consists in the belief that we must come to see others as like ourselves if we are to have any chance of behaving decently in the world.[22] But attention to the rule-governed nature of literary discourse may enable us to see that others are unlike us – that they do not conform to the rules, or that the rules exclude them altogether.

There are two familiar responses to this, but ultimately they involve the same mistake: with Taylor and the philosophers we may conclude that a 'soul' can be discovered, or with Rorty and the poets we may conclude that a 'soul' may be invented. But this choice, the choice between a good independent of us and a good which we may create through increased solidarity, is false. Our problem is not to live with others by coming to see them as like us. Our problem is to live with others despite the fact that they are not like us. Here, the notion of moving back and forth between literature and philosophy is at its most instructive: the philosopher's search for Truth, *Geist*, or the Good reflects an anxiety about the exclusion which may occur if we concentrate on detail; the poet's emphasis on particularity notes the temptation to suppose that there is a single answer to problems of diversity. Philosophy therefore must draw attention to the theory which underpins even the detail of the novel, and the novelist must draw attention to the divergence which is masked by the generality of philosophical theory. The poet asks what we can imagine and the philosopher indicates that the 'we' who do the imagining are a certain sort of people.

Rorty urges that we redescribe both intellectual and moral progress by 'substituting metaphors of evolutionary development for metaphors of progressively less distorted perception'.[23] But the arguments adduced above suggest that perhaps it is a matter of wider, rather than less distorted perception: not perception which conforms with reality (or not) but perception which includes more within its compass. Seeing more will involve *both* literary attention to detail (the text may indeed enhance sympathy by its description of detail) *and* philosophical frameworks (the recognition that we cannot see at all unless we have concepts under which to bring our perceptions). This metaphor of seeing of course retains the assumption that there really are things to see, and possibly for that reason it will not commend itself to Rorty. On the other hand, it also includes the contention that what we see is determined by our own conceptual framework as much as it is determined by what is 'really' there. In one sense, there must be things which are really there in order for us to see them, but in another sense, our seeing *them*, rather than other things, is a function of our own conceptual scheme.

This relationship between perception and reflection in the case of the external world is paralleled by the relationship between poetry and philosophy in the ancient quarrel: the poet draws our attention to things which are really there, and the philosopher draws our attention to the conceptual scheme which enables us to see them. Thus, Rorty the poet draws our attention to the detail which denies that there is any such thing as an Essential Core, a Soul, or What Human Beings Really Are. But Rorty the philosopher should also be alert to the conceptual scheme which dictates that pain and humiliation are universal harms. In prioritising pain and humiliation he suggests that there is, after all, something which we really are – and that that thing is damaged by humiliation. His evolutionary metaphor suggests that we may improve by inflicting less humiliation, but the metaphor of wider vision suggests that humiliation itself is part of the philosopher's conceptual scheme. What counts as humiliation may differ from one society to another: we should be alert, therefore, to the possibility of inadvertently humiliating others. Moreover, even humiliation presupposes that there is someone there to be humiliated, and therefore we should be alert to the possibility that our conceptual scheme (in so far as it is only *our* conceptual scheme) itself humiliates by, for example, excluding women or conceptualising them in a certain way.

My question was 'What of soul was left, I wonder?' and my answer is 'not very much'. In the end, both the philosopher and the poet assume that a soul must be either created or discovered by, respectively, appeal to a good which exists independent of us or the creation of solidarity by conversational success. The yearning for soul cannot be satisfied, yet, as we have seen, it persists in both poet and philosopher. When philosophy and poetry are assigned their separate tasks, the poet (*à la* Rorty) will direct our attention to the forms which pain and humiliation may take; the philosopher (and this too is Rorty) should direct our attention to the fact that it is a specific conceptual and philosophical scheme which determines both that pain and humiliation are bad and that some things rather than others count as pain and humiliation. The equilibrium between detail and theory, or between perception and reflection, may enable us to adopt a narrative turn without prematurely announcing the death of philosophy itself.

NOTES

1 R. M. Hare, *Moral Thinking*, Oxford, University Press, 1981, p. 48.
2 Martha Craven Nussbaum, *Love's Knowledge: Essays on Philosophy and Literature*, Oxford, Oxford University Press, 1990, p. 3. Nussbaum's views are discussed in detail in John Horton's contribution to this volume.
3 Michael Fischer, 'Redefining Philosophy as Literature: Richard Rorty's "Defence" of Literary Culture' in Alan Malachowski (ed.), *Reading Rorty*, Oxford, Blackwell, 1990, pp. 233–43.
4 Richard Rorty, *Consequences of Pragmatism*, Brighton, Harvester, 1982, p. 167.
5 Some further problems with the 'narrative turn' are discussed by Maureen Whitebrook in her contribution to this volume.
6 Charles Taylor, *Sources of the Self*, Cambridge, Cambridge University Press, 1989, p. 518.
7 Alasdair MacIntyre, *Whose Justice? Which Rationality?*, London, Duckworth, 1988, p. 170.
8 Quentin Skinner, 'Who are "We"? Ambiguities of the Modern Self', in *Inquiry*, vol. 34, no. 2, June, 1991, p. 137.
9 Charles Taylor, 'Comments and Replies', in *Inquiry*, vol. 34, no. 2, pp. 237–54.
10 Quentin Skinner, 'Who are "We"? Ambiguities of the Modern Self', p. 146.
11 Richard Rorty, *Contingency, Irony and Solidarity*, Cambridge, University Press, 1989, p. 192.
12 This point is made forcefully by Martin Hollis in 'The Poetics of Personhood', in Malachowski *Reading Rorty*, pp. 244–56.
13 Onora O'Neill, 'The Power of Example', in *Philosophy*, vol. 61, no. 235, January 1986, p. 18.
14 Richard Rorty, *Contingency, Irony and Solidarity*, p. xvi.
15 James Cameron, *An Indian Summer*, London, Penguin, 1987, p. 42.
16 Richard Rorty, *Essays on Heidegger and Others: Philosophical Papers*, Volume, 2, Cambridge, Cambridge University Press, 1991, pp. 75–6.
17 Stein Haugom Oleson, 'Thematic Concepts: Where Philosophy Meets Literature' in A. Phillips Griffiths (ed.), *Philosophy and Literature*, Royal

Institute of Philosophy Lecture Series, 16, Supplement to *Philosophy*, 1983, pp. 75–93.

18 Richard Rorty, *Essays on Heidegger and Others*, p. 74.

19 For an extended discussion of this point see Anne Cranny Frances, *Feminist Fiction*, Oxford and Cambridge, Polity, 1990, especially pp. 193–208.

20 For more on this see Roger Webster, *Studying Literary Theory*, London, Edward Arnold, 1990, Chapter 4, 'Society and the Individual'.

21 John Rawls, *A Theory of Justice*, Oxford, Clarendon, 1971, p. 48.

22 Jean Grimshaw makes reference to the covert essentialism in Rorty in her editorial discussion of his 1990 Tanner Lecture in *Radical Philosophy*, vol. 59, Autumn 1991, p. 1.

23 Richard Rorty, 'Feminism and Pragmatism', Tanner Lecture, 1990, as published in *Radical Philosophy*, vol. 59, Autumn, 1991, p. 4.

4 Life, literature and ethical theory
Martha Nussbaum on the role of the literary imagination in ethical thought

John Horton

Many people, including some philosophers, when they read one of the great novels often have the feeling that it has something of 'philosophical' importance to communicate. Many such novels seem to speak, and some profoundly, about questions concerning the nature of human experience, and in particular what might loosely be called 'ethical questions'.[1] It is not that, generally speaking, novels tell us how to live, how society should be organised or what is right or wrong, though a few purport to; but that they in some way deepen, broaden or challenge our sense of the ethical and its place in our lives. One might, therefore, expect that there would be a close relationship between such works of literature and philosophical enquiry, and perhaps especially ethics. Yet, not only is this not the case but the two forms of writing and thinking seem curiously resistant to each other.

Novelists and literary critics are frequently suspicious of philosophical abstraction, and inclined to see anything resembling philosophy as an alien intrusion into the aesthetic imperatives of imaginative literature. Philosophers typically see novels and other fictions as at best providing vivid illustrations of moral maxims or rules independently arrived at or justified, and which may have a moderately useful role in moral education. From the philosophical point of view novels are often viewed as unnecessarily complicating moral theorising or as a seductive form of dangerous special pleading.[2] Nor is this mutual wariness between the practitioners and advocates of philosophy and imaginative literature (including drama, poetry and fiction) of recent origin – entirely explicable as merely another manifestation of the division of labour and increasing specialisation of modern life. Although it has become more marked in the modern world, it is an antagonism which seems to have emerged with the very beginnings of philosophy as a form of systematic enquiry, in the 'ancient quarrel' between poets and philosophers referred to by Plato in his *Republic*.[3]

My purpose is to undertake a preliminary exploration of some dimensions of this 'ancient quarrel' in a modern context, and to consider one particular attempt to incorporate imaginative literature into ethical enquiry. One concern will be to try to identify some of the difficulties which lie in the way of any attempted philosophical appropriation of the form or content of literature, and in particular literary narratives. This is not because I am sceptical or hostile to such an endeavour, quite the reverse. As is suggested towards the end of the chapter, I am convinced that the enrichment of philosophical argument by literary narratives is essential to remedying some of the inadequacies of much modern moral and political theorising. These inadequacies are both substantive and stylistic; indeed, I shall shortly recount an argument according to which there is an intimate connection between the form in which modern moral and political philosophy most commonly expresses itself (the abstract argumentative treatise) and its content (the exclusive and narrow concern with general rules and abstract principles). But, if any *rapprochement* between philosophy and literature is to be rewarding, then a number of important questions need to be addressed. My main aim will not be to answer these questions so much as to identify some of the more important of them.

I shall limit my discussion to ethics, including social and political philosophy, though this is not the only area of philosophy to which literature can contribute. It may also illuminate questions about freewill, personal identity, our knowledge of other minds and a whole range of metaphysical issues; even if there are more technical aspects of philosophy, most obviously formal logic, to which literature seems to have little relevance. However, it is with respect to moral and political theory that the lack of engagement between literature and philosophy is most surprising and its remedy potentially most fruitful. Moreover, I shall concentrate on narrative fiction when discussing literature, though much of what I say is also relevant, *mutatis mutandis*, to plays, poems, films and perhaps other ways of expressing the artistic imagination. Although I shall often write of novels without any qualification, it is important to recognise the immense diversity of the novel form and the fact that some novels cannot properly be understood as *narrative* fictions at all.

Before proceeding, however, there are a number of preliminary points worth noting. First, there are those for whom this entire project will seem misconceived. Potential objections may be various but among them is likely to be the argument that literature or the aesthetic, on the one hand, and philosophy, on the other, represent categorically distinct forms of cognition or modes of experience.[4] There is *some* truth in this claim, and it is certainly not my intention to suggest that literature and philosophy should simply be assimilated, or that one is reducible to the other, or that they necessarily have the same purposes. Indeed, the argument that there are fruitful connections between them is not only consistent with acknowledging differences but depends in part upon a recognition that they are substantially separate and distinct (though this is not to preclude the possibility of hybrid forms). However, the argument does reject that kind of conceptual purism according to which types of discourse exist as entirely self-enclosed and between which there can be no intelligible interaction or communication.

Moreover, and this is my second point, one should not understate the extent to which there has been some mutual influence between literature and philosophy. Just as some novelists have employed philosophical ideas in their novels, so some philosophers have used novels for philosophical purposes, including the use of fictional forms to express their philosophy. It is pointless to ask whether, for example, Sartre's *Nausea* or Ayn Rand's *The Fountainhead* is really a work of fiction or a work of philosophy, as if they could only be one or the other. It is interesting, however, that these works tend to be viewed with suspicion by both literary critics and philosophers, and that it seems to be widely, though not universally, agreed that they are not very successful as either novels or philosophy. My concern though is not principally with something which might be called 'the philosophical novel' in which a writer consciously tries to express a philosophy in fictional form, it is rather with a wide range of narrative fictions and their relevance to ethical reasoning and theorising.[5]

Finally, I shall not take as the focus of my discussion those philosophers such as Alasdair MacIntyre, Charles Taylor and Richard Rorty most closely associated with what has been called 'the narrative turn' in recent moral and political theory.[6] One reason for this is that, with the partial exception of MacIntyre, all three, despite their many differences are united by a surprising naivety in their treatment of literature. Although, for example, MacIntyre has some important things to say about the role of narrative and story-telling and Rorty makes some interesting claims about the edifying function of novels, none of them systematically address questions about how and why specifically fictional narratives should be integrated into our moral and political theorising; certainly none of them make any very serious attempt to address the problems to which such a project gives rise. Instead I shall look at some of the work of a philosopher who has attempted to define a specific role for literature within ethical theorising, Martha Nussbaum, and especially at her recent impressive collection of essays, *Love's Knowledge*.[7]

It is perhaps appropriate to note that this book comprises 15 distinct and separately published essays, but in no sense is the volume merely a miscellaneous collection of the authors' occasional writings masquerading as a book. It consists of a connected series of intelligent and thoughtful discussions of the relationship between philosophy and literature, and especially of how literature makes an essential contribution to an adequate ethical understanding. It is also something of a sequel to Nussbaum's earlier work, *The Fragility of Goodness*, to which it makes frequent reference.[8] The principal relevance of the earlier book, and a number of subsequent papers not included in *Love's Knowledge*, to my enquiry is that they provide a much fuller account of her Aristotelian conception of ethics within which literary narratives have their place.[9] Although it will be impossible to consider this conception in any detail, I shall have cause to return to it later.

While *Love's Knowledge* has a genuine unity of concerns, however, it is largely resistant to straightforward summary. In part this is because of the essay form; in part it is because of qualifications and elaborations of the author's views in the decade during which the essays were written; but most importantly it is because of the close connection which Nussbaum herself argues must obtain between form and content in writing about ethics. Moral philosophy needs to be more sensitive to the context and particulars of ethical reasoning and deliberation than is commonly the case, and part of this sensitivity needs to be reflected in the way in which ethical issues are discussed.

> Style itself makes its claim, expresses its own sense of what matters. Literary form is not separable from philosophical content, but is, itself, a part of content – an integral part, then, of the search for and the statement of truth. (p. 3)

Nussbaum's own practice is, quite properly, an exemplification of this claim, and since she is an admirer of Proust and the later novels of Henry James we should expect some of the writing to be complex and extremely difficult. In fact, she writes more accessibly than either of them, and though her prose is often dense it is mostly marked by a refined and delicate lucidity. She generally presents her arguments through careful and searching commentaries on specific novels – in particular *The Ambassadors, The Golden Bowl, The Princess Casamassima, A la Recherche du temps perdu, Malone* and *David Copperfield* – or through reflections on themes derived from classical Greek sources – primarily Aristotle and Plato. My focus will be specifically on those essays which concern the role of the literary imagination in ethical thought.

Nussbaum clearly has strong views about recent moral theorising but she rarely directly engages with it. Her approach tends to be more oblique. Furthermore, apart from a few passing references, mostly to Cavell, she does not seriously discuss any work on philosophical style, such as that of Berel Lang, nor any of the attempts which have been made within recent philosophy to use literature to enrich our moral understanding – Peter Winch, for example, surely one of the most interesting, is never mentioned.[10] Nor does she consider the phenomenological or existentialist traditions which have often shown a much more sustained philosophical interest in literature than the Anglo-American analytical tradition.[11] Nussbaum is in fact slightly less of a lone voice than one might infer from her book. But, more importantly, her failure to engage explicitly and directly with contemporary moral philosophy sometimes leaves the import of her argument less clear than it need be. In particular, it is unclear precisely how deep her implied critique of much modern moral philosophy really goes, and how a suitably reformed ethical theorising should be conducted. Sometimes she seems to advance a fairly radical argument which suggests that fundamental change is required in both the form and content of moral theorising, but at others she seems to step back from this and suggest a more modest, essentially supplementary, role for literature which requires only moderate reform and which might be broadly accommodated within present practice.[12]

Nussbaum herself, following Michael Tanner, quotes a good example of the kind of writing which, perhaps in less extreme forms, is all too characteristic of the style of modern philosophy which she is concerned to challenge. The passage comes from W. Newton-Smith's aptly entitled 'A Conceptual Investigation of Love', where he writes:

> Having defined the field of investigation, we can now sketch the concepts analytically presupposed in our use of 'love'. An idea of these concepts can be gained by sketching a sequence of

relations, the members of which we take as relevant in deciding whether or not some relationship between persons A and B is one of love. These are not relevant in the sense of being evidence for some further relation 'love' but as being, in part at least, the material of which love consists. The sequence would include at least the following:

(1) A knows B (or at least knows something of B)
(2) A cares (is concerned) about B
     A likes B
(3) A respects B
     A is attracted to B
     A feels affection for B
(4) A is committed to B
     A wishes to see B's welfare promoted.

The connection between these relations which we will call 'love-comprising relations' or 'LCRs' is not, except for 'knowing about' and possibly 'Feels affection for', as tight as strict entailment (quoted on p. 20).

Nussbaum endorses Tanner's judgement on this passage that 'what is needed is a recognition that there are other modes of rigour and precision than quasi-formal ones' (p. 20). It is not merely that Newton-Smith's article is less illuminating about love than *Wuthering Heights* or Shakespeare's *Sonnets*, for that is to be expected, but that it is hard to see how anything written in such a form could make a significant contribution to our understanding of love: the very language and style of the writing seem to preclude it. And in so far as this *is* the style of contemporary philosophy, then ethically important aspects of our experience are unavailable to it without distortion or deformation.

Nussbaum's most fundamental claim is closely connected to this point. It is that 'certain truths about human life can only be fittingly and accurately stated in the language and forms characteristic of the narrative artist' (p. 5). These truths relate broadly to the question which guides her reflections, and from which ethical enquiry should begin, of 'how a human being should live'. Her explicit aim

is to establish that certain literary texts (or texts similar to these in certain relevant ways) are indispensable to a philosophical inquiry in the ethical sphere: not by any means sufficient, but sources of insight without which the inquiry cannot be complete. (pp. 23–4)

And for Nussbaum a certain class or type of novels are the literary texts which most clearly possess the necessary qualities. What such novels contribute to ethical enquiry is principally an appreciation of the non-commensurability of values; a recognition of the priority of the particular (a special kind of perception); an adequate understanding of the role and value of the emotions; and an acknowledgement of the place of contingency and uncertainty in human life. These features of ethical reflection can only properly be appreciated within the literary form of a narrative. Such narratives, therefore, provide at least a necessary complement to a style of moral theorising which, in either its Kantian or its utilitarian forms, has become distorted by too narrow a focus on rules and general principles and informed by a correspondingly etiolated conception of rationality.

The need that ethical enquiry has specifically for literature, and especially the narrative novel, takes a number of closely interrelated forms. First, novels give expression to 'our sense of life' which is the essential point of reference for such an enquiry. Second, in giving expression to this sense of life they foreground features of our lives which are typically ignored or marginalised in most ethical theorising. Novels provide a much richer understanding of life and its complexities than are afforded by a narrow emphasis on concepts like duty, obligation and rights, and the kinds of examples philosophers commonly use to explore moral issues. Finally, the narrative form of the novel reflects the shape and structure of our lives: we understand our own life and the lives of others in terms of narratives from which specific actions and events derive their meaning and within which they have an intelligible place. In all these ways novels can contribute to our ethical understanding and help to provide a more adequate account of what is involved in mature moral reflection.

The style of reflection which is most hospitable to these neglected features of ethical life is, according to Nussbaum, a broadly Aristotelian understanding of practical reasoning. This conception combines

> an attack on the claim that all valuable things are commensurable; an argument for the priority of particular judgements to universals; and a defence of the emotions and the imagination as essential to rational choice (p. 55).

The Aristotelian rejects the view that practical reasoning can be satisfactorily understood as either simply a calculating or computational faculty or as a straightforward process of deduction from abstract principles or general rules. What is most conspicuously added to this Aristotelianism in *Love's Knowledge* is what might loosely be called a 'Jamesian sensibility', about which more will be said later – a superficially unlikely combination but one presented with considerable imagination and persuasiveness, though the ultimate faithfulness of the synthesis to Aristotle's thought is not a question I shall pursue.[13]

The point of connection between James and Aristotle is provided by the latter's conception of practical wisdom. An important part of practical wisdom is possessing the kind of judgement of particulars which for Nussbaum can only be cultivated through the reading of narrative texts. What the reading and interpretation of the appropriate novels can do is develop a certain sensitivity and capacity for discriminations in the reader; qualities which are also essential to an adequate ethical understanding. In the words of Henry James, to which Nussbaum frequently adverts, we must make ourselves people who are 'finely aware and richly responsible'; people 'on whom nothing is lost'. This requires a careful attentiveness to the particulars of a situation; an openness and generosity of response to human beings and their circumstances; and ultimately a knowledge which is inseparable from a certain sort of love (though it may also require a refusal of some other sorts of love – principally the erotic sort). These cannot be represented within, or acquired through, a style of moral philosophising couched exclusively in terms appropriate for an abstract theoretical treatise – though general rules and principles have their place – but only through the reading and assimilation of certain sorts of literary texts, of which some of James' novels are paradigm examples. And a broadly Aristotelian framework can accommodate these necessary features of ethical reflection much better than Kantian or utilitarian alternatives, with their inclination towards abstraction, generality and complete commensurability.[14]

Nussbaum argues that we should aspire towards what she calls a 'perceptive equilibrium', somewhat analogous to Rawls's reflective equilibrium though not a mere extension of it. Perceptive equilibrium deals with 'impressions, emotions, and, in general, with particulars' and is

> an equilibrium in which concrete perceptions 'hang beautifully together', both with one another and with the agent's general principles; an equilibrium that is always ready to reconstitute itself in response to the new. (p. 183)

Perceptive equilibrium lies at the heart of moral judgement and understanding which consists of knowing much more than a system of rules and principles which are then simply 'applied'. This process of perceptive equilibrium, the details of which are perhaps less than transparent, must also be related to a philosophical commentary on the narrative texts. Novels cannot be simply a substitute for philosophy but themselves need to be elucidated through philosophical commentary. For Nussbaum 'both the literary works and the "philosophical criticism" that presents them are essential parts of the overall philosophical task' (p. 49). In this way she seeks to show how a particular kind of sensibility, which is acquired from an attentive reading of the appropriate novels, is integral to any adequate conception of ethical reasoning; and that this is an element of human life to which recent moral and political theorising, in part because of its form, has been blind.

In general terms I have considerable sympathy both with Nussbaum's strictures about the inadequacy of a good deal of modern moral and political philosophy and with the importance she attaches to literature as an essential resource for ethical reflection and understanding. I further agree with her about the importance of particularity, contingency, the role of the emotions and the non-commensurability of values to any adequate understanding of ethics. Yet, I am also troubled by several features of her own attempt to integrate literature within ethical theorising, and surprised by her failure to give much consideration to a number of problems which any such attempt surely needs to confront. The effect of these failings is to raise some serious doubts about the success of her enterprise. It is some of these doubts that I shall explore in what follows, though I hope the rather negative tone of much of the subsequent discussion does not suggest that Nussbaum's work is merely misguided or without interest. At the very least, it seems to me, she both sets an agenda for debate and makes a serious and substantial contribution to that debate.

One significant cluster of issues about which Nussbaum has surprisingly little to say in a work which places such importance upon the attentive reading of texts are the very considerable difficulties of appropriating fictional texts for philosophical purposes. For example, fictional narratives typically employ a vast array of literary devices and techniques – metaphor, allegory, symbolism, imagery, allusion, ambiguity, irony and multiple narrative perspectives to mention only a few of the most common – which make novels resistant to straightforward incorporation within other discursive contexts. So, while agreeing with Nussbaum about the fundamentally important role of philosophical commentary in the process of appropriation, we need to be told rather much more about the relationship between a novel and any philosophical commentary on it. Novels, especially good ones, do not just tell a story, they also tell it in a particular way; and how the story is told is integrally connected to what the story is. Novels, as Nussbaum herself insists, do not consist of neutral reports on the real world. If we are to be sensitive to the relationship between form and content we have to be alert to more than the fact that a novel tells a story and that the story is likely to be more richly detailed than any philosophically constructed example. There is *always* more to any interesting novel than can be contained within any commentary on it and novels rarely if ever permit of only one plausible reading. Hence, there are inevitably questions which need to be asked about the authority of any particular reading of a novel; about the relevance and legitimacy from a philosophical perspective of the rhetorical strategy and textual devices employed in the narrative; and about the relationship between the reading of a novel and its role in interpreting our experience of life.

Before briefly considering each of these questions, there is an important objection to the way in which I have formulated the issue that needs to be noted, though it is not an objection which is likely to be raised by Nussbaum, and in any case I cannot pretend to deal with it adequately here. It is, however, an objection which is especially likely to be embraced by postmodernist literary critics, deconstructionists and others of their ilk. This objection is simply that many of the the techniques I have ascribed to literary narratives are in fact features of textuality as such. Thus, to take only one example, metaphor is not a literary device which is the special province of novelists but is ubiquitous, a feature of all but the most simple of texts. The particular point being that philosophical writing too has these features; and it is one of the achievements of Derrida to show just how pervasive and ineliminable metaphor appears to be in philosophical texts.[15] Whatever one thinks of Derrida's more ambitious claims about the metaphorical character of all writing – since all writing is a form of re-presentation even the most apparently literal of writing is unavoidably figurative – one has only to think, for example, of the role of 'seeing' in philosophical discussions of epistemology to appreciate (or as I could have said 'see') how deeply embedded metaphor is in philosophical discourse. It may be argued against me, therefore, that in claiming that these literary devices pose particular problems for philosophy I am, at least implicitly, subscribing to a model of philosophical argument which I purport to criticise.

There is undoubtedly something to this objection, and one way in which it is possible to bring philosophy and fiction closer together – or more accurately to recognise some of their affinities – is by emphasising common features of their textuality. This indeed is a significant part of Derrida's larger project in deconstructing Western metaphysics. However, though this is not an issue that can be treated adequately here, and I do not pretend so to deal with it, three points are perhaps worth observing. First, Derrida's views are of course highly controversial, especially among philosophers. Most would strongly resist any unqualified assimilation of philosophy to other forms of writing or reduction of philosophy to textuality. Second, Nussbaum herself evinces no sympathy with 'deconstructionist' approaches and is consistently fiercely hostile to them. Hence, this issue is not likely to figure in any disagreement she may have with my criticisms. Finally, even if one concedes that the textuality of philosophy connects it much more closely to fictional discourse, it does not follow that the canons of argument which are generally supposed to govern philosophy are not very different from those considered relevant to fictional narratives. It could scarcely be denied that such differences have been integral to the way in which the two discourses have been constructed.

To return then to the first of my earlier questions: how does the fact that there are invariably many plausible readings of any novel affect the claims to authority of any particular philosophical commentary on it? One set of issues here concerns the degree of independence that a philosophical commentary on a novel has from either the philosophical assumptions which inform the commentary or the way in which the novel is interpreted. It would be silly to suggest that novels are open to *any* interpretation – though sometimes this is suggested – but often what they are taken to show, perhaps especially in an ethical context, will be partly a reflection of what the *reader* brings to the interpretation, and of course a philosophical commentary inevitably depends in part upon an interpretation of the novel. Moreover, the interpretation may itself be driven by a philosophical theory or argument.

Thus, for example, Peter Johnson in his *Politics, Innocence and the Limits of Goodness* interprets Pyle's behaviour in Graham Greene's novel, *The Quiet American*, as showing the limits of a certain sort of moral innocence in political contexts.[16] Yet this interpretation depends upon a specific understanding of Pyle's character and its relationship to a particular conception of moral innocence, a conception shaped by Johnson's own argument, which is, to say the least, contestable: it is possible to 'read' Pyle differently from the straightforward moral innocent, in Johnson's sense of the term, of his account. What then is the standing of Johnson's claim that Pyle in *The Quiet American* exemplifies his argument about the limits of moral innocence in politics? Suppose it is possible to make sense of Pyle in Johnson's terms, as indeed I would accept, what does this show, if it is also possible to make sense of him in significantly different terms? What is the source of the authority of a particular philosophical reading of a literary narrative over those who either deny it or incorporate it, more or less effectively, within their own ethical understanding?

Of course, an insightful reading of a literary text, such as Nussbaum's discussion of the tangled web of personal relationships in *The Golden Bowl, may* help to us to see a particular ethical significance in what is being described. It may, once we have come to understand, do what we would regard as deepening or enlarging our moral understanding. But what if we do not see things differently at all, or do see them differently, though not in the way suggested by Nussbaum's commentary? My point is not that there are not good and bad arguments about the interpretation of specific novels or the philosophical commentaries based on them. Rather, it is first that these arguments are themselves often partially theory-dependent, and second that in any case they usually radically underdetermine any particular moral conclusion.

The second question concerns the relevance and legitimacy of various rhetorical strategies or literary techniques from a philosophical perspective. For instance, to take a very simple case, Bounderby in Charles Dickens' *Hard Times* is representative of a kind of (allegedly) self-made capitalist, and he is presented as among other things both a brazen liar and physically repellent.[17] Yet these characteristics are clearly not integral to being a self-made capitalist, and the latter characteristic would normally be thought to be of no moral significance whatsoever. And in so far as our attitude to Bounderby and what he stands for is in part shaped, as it will be, by these considerations, how should we respond? There are some features of the literary narrative that influence our responses which seem morally and philosophically dubious, in this case because they are irrelevant, or because they have an *ad hominem* quality or because they appear to possess a generality which is illusory. In the context of the novel the caricature of Bounderby works well enough

– caricature can be an effective literary device – but how should any philosophical commentary on the novel deal with it? This question can take a specific and a general form. How should we respond to *this* particular deployment of caricature in the context of *this* narrative; and what should we think more generally about caricature as a literary technique employed for moral purposes?[18] This is a very simple example, and the problems are compounded when dealing with a dense and difficult literary narrative, Dostoyevsky's *The Devils*, for example, simultaneously working at several different levels and through a complex web of metaphors, allusions, symbols, images and such like, with a variety of narrative perspectives and its polyphonic structure. What is a philosophical commentary to make of such a panoply of textual strategies?

Another aspect of this problem, though it is also closely related to the first question, is the more general issue of persuasiveness in literature, of truth and falsity in fiction. It is an important feature of fiction that it can be found truthful or false, authentic or artificial, convincing or unconvincing; that novels can be criticised as inconsistent, unrealistic or unbelievable. But these qualities are to be found in a text at least in part by virtue of its literary properties. This is not simply, and sometimes not at all, a matter of the literal accuracy of reportage. Take, for example, another novel by Dostoyevsky, *Crime and Punishment*. In this novel, which is often taken to be one of the classics of realism, there are a large number of literally unbelievable coincidences yet these seem not to undermine the truthfulness of the novel, and they have no adverse bearing on Dostoyevsky's moral and psychological analyses. In fact, some of them are an important part of the symbolic structure of the novel which contributes to its overall cogency – for example, through Dostoyevsky's technique of 'doubling' – though in the context of another novel such coincidences might seem strained, contrived or utterly unconvincing. On the other hand many critics find Raskolnikov's relationship with Sonya, particularly as depicted towards the end of the novel, sentimental and false; although the element of cliché it contains – the reform of a sinner through the love of a 'fallen' woman – may be rather more plausible, in a statistical sense, than some of the extraordinary coincidences which, in the context of the novel, are accepted without demur.

The point is that in these kinds of cases – of course they are not the only ones, for sometimes literal truth or statistical probability does matter – it is the *writing* which convinces or fails to convince. The coherence, sense or logic of a novel is not straightforwardly determined by the kinds of consideration which would be relevant, for example, in a court of law. The nature of fictional 'truth' has been much discussed and my purpose is not to add to those discussions.[19] However, that fiction can seem true or false is something with which we are all familiar; and it is a significant dimension of the textuality of a specific novel of which account needs to be taken in understanding how and what we learn from fiction.

Finally, the third question concerns the relationship between reading a novel and its role in interpreting our experience. In particular, what are the differences between the two, do they matter and, if they do, how and what can one learn from the former of relevance to the latter? In fact, this is a very large cluster of questions and I shall return to some of them later. Here I shall focus on only one issue. Literary texts such as novels confront us quite differently from our everyday experience.[20] Texts are characteristically complete and composed, while life is neither – the author describes a situation and there is nothing more to that situation than that which is contained in the text. If Dostoyevsky does not mention that Raskolnikov has a grandfather, it makes no sense to ask what kind of man he was or whether Raskolnikov's actions were influenced by his childhood relationship with him. There is nothing to be known about Raskolnikov's grandfather and he cannot be relevant to any question which we can sensibly ask of the novel. All that there is to know about Raskolnikov is to be found within the pages of *Crime and Punishment*, for Dostoyevsky's Raskolnikov 'exists' only in those pages. (There is an intriguing issue about what can be inferred from a text: for example, is it reasonable to infer that Raskolnikov must have had a grandfather, because his mother must have had a father even though he is never mentioned? But this kind of question is irrelevant to my concerns.) The world that Dostoyevsky creates in *Crime and Punishment* is a complete world and, in an important sense, all that there is to be known about it is what we can find in the novel.

Much recent literary theorising stresses the 'infinite openness' of literary texts, but there is also about the novel a closure which is not present in our ordinary experience. While there is scope for disagreement about what within the novel is relevant to the understanding of any situation it depicts, it is generally the case that the range of possibilities is significantly circumscribed relative to any situation which confronts us in everyday life. One aspect of this is that, though one can be surprised by literature, once one has read a novel carefully it cannot contain the kind of surprises which are all too common in our ordinary experience: we cannot discover, for example, facts about Raskolnikov which were previously unknown to us. Moreover, once we have read a novel we know how things turn out (in so far as they turn out at all) but it is a rather significant feature of our deciding and acting in the world that it is always accompanied by a host of uncertainties. One does not need to be a thoroughgoing consequentialist to recognise that these uncertainties are a crucial dimension of our ethical experience and often central to our moral perplexity when faced with even mildly troubling moral choice. Literary narratives do not possess *that* quality even when they are at their most opaque, ambiguous or open-ended.

This is only one respect in which reading a text is unlike moral deliberation and action in real life. Other questions, for example, those to do with authorial intention, I shall ignore, while still others will be taken up shortly, specifically in the context of assessing some of Nussbaum's arguments. However, it may be worth noting that many of these questions arise from what might be presented as a general dilemma for anyone claiming a special role for narrative fictions in moral deliberation. The more such narratives are assimilated to other forms of writing about ethical issues the less clear it is that they have anything distinctive, which cannot be found elsewhere, to contribute to moral thinking and reasoning. On the other hand, the more one emphasises the distinct and special qualities of fictional narratives, which are not to be found elsewhere, as Nussbaum does, the more imperative and difficult it becomes to explain how something so qualitatively different from our ordinary moral experience can make a significant and indispensible contribution to it.[21]

My purpose in raising these and the other issues I have so far mentioned has been simply to identify some questions which need to be addressed.[22] However, I certainly do not want to suggest that I have identified a series of insuperable difficulties which effectively disqualify novels for any useful ethical or philosophical purpose. But I do believe that there are important and difficult questions about how they can serve such purposes – about the limits and possibilities for which narrative fiction can be used in the context of a philosophical enquiry into ethics. Furthermore, Nussbaum is not alone in neglecting them, for most of those who take seriously the role of literary examples in moral or political theory rarely seem to consider these issues either. Characteristically, such philosophers, some Wittgensteinians would be good examples,[23] tend to read innocently (which is not all the same as insensitively), ignoring the complex literary qualities of what they read. In Nussbaum's case, such innocence is undoubtedly 'knowing'; she is fully aware of the kinds of question I have raised, though she chooses to say little about them. However, the crucial question is whether her relative neglect of most of these issues has damaging consequences for her own argument. I think that it does.

It would be absurd to suggest that Nussbaum is unaware of the differences between life and art; between living and reading; or between real people and fictional characters – she herself makes similar distinctions, for example, when discussing Wayne Booth's *The Company We Keep: An Ethics of Fiction* and in her insistence that novels do not function 'as pieces of "raw" life' (p. 47) – but she sometimes seems to me to be insufficiently attentive to some of these differences and the problems to which they give rise. It may be illuminating on occasion to speak of novels as 'friends', or of 'falling in love' with fictional characters, as she does, but these seductive metaphors also carry with them real dangers. In particular, they point to a recurrent failure on Nussbaum's part to distinguish adequately the kind of engagement which is appropriate with novels and fictional characters from relationships with real people. A small but symptomatic example of this tendency is the way in which Dickens' reference to the young David Copperfield 'reading as if for life' is overenthusiastically truncated into 'reading for life'. (Indeed she sometimes conveys the impression that a childhood spent in the company of Roderick Random, Peregrine Pickle et al. might provide an adequate, perhaps even rather superior, substitute for relationships with real children, and it is worth pondering why that is not the case.) In short, there are a variety of issues concerning the relationship between life and literature, and the role literature might play in our lives and our judgements, which Nussbaum needs to address more directly than she does. Her reluctance to do so is of both ethical and philosophical significance.

Thus, to focus on only one such issue, and to put the point too bluntly, being 'richly responsive' to a situation in a novel does not require us to *do* anything. We may experience certain thoughts and feelings in response to a fictional description but we do so only in a way which significantly detaches them from their 'normal' context in our lives. We may be moved by the fate of Anna Karenina but we cannot sensibly mourn for her or be grief-stricken by her death.[24] The possibilities with which literature presents us are importantly circumscribed, and in a variety of ways. It is not merely that we are not caught up in the 'vulgar heat' of our own involvement, as

Nussbaum says, but that our very sense of what the possibilities are is shaped by our acknowledgement that we cannot benefit or harm, help or hinder, comfort or dismay the objects of our attention in reading novels. There is an important sense in which novels are *just* stories. For, while it would be wrong to reduce the ethical to too simplistic a conception of its being 'action-guiding', an ethic is, on Nussbaum's own understanding, a practical matter – it concerns how we should *live* our lives. The practically passive character of reading – of course it involves the mind actively – is something which crucially distinguishes our response to a novel from our response to real situations. It is for this reason too that literature may allow us to experience our emotions 'on the cheap', and ultimately encourages a peculiarly aesthetic deformation of our moral sensibilities. There is, for example, something morally corrupt, and alas all too common, in the responses of a man who is moved to tears by a dramatisation of *The Ragged Trousered Philanthropist* but is stonily indifferent to the vagrants he passes on his way from the National Theatre. Nussbaum never ponders this possibility.

There is a real danger that Nussbaum's excessive concern for what makes a good reader sometimes leads her into moral obtuseness: the high-minded can degenerate into the sanctimonious. Consider, for example, some comments she makes about political ethics, an area in which her views are generally unconvincing, in the context of her defence of Henry James' *The Princess Casamassima*.[25] After quoting a long passage from Auden's 'At the Grave of Henry James', written in 1941 after his escape from the war in Europe, Nussbaum eulogises that:

> the essential point is wonderfully made: that war is from the Jamesian viewpoint, the easy, crude, cowardly way with the problems of moral and political life, whereas a patient lucid confrontation with difficulty is the way of true courage. War doesn't confront, doesn't *see*, our humanity, it simply breaks in on it. It appears to be strong, vigorous, passionate; but it avoids passionate engagement with the reality, the complexity of each thing. The James novel, on the other hand, confronts those complexities and ambiguities, opening its arms, passionately and tenderly, to humanity's hopes and conflicts as to a child, with all the love, patience and gentle interest in the difficult that this parental relation entails (p. 214).

For what it is worth I share Nussbaum's lack of enthusiasm for the brutality of warfare, but this passage surely veers between the comic and the offensive. Nussbaum almost makes it sound as if, when confronting a murderous enemy, the choice facing us is between war and sending them a copy of *The Princess Casamassima*! This response is no doubt somewhat unfair, but it would be interesting to know exactly what would have constituted 'a patient and lucid confrontation' with the evils of Hitler and Nazism? And even the most committed pacifist would cavil at the apparent implication that all those men and women who sacrificed their lives in the struggle against those evils were taking 'the easy, crude, cowardly way'.

This degree of moral obtuseness is untypical of Nussbaum's thinking, but it is an extreme manifestation of a more persistent inadequacy, particularly apparent in political contexts. She is careful not to deny that there is a place for rules and principles in ethical deliberation, but she is inclined to both underestimate and misconstrue their importance in matters of public policy. It is not that there is no role in public life for judgement, discretion and sensitivity; and the inadequacies of crude calculative conceptions of cost-benefit thinking have been well documented.[26] However, there are many situations in which impersonality is unavoidable and it is not at all clear how well Nussbaum's approach is suited to such contexts. The point is clearly made by Jesse Kalin:

> The vision of morality and of moral thinking and dialogue she offers is of something that holds between friends. And this does capture a side of morality, particularly in its aspiration towards the good and the best. But there is a quite different side and ground to moral thinking: this is the distance of strangers and the need to protect both ourselves and them. Much of morality and our moral thinking originates here and is designed to meet these concerns and as a result is quite different from most of what Nussbaum focuses on.[27]

Interestingly it is almost exactly what Nussbaum most values literature for – its richness, detail and concrete particularity – which distinguishes it from the kind of knowledge that we can have of most people and situations, especially when we are dealing with large numbers of people or people with whom we have only distant relations.

The dangers of trying to apply Nussbaum's conception of ethical deliberation in the public realm are all too evident in her remarks about the good judge who, she says, 'rather than being unreflectively subservient to law, will apply it in accordance with his very own ethical judgement' (p. 99). As is not uncommon at key points in her argument, the rhetorical force of this claim derives largely from contrasting her conception with a too simple-minded alternative – unreflective subservience in this case – but it is far from clear that these are the only options. (Moreover, even if they were, given what little I know about the judiciary in Britain, I might prefer unreflective subservience to the law to the ethical judgement of some judges.) At a deeper level, though, it can be argued that the law is precisely intended to render irrelevant many features of a given situation, including the moral failings of people which it would be wholly reasonable to take into account in choosing them as friends, or deciding whether to entrust to them the care of one's child or whether or not they are likely to give one good advice about a troubling personal relationship. The morally odious are as entitled to the protection of their rights and the impartial application of the law as those with whom we sympathise or those whom we admire.

Probably Nussbaum would agree with this, but her conception of ethical reasoning is sometimes afflicted by a worrying preciousness which occasionally lapses into sentimentality. In saying this I do not wish to be understood as endorsing some kind of hard-nosed utilitarianism; nor as denying the relevance of the literary imagination to the public realm. However, Nussbaum gives the impression of a person who has spent rather too much time in the company of the novels of James and Proust and not enough with those of, say, late Tolstoy or Zola. Her discomfort with a distinctly bleaker view of life is also evident in her somewhat uneasy discussion of Samuel Becket's novel trilogy.

Nussbaum's own moral understanding seems to be unduly influenced by the reading of her preferred authors and her emphasis on the qualities necessary to be a good reader of complex narrative texts. The qualities which are most valuable in this context are those of openness, subtlety of discrimination, a delicately nuanced understanding and a precisely graded emotional responsiveness. In short they are, perhaps not surprisingly, the virtues of a liberal literary intellectual. While acknowledging the importance of these virtues, however, one may also wonder whether there are other virtues which are likely to be ignored or undervalued by such an emphasis. For example, there are at least two sets of values which might be counterposed to those which Nussbaum seems to privilege. First, there are those of innocence, simplicity and spontaneous affection unmediated by the excessively cognitive processes that she describes. (Although Nussbaum herself attaches considerable importance to the emotions, she has a highly rationalistic understanding of them.) Second, there are values, which may be especially appropriate in political life, to do with decisiveness, toughness and perhaps even a degree of emotional bluntness which makes possible the undertaking of necessary but disagreeable actions.[28] One need not go all the way with Machiavelli or Lenin to agree that the person with a highly tuned moral sensibility and reared on the novels of Proust and Henry James may not in all circumstances make the best political leader.

There are two complementary truths which it is important to hold on to in assessing Nussbaum's claims about the values to be derived from the literary imagination and the attentive reading of fictional narratives. First, though this claim might be contested, one can be a highly discriminating reader of such texts while being morally shallow and corrupt. Second, and this claim is surely incontestable, one can be a person of considerable moral sensitivity and depth without having the literary skills to fully comprehend the refined and elaborate prose of Proust or late James. Moreover, perhaps paradoxically, these are both truths we can learn from literature. For example, Humbert Humbert in Nabokov's *Lolita* provides us with a fine literary delineation of the former and, in some of the later stories of Tolstoy, we are confronted with incomparable portraits of the latter. (Indeed, in Tolstoy's view the kind of literary sophistication embraced by Nussbaum is most often an *obstacle* to moral goodness, but we need not share Tolstoy's view to doubt Nussbaum's.) In short, there is certainly no necessary connection, and perhaps no connection at all, between a vivid sense of the literary imagination and being a good person.

To further support this last contention let us return once again to *Hard Times* and to the character of Bounderby. Nussbaum reads this novel, very plausibly, as a defence of the role of the literary imagination ('fancy') in the ethical deliberations of public life against attack from a reductive, mechanical and philistine conception of political economy.[29] Moreover, she sees the novel as not merely asserting this but as showing it through Dickens' language, in particular through the contrast between the rich and imaginative language associated with Sissy Jupe and the world of the circus and the flat and harsh language of Mr Gradgind and the M'Choakumchild school. But how, we might ask does Bounderby fit within this account of novel? Bounderby is surely one of the most imaginative and creative story-tellers, employers of 'fancy', in the novel. Of course, in part this supports Nussbaum's reading in that it shows how Bounderby too cannot avoid a kind of imaginative engagement with his life that his avowed philosophy denies. Yet, Bounderby's attachment to fancy surely undermines Nussbaum's larger claim about the intimate connection between the ethical and the imaginative. For Bounderby, apart perhaps from Bitzer, is the most straightforwardly reprehensible character in the book – a pompous, selfish fraud. His representation, however, reminds us of another, less morally wholesome connection, that between imagination and fiction on the one hand and falsity, lying and dissimulation on the other.

So *Hard Times*, whatever Dickens' intentions, tells a rather more complex and morally ambiguous story about the relationship between the ethical and the imaginative than Nussbaum's reading indicates. The story-telling of Sissy Jupe needs to be set against that of Josiah Bounderby. Of course, further elaboration may be possible here and some, including Nussbaum, might wish to distinguish Bounderby's imagination from that of Sissy Jupe. Be that as it may, however, two points seem clear. First, Nussbaum's discussion of the novel is in fact blind to the connection I have suggested. It is not that she considers and rejects it, but that it does not appear to occur to her at all, and her silence about Bounderby tells its own story. One cannot help wondering if this blindness is not a function of her coming to the novel with a view already formed about the relationship between ethics and the literary imagination. Second, whatever alternative reading of Bounderby is proffered, it is very hard to see how it can do other than require at least a much more nuanced and qualified defence of the imagination than that essayed by Nussbaum.

It is unclear quite how damaging the kinds of criticism I have been advancing are to Nussbaum's overall argument, though they are surely more than peripheral. Moreover, I suspect that they are also connected to another difficulty in her position. For there seems to be something of a tension between the way in which literature can enlarge our moral understanding and the subterranean but robust strand of moral realism, in the form of an Aristotelian essentialism, which she also embraces. This is never fully articulated and little is said directly in its defence in her essays dealing with literature – though it is treated in a more extended fashion elsewhere – but it does make important appearances at some junctures in the argument.[30] It is made explicit mostly in the form of bare, and sometimes peremptory, assertions about 'human nature', 'human beings', 'truth' and 'the right way to live'. Nussbaum is firmly committed to the idea of moral truth and believes that the concept of human being provides the necessary grounding for its pursuit.

Indeed, both these features are fundamental to her account of an Aristotelian ethical conception.

The way in which Nussbaum pursues her enquiry is, as she recognises, intimately bound up with her starting point in the question, 'How should one live?' As she further notes, this question is different from that with which a Kantian or a utilitarian might begin, but she claims it is none the less neutral because her question leaves room for theirs within the enquiry. For Nussbaum 'the point is to state the opening question in a general and inclusive way, excluding at the start no major story about the good life for human beings' (p. 173). Yet it is the very generality of the question which may give rise to some unease. Is it possible to say what it is for a human being to live well, apart from any specific social and historical context and in entirely general terms? Probably there are some very basic conditions which have to be met 'for a human being to live well', but one is also likely to be struck both by the immense diversity in what human beings have believed it is to live well, and by the extent to which disputes about this issue have proved rationally irresolvable.

Nussbaum is of course aware of this kind of objection and she is insistent that the concept of human being must be sufficiently broad to allow for a wide variety of valuable ways of living. She understands her Aristotelian conception of ethics not as a form of metaphysical or transcendental realism but as an historically grounded empirical essentialism which she calls 'internalist essentialism'. And it is through historical experience that we learn that there can be many, though not an unlimited number of, forms of the Good Life. In this way she argues that there is no real conflict, only a fruitful and illuminating interrelationship, between the Aristotelian commitment to a general conception of the human being and a recognition of the role of particularity and plurality in moral life. However, this reconciliation is achieved only by insufficiently attending to the distinction between what might be regarded as common features of the human condition on the one hand, and the very different ways in which human beings can respond to and make sense of these features on the other. And it seems hopelessly to beg the question for Nussbaum to assert that 'surely the use of the concept "human being" will play an important role in . . . cross-cultural judgements and ground a cross-cultural debate' (p. 96), since what it is to be a human being is itself likely to be central to any such debate.

The point, therefore, is not that Nussbaum is committed to one simple answer to the question of what it is to live well. As she explains, it is a fundamental feature of her account of ethical reasoning that it includes a recognition that there is a diversity of noncommensurable goods, not all of which can be realised within one life. But it is much less clear that Nussbaum allows for the possibility of radically different and conflicting ethical perspectives issuing in irresolvable disputes about what is and is not valuable. Nussbaum's Aristotelianism naturally leads her to locate such differences within a context where they are part of a rational argument seeking an answer to the question of what the Good Life is for a human being. She stresses that

> the Aristotelian view does not imply subjectivism, or even relativism. The insistence that deliberation must take contextual features into account does not imply that the deliberated choice is correct only relative to local norms. Aristotelian particularism is fully compatible with the view that what perception aims to see is (in some sense) the way things are (p. 96).

On some interpretations this claim is unexceptionable, but much hangs on how the 'in some sense' is to be interpreted. I think the interpretation she places on it is too strong.

This can be seen in some comments Nussbaum makes on Wayne Booth's conception of ethical criticism in his book, *The Company We Keep: An Ethics of Fiction*.[31] In general, she is sympathetic to his work but she also has a serious worry that what she calls his 'open-minded pluralism' leads him to bend over too far 'to answer his real or imagined critics in the literary world'. She comments:

> Early in the book he appears to say that he holds both Aristotle's view of friendship and the Christian account (p. 173) – although in many essential respects the two are in direct contradiction (over the worth of the person, the proper basis for love and so forth). This is pluralism that leads to ethical confusion ... Wanting to accept and believe all candidates for truth, he reaches the verge of giving up on reason-based ethical judgement. (p. 243).

If this last sentence is true, though I rather doubt that it is, then Nussbaum's criticism of Booth is apt, but it certainly does not follow from the first sentence. Literature may well help us to see the ethical validity of both Aristotelian and Christian conceptions of friendship, even though they may be in some respects contradictory. Why *must* there be only one 'correct' conception of friendship? It is true that each of us can only live out one or other of these conceptions and in *that* sense we cannot accept both, but it does not follow that we cannot acknowledge both as conceptions of friendship or that there must be some way of rationally demonstrating one to be superior to the other.

In her desire to repudiate both relativism and subjectivism Nussbaum frequently invokes what she calls 'our sense of life'. But she constantly runs together acceptable and unacceptable uses of this expression so as to coercively constrain the possibility of moral disagreement. In the acceptable sense it simply draws attention to structural features of our lives which are indeed broadly shared, and are such that we could only doubtfully comprehend someone who thought they were morally unimportant – features of our lives such as birth, death and human sexual relations. However, it does not follow from this that people will or must agree about the form in which this importance should be manifested. Nor does it follow that people must agree about the relative significance of these common features of the human condition one to another or with respect to features of their lives which are not common. In short, there is no one 'sense of life' to which legitimate appeal can be made, nor is there one moral sensibility to which we should all aspire.[32]

Perhaps the closest Nussbaum comes to acknowledging the force of such an argument, and it is not very close, is in her discussion of romantic or erotic love. She, herself, now finds unsatisfactory her earlier attempt to straightforwardly incorporate the value of erotic love within an Aristotelian ethic. Instead, it is now seen as possibly marking a limit to the ethical, as leading 'the lover at times beyond the ethical stance into a world in which ethical judgement does not take place' (p. 52). Yet Nussbaum fails to follow through the implications of this thought; and she cannot resist the urge to re-establish harmony. For she still maintains that though 'love and ethical concern do not exactly have an equilibrium ... they do support and inform one another; and each is less good, less complete without the other' (p. 53). But surely our whole experience, both directly and as mediated through literature, resists this comfortable conclusion. It altogether ignores the destructiveness and unfairness which characteristically lurks within such love. Deep, partisan emotional attachments are always a potential threat to an ethical order in which treating people in accordance with their deserts plays a fundamental role.[33] Of course while love, especially of the erotic (or parental) sort, is in our culture typically the deepest of such attachments it is not the only one. We might, for example, consider the very different case of passionate commitment to a cause. And when we start to open up all these possibilities the prospects for a comprehensive and inclusive structure of values seem slim indeed.

It is surely one of the most remarkable, and I would argue philosophically valuable, features of literature that it helps us to understand divergent and conflicting human impulses, and perhaps to come to see the value in commitments and ways of life which from our own moral perspective may seem empty and worthless. Conversely, it may also help us to see inadequacies or limits in our own moral commitments. Ultimately I very much doubt that literature can be captured by any one ethical conception – Aristotelian or any other. It may be that this is one of the sources of tension between literature and philosophy, at least as the latter is commonly understood: literature perceives truths, philosophy pursues Truth.[34] (From his perspective Plato was no doubt right to be suspicious of the poets.) But it is *this* which I believe is probably literature's most significant contribution to reforming the dominant conception of moral and political theory.

Inevitably there will be limits to how far our understanding can be extended, and an exploration of these limits is a worthwhile philosophical undertaking. It is also something we are constantly testing and probing in reading narrative fictions. However, to deny that literature can enlarge and challenge our understanding of the ethical possibilities in this way, to appreciate conflicting and contradictory ethical conceptions, is itself a refusal of attention to what we can learn from literary narratives. It is a refusal which can be seen to have both philosophical and ethical consequences. But of course to make such claims is already to take a stand on a number of controversial philosophical and ethical issues. It also takes us back to some of the questions about the philosophical appropriation of the literary imagination which were raised earlier; questions which have only been raised not answered.

While in these closing remarks I have indicated very briefly something of *what* I believe literature can contribute to our ethical understanding, I have only asked questions about *how* it does it. And in the absence of a better understanding of the latter, on which philosophers probably have a lot to learn from literary critics, it might be wiser to remain tentative in one's claims about the former. Perhaps when we have a better understanding of the *how* we will also have a better understanding of *why* it is so difficult to appropriate the literary imagination for philosophical purposes in a way that does justice to both what is distinctively literary and to our philosophical concerns. Nussbaum's work certainly helps us to see why this matters, whether or not we find her own treatment convincing.[35]

NOTES

1 The 'ethical' includes matters of political morality such as justice, freedom and equality.
2 See, for example, R. M. Hare, *Moral Thinking*, Oxford, Oxford University Press, 1981, p. 48. The 'seductiveness' of literature is discussed by Susan Mendus in this volume.
3 For a discussion of this issue see Thomas Gould, *The Ancient Quarrel Between Poetry and Philosophy*, Princeton, NJ, Princeton University Press, 1991.
4 This kind of objection is suggested by Michael Oakeshott, 'The Voice of Poetry in the Conversation of Mankind' in his *Rationalism in Politics and Other Essays*, London, Methuen, 1962.
5 In the subsequent discussion no sharp distinction is observed between moral and political philosophy on the one hand, and ordinary moral and political thought on the other. It is important on occasion to make distinctions along these lines but it is doubtful that there is only *one* distinction to be made and there are also significant continuities. My focus, however, will be on the kinds of systematic and reflective thinking typical of philosophical enquiry.
6 See Alasdair MacIntyre, *After Virtue*, London, Duckworth, 1981; Charles Taylor, *Sources of the Self*, Cambridge, Cambridge University Press, 1989; and Richard Rorty, *Contingency, Irony and Solidarity*, Cambridge, Cambridge University Press, 1989. The 'narrative turn' is discussed by Maureen Whitebrook and Susan Mendus in their chapters in this volume.
7 Martha Nussbaum, *Love's Knowledge: Essays on Philosophy and Literature*, New York, Oxford University Press, 1990. All page references in the text are to this volume. An important supplementary essay is 'The Literary Imagination in Public Life', *New Literary History*, 22, 1991, pp. 877–910.
8 Martha Nussbaum, *The Fragility of Goodness: Luck and Ethics in Greek Tragedy and Philosophy*, Cambridge, Cambridge University Press, 1986.
9 Among the more important of these uncollected papers are 'Non-Relative Virtues: An Aristotelian Approach', *Midwest Studies in Philosophy*, 13, 1988, pp. 32–53; 'Nature, Function and Capability: Aristotle on Political Distribution', *Oxford Studies in Ancient Philosophy*, Sup. Vol. 1, 1988; 'Aristotelian Social Democracy', in R. B. Douglass, G. Mara and H. Richardson (eds), *Liberalism and the Good*, New York, Routledge, 1990; and 'Human Functioning and Social Justice: In Defence of Aristotelian Essentialism', *Political Theory*, 20, 1992, pp. 202–46.
10 See, for example, Berel Lang, *The Anatomy of Philosophical Style*, Oxford, Basil Blackwell, 1990 and *Writing and the Moral Self*, London, Routledge, 1991; and Peter Winch, *Ethics and Action*, London, Routledge and Kegan Paul, 1972.
11 Consider, for example, the role of Arthur Koestler's *Darkness at Noon*

in Maurice Merleau-Ponty's *Humanism and Terror*, Boston, Beacon Press, 1969.

12 The 'Introduction' for example is generally much more cautious than some of the essays. See also her comments in 'A Reply', *Soundings* 72, 1989, pp. 727–8.

13 It is an issue which has been extensively pursued in discussions of *The Fragility of Goodness*. See, for example, the review by John Cooper in *Philosophical Review* 97, 1988, pp. 543–64, and the symposiums in *Soundings* 72, 1989 and *Philosophical Investigations* 16, 1993.

14 These claims are of course controversial. For an interesting argument that the insights of literature support a Kantian ethic see Richard Eldridge, *On Moral Personhood. Philosophy, Literature, Criticism and Self-Understanding*, Chicago, University of Chicago Press, 1989.

15 See Jacques Derrida, *Margins of Philosophy*, Brighton, Sussex, The Harvester Press, 1982.

16 Peter Johnson, *Politics, Innocence and the Limits of Goodness*, London, Routledge, 1988, Chapter 9.

17 In 'The Literary Imagination in Public Life' Nussbaum discusses *Hard Times* at more length but she has very little to say about Bounderby. I shall return to another difficulty for Nussbaum to which Bounderby gives rise a little later.

18 It is interesting that in a philosophical context to characterise someone's argument or account of a position as a 'caricature' is almost always to condemn it.

19 See for example K. K. Ruthven, *Critical Assumptions*, Cambridge, Cambridge University Press, 1979, Chapter 11 for a literary critic's treatment of the issue; and Joseph Margolis, *Art and Philosophy. Conceptual Issues in Aesthetics*, Brighton, Sussex, The Harvester Press, 1980, Chapter 12 for that by a philosopher.

20 See also the chapter by Susan Mendus in this volume.

21 Though I cannot argue the point here, I suspect that Nussbaum undervalues the ethical potential of non-fictional forms of narrative, such as history, biography and personal testimony. Acknowledging these other forms of narrative would help to connect fictional narratives to a more general narrative self-understanding.

22 A useful beginning is made in Frank Palmer, *Literature and Moral Understanding*, Oxford, Clarendon Press, 1992.

23 In addition to Winch, *Ethics and Action*, see, for example, D. Z. Phillips, *Through a Darkening Glass: Philosophy, Literature and Cultural Change*, Oxford, Basil Blackwell, 1982 and the essays by R. W. Beardsmore and Ilham Dilman in A. Phillips Griffiths (ed.), *Philosophy and Literature*, Cambridge, Cambridge University Press, 1984.

24 Some have doubted that we can be intelligibly moved by the fate of Anna Karenina. See the extensive debate initiated by the exchange between Colin Radford and Michael Weston, 'How can we be Moved by the Fate of Anna Karenina?', *Proceedings of the Aristotelian Society*, Sup. Vol. 69, 1975.

25 Nussbaum's account of the role of literature in political deliberation is more fully explored in her 1991 Alexander Rosenthal Lectures. These

are due to be published as *The Literary Imagination in Public Life* but had not appeared at the time of writing.

26 See for example Stuart Hampshire, 'Morality and Pessimism' and 'Public and Private Morality' in S. Hampshire (ed.), *Public and Private Morality*, Cambridge, Cambridge University Press, 1978.

27 Jesse Kalin, 'Knowing Novels: Nussbaum on Fiction and Moral Theory', *Ethics* 103, 1992, p. 144.

28 Bernard Williams, 'Politics and Moral Character' in Hampshire, *Public and Private Morality*.

29 See Nussbaum, 'The Literary Imagination in Public Life'.

30 See the references in note 7 above.

31 Wayne Booth, *The Company We Keep: An Ethics of Fiction*, Berkeley, CA, University of California Press, 1988.

32 This is a dimension of Nussbaum's thought which seems to be neglected in the highly sympathetic and illuminating discussion of it by Cora Diamond. See Cora Diamond, 'Martha Nussbaum and the Need for Novels', *Philosophical Investigations* 16, 1993.

33 Nussbaum shows somewhat greater awareness of this in a recent piece, 'Ethics as Judgements of Value', *The Yale Journal of Criticism* 5, 1992.

34 In his *Essays in Ethical Theory*, Oxford, Oxford University Press, 1989, p. 57, R. M. Hare claims that 'it would not be too much of an exaggeration to find, in the current prevalence of fiction as an art-form, the principal cause or at least symptom, of the decline of moral standards which occasions so much concern'.

35 Earlier, substantially different, versions of this chapter were presented at the Political Theory Workshop at the University of York and the annual Political Studies Association Conference at Leicester University. I am grateful for the helpful discussion it received on both occasions, and for the detailed comments of Andrea Baumeister, Susan Mendus and Peter Nicholson.

5 Modes of political imagining

Martin Warner

PART 1

Much recent political thinking can be organised under three concepts: justice, utility and community. Each represents a particular range of options for theorising about ethics, politics and their integration, ranges which in current discussion are often thought to be incompatible. Thus, Rawls introduced his seminal conception of 'justice as fairness' by contrasting it with 'classical utilitarianism' according to which justice is understood as an executive decision in the service of efficient promotion of the general welfare. Such an approach he criticises for

> its profound individualism, in one sense of this ambiguous word. It regards persons as so many *separate* directions in which benefits and burdens may be assigned; and the value of the satisfaction or dissatisfaction of desire is not thought to depend in any way on the moral relations in which individuals stand.[1]

Somewhat ironically it is individualism with which 'communitarian' critics frequently charge Rawls. Rawls analyses justice in terms of an imaginary 'original position':

> We are to imagine that those who engage in social cooperation choose together, in one joint act, the principles which are to assign basic rights and duties and to determine the division of social benefits.

This decision is imagined both as a rational one and as taking place behind a 'veil of ignorance' in which

> no one knows his place in society, his class position or social status, nor does anyone know his fortune in the distribution of natural assets and abilities, his intelligence, his strength, and the

like. I shall even assume that the parties do not know their conceptions of the good or their special psychological propensities.[2]

But an individual abstracted from all such identifying features is hardly a human agent, and it may be asked how far rational choice can find a foothold in such an imagined situation. For Rawls 'the self is prior to the ends which are affirmed by it', thus it is intelligible to abstract from rational agents their 'conceptions of the good', but writers such as Sandel, for example, have objected that the boundaries of the self are themselves partially determined by commitments and interpersonal relationships and these bear on rational choice; the 'radically disembodied' subjects of the 'original position' are incapable of rational choice, which depends on self-knowledge, and in practice Rawls has to rely on an intersubjective conception of the self abstracted in such a way as to guarantee the liberal conclusions Rawls seeks – the 'original position' is rigged.[3]

The past decade has seen a ramifying debate over such issues as Rawls's own thinking has developed and philosophers such as MacIntyre and Taylor have developed their own 'communitarian' conceptions of ethics and the self, with significant implications for political theorising. I am not concerned here to trace the details, though I shall consider certain aspects of Rawl's most recent contribution in the final section of this chapter. In general, the Rawlsian invocation of justice conceived in terms of rational principles abstracted from empirical circumstances and 'psychological propensities' has Enlightenment – indeed Kantian – associations, while the opposing insistence on the embeddedness of our moral life in interpersonal relationships and the particularities of our human dispositions is closely associated with the contemporary revival of interest in the sort of virtue-based ethics associated with Aristotle (for whom justice, of course, was a virtue); further, in MacIntyre and Taylor this deconstruction of the Enlightenment is seen to reveal the continuing power of Judaeo-Christian theism 'in its central promise of a divine affirmation of the human, more total than humans can ever attain unaided'.[4] In the present context I wish to highlight just three features.

The first concerns Rawls's 'anti-perfectionism'. This connects with his proposal that in the 'original position' the parties do not know their conceptions of the good, those perfectionist ideals that guide their aspirations; a consequence is that the conception of justice that arises from this situation is supposed to have no determinate conception of the good and thus a just state should be neutral between such conceptions. To this it has been objected that the overall account of justice as fairness can only be defended by treating human autonomy as itself such a good, thus the supposed neutrality is a mirage. However this may be, Cavell provides a distinctive perfectionist counter to Rawls. On his Emersonian account the notion of 'perfection' as an achievable goal is a mirage, it functions more as a regulative ideal but as such is humanly important; it 'spans the course of Western thought and concerns what used to be called the state of one's soul';[5] it understands that soul as on an upward journey and makes sense of such notions as that of an individual's truth to him or herself. Now, on Rawls's account, justice is expressed through principles capable of being rationally articulated in the form of a contract such that 'those who express resentment must be prepared to show why certain institutions are unjust or how others have injured them'.[6] But Cavell queries whether the requisite consent to such principles is determinable in advance of particular circumstances and our developing conceptions of what we are and would become – the reach of our consent is in part a matter of discovery, not simply of choice. He instances Nora in *A Doll's House*:

> My question is, Do we feel that Nora's expressions of dishonor and outrage at the state of her so-called marriage require that she be prepared to show why certain institutions (here the institution of marriage), are unjust or how others have injured her?

The whole thrust of Ibsen's play shows why this is precisely wrong, allying Rawls with the uncomprehending Torvald. What is required is neither quasi-contractual argument within the Rawlsian 'conversation of justice', let alone a utilitarian defence of marriage in terms of the efficient promotion of general welfare, but rather radical personal – and by implication social – transformation.

> I am taking Nora's enactments of change and departure to exemplify that over the field on which moral justifications come to an end, and justice, as it stands, has done what it can, specific wrong may not be claimable; yet the misery is such that, on the other side, right is not assertible; instead something must be shown. This is the field of Moral Perfectionism, with its peculiar economy of power and impotence.[7]

The showing, it would appear, is only possible in terms of the particularities of lived experience in communities.

This raises, in the second place, the radical question of where else any form of political reasoning or legitimation can arise. Writing out of a different set of preoccupations, concerning the 'decay of Marxism', Castoriadis assaults 'the illusion of *theoria*':

> the evil commences when Heraclitus dared to state: Listening not to me but to the *logos*, it is wise to agree that ... To be sure, one must struggle against personal authority as well as against mere opinion, incoherent arbitrariness ... But do not listen to Heraclitus. His humility is but the height of arrogance. It is never the *logos* that you are listening to but always *someone*, such as he is, speaking from the place where he is at his own risk, but at yours too.

One can only speak authentically from what one perceives as one's own 'place', but risk here remains unavoidable. One may believe that one recognises one's self and one's situation in a particular articulation, but

> what is said may and sometimes does induce a 'recognition' which nothing permits us to assert that it would have existed without this discourse, or that it validates it. Millions of Germans 'recognized themselves' in Hitler's discourse, millions of 'communists' in that of Stalin.

Not every wife who 'recognizes' herself in Nora, it would seem to follow, is thereby 'shown' her true situation; the discourse needs to be tested, but not by reference to principles generated out of the 'conversation of justice' between the radically disembodied subjects of Rawls's 'original position' nor, indeed, by any 'prior criteria belonging to instituted reason', any authoritative *logos*.[8]

So, third, the pressing question is in what such testing can consist; where there is no possibility of failure there can be no risk – but what are the criteria here for judging failure, practical, intellectual or other? If one can only speak from one's place, not from principles of reason which transcend it, but one's perception of one's own place may be flawed as may be that of the 'millions' in one's own community who share one's perception, what counts as testing? The general shape of the dilemma is familiar: if neither 'principles of reason' nor 'facts of experience' provide hard data, how can we test our judgements? The Kantian answer involves looking to the judging subject as itself partially constituting the field within which judgement must take place and as possessing a certain form of autonomy.

Analogues can be found in Castoriadis. For him, social institutions operate within a 'symbolic network' and every symbol has an 'imaginary component' which is 'separate from the real'; the existence of the imaginary is dependent on the symbolic but 'conversely, symbolism too presupposes an imaginary capacity. For it presupposes the capacity to see in a thing what is not, to see it other than it is.' Institutions are socially sanctioned symbolic networks which combine functional and imaginary components; alienation is in part a function of the imaginary element becoming autonomous and predominating, but we cannot do without it for our capacity to solve functional problems depends on our imaginary capacity – our ability to see things as they are not – and problems can present themselves to us as such 'only in relation to an imaginary central to a given epoch or society'. This bears on our self-understanding:

> Man can exist only by defining himself in each case as an ensemble of needs and corresponding objects, but he always outstrips these definitions ... because he invents them (not arbitrarily, to be sure, for there is always nature, the minimum of coherence required by rationality, and previous history), and ... because no rational, natural or historical definition allows us to establish them once and for all.[9]

Fetishisation may mask from us the reality that society is essentially a form of self-creation, but particular historical formations may be apt for enabling us to do the unmasking. The reflective questioning, both theoretical and practical, of instituted traditions has its origin, we are told, in ancient Greece where we find the foundations of the unique Western project of autonomous political activity.[10] But autonomy is not the only 'social imaginary signification' of the modern West; the other is 'the unlimited expansion of "rational" mastery' which now faces us with ecological destruction. The two are intimately linked but the second is ultimately delusory if understood as representing a heteronomous *logos*, for

> The imaginary ... is the unceasing and essentially *undetermined* (social-historical and psychical) creation of figures/forms/images, on the basis of which alone there can ever be a question *of* 'something'. What we call 'reality' and 'rationality' are its works.[11]

The obvious riposte is to ask how we are to tell that this is not itself to make a fetish of autonomy. The claim that some empirical configurations are more conducive to unmasking delusions than others is not incompatible with the perception that all thought is socially, historically and psychologically situated – indeed, it may presuppose it. But unless some sense can be made of the notion of delusion the claim collapses. But this notion depends on that of 'reality' which, with 'rationality', are functions of the 'imaginary' – of what is not real. A familiar vicious circle is here developing. Further, the project of autonomy is said not to be arbitrary because it is constrained, *inter alia*, by 'the minimum of coherence required by rationality', but what counts as minimal here is presumably contestable and it is the rules of the contest that are in question. What is to determine arbitrariness here and hence delimit the proper scope of autonomy? If one rejects the *logos* one is left with the individual or the community, but these may be Hitler or Stalin or the millions who 'recognized themselves' in their discourses. Castoriadis rejects these discourses as heteronomous, but without clear warrant for and/or clarification of the proper scope for his leading value of autonomy we are once more involved in a circle.

The underlying problem is not so much political or even ethical as logical and epistemological. To distinguish between reality and delusion one needs a concept of truth that is independent of judgement, whether of individuals or of communities. This perception has powered the Kantian appeal to principles of reason which transcend 'step-mother Nature' and (probably) the Heracleitian appeal to the *logos*. Those who reject such appeals while still wishing to invoke some such notion as 'the minimum of coherence required by rationality' need to give an account of truth which is both socially contextualised and independent of judgement. Some help here is given by Wiggins's recent account of the 'marks' of a minimal concept of truth, which includes its independence of judgement, its ruling out of something, and also its propensity to 'convergence', including convergence of belief:

> If x is true, then x will under favourable circumstances command convergence, and the best explanation of the essence of this convergence will require the actual truth of x.[12]

If truth is independent of judgement, in maintaining that x is true one is ruling out a state of affairs which is independent of one's own judgement; hence, one must be able to conceive how others could in principle recognise such a state of affairs as obtaining and claim that if they held that it did so there would be something defective in the circumstances; under favourable circumstances beliefs should converge. But convergence of belief is only a mark of truth where there are not better explanations available (habit, deference, group dynamics, fear, and so on); it may be that the notion of the 'best' explanation here may only be sustainable as a regulative ideal, but this is no objection so long as the requirement is taken to imply that for this mark of truth to be present the cultural story (or whatever) told by way of explanation must be such that the 'actual truth of x' plays an integral role in its putative acceptability. On such an account a truth predicate for beliefs may well be contextualised in the sense that it carries no commitment to an Enlightenment, 'absolute', concept of truth, without making it subject to the totalising – even totalitarian – imaginary of a given community.

Whether such a *via media* can be sustained is still unclear, but one way of assessing the hypothesis is to consider the light it throws on the problems we have been considering in political thinking. Here, literary modes of imagining are helpful. Harrison has plausibly argued for the power of literature 'to rebuke and discipline the products of our purely theoretical intelligence',[13] and we have seen how Ibsen's play can be used to question Rawlsian theory, not least through the capacity of dramatic narrative (one of several subversive literary modes) to present lived experience in its complex particularity. Further, such presentations can make imaginatively accessible to us cultural formations significantly different from our own and thereby enable us to widen the range of our assessment. Given a significant degree of cultural resonance, the conceptual and temporal distance from today's standard categories that is available to works of the literary imagination can assist us in the radical rethinking required if we are to seek to avoid the contemporary logical and epistemological impasse of political theory.

PART II

The *Oresteia*

I start with quotations from three leading commentators:

> The *Oresteia* is our rite of passage from savagery to civilization.
> (Stanford, 1976)

> The cliché we have heard repeated all our lives, that the *Eumenides* depicts the transition from the vendetta to the rule of law, is utterly misleading. Even in the *Iliad*, the blood feud is regulated by the justice of Zeus administered through kings; even in the law of the Athenian polis in the fifth century, the blood feud and

the Erinyes have their allocated place. When the Erinyes become Eumenides, there is not the least question of their giving up their function; we have been assured that if they did the government both of the state and of the universe would collapse.

(Lloyd-Jones, 1971)

The trial [in the *Eumenides*] solves nothing;... [it] presents us with a dramatic image of deadlock, which liberalising commentators spoil by reading into... the whole trilogy an Aeschylean intention to oppose civilised principles of equity and morals to the savagery of blood-guilt, pollution and ritual purgation.... [The trial] *decides* something certainly; a verdict is reached, the knot is cut. But it solves nothing. The image of deadlock recovers its massive simplicity when we cease to believe that it is transcended.

(Jones, 1962)[14]

The tension between these perceptions is not, I think, primarily a matter of ambiguities in the text or the 'reading in' of civilised (or other) principles. It is rather, at least in part, a function of the ambiguities, paradoxes, and perhaps even 'deadlock', we have already noted in our contemporary conceptions of the rules of law, of justice and hence of civilisation.

Even Jones concedes that Aeschylus 'is celebrating the victory of State justice over family justice... a more efficient juridical instrument than the bloody and protracted vendetta', and Stanford that the rule of Zeus is operative from the start and the Erinyes retain their function to the end: '*Dikë* must evolve from the blood vendetta of the tribe to the social justice of our hopes... The furies will temper Zeus and make his *Dikë* just.'[15] Whether the transition 'solves' anything depends on what will count as a solution, whether it indeed points to 'the social justice of our hopes' on the content of those hopes, and whether to 'the rule of law' on whether that law can encompass the communal fury and 'special psychological propensities' the Erinyes represent.

The justice of Zeus no doubt regulates the vendetta and much else from the start: 'So towering Zeus the god of guests / drives Atreus' sons at Paris' (*Agamemnon*, lines 66–7[16]), but its recognition and enforcement is another matter – as is shown by the differences between the gods. Artemis is in general the patron of Troy, and angered by the project of Atreus' sons – with dire consequences for Iphigeneia – and Apollo the patron of Orestes: 'Zeus, Zeus, watch over all we do' is the general plea, but for specific guidance: 'Apollo will never fail me, no, / his tremendous power, his oracle charges me / to see this trial through. I can still hear the god' (*The Libation Bearers*, lines 250, 273–5). Against Apollo, representing, *inter alia*, purification and law, stand the Erinyes, the principle of vengeance. Further, in *The Eumenides* this latter opposition is further polarised in terms of gender, Apollo representing the masculine principle and the Erinyes the feminine; Aeschylus dramatises a resolution in which the female but virgin and motherless Athena upholds Apollo in the name of Zeus while seeking to incorporate the Erinyes in the new order through persuasion rather than lightning-bolt. Whether any such resolution is credible will depend in part on whether justice can properly be seen to include what Lloyd-Jones[17] refers to as 'the punitive element', whether vengeance can intelligibly be transformed under the rule of law into retribution. If not, then the fact that the Erinyes retain their function at the end of itself shows that the notion that 'the *Eumenides* depicts the transition from the vendetta to the rule of law is utterly misleading'; but Aeschylus appears to have believed otherwise.

Just under halfway through the second play of the trilogy the 'deadlock' Jones speaks of is sharply articulated: 'Now force will clash with force, right with right' (*Dikai Dika; The Libation Bearers*, line 447).[18] By the close the tutelary goddess of wisdom has apparently unified these competing rights, each associated with different communal perceptions, in the all-encompassing justice of Zeus. At the start this justice is an apparently unrealisable ideal under cover of which different communities play out their murderous rivalries; in Castoriadis's terms, 'it is never the *logos* that you are listening to but always *someone*' (on occasion that projection of one's community, the tutelary deity), but by the end the drama purports to enact the achievement of universal justice through the transcendence of partiality. Justice, like Wiggins's truth, rules out some possibilities (the destruction of Orestes), it transcends the judgement of a particular community (for the lots are equal) and, under the favourable circumstances of Athena's presidency and persuasion, it commands convergence through its integration of the 'special psychological propensities' that had provoked the deadlock. The suspicion that the deadlock remains nevertheless derives largely from the perception that the persuasion employed is less than rational and hence the integration celebrated bogus. But this issue turns on the conception of rationality with which Aeschylus is working – of what count as Wiggins's 'favourable circumstances' which should command convergence and as the 'best explanation' of such convergence. And here Aeschylus is very far removed from the Enlightenment paradigm.

> Zeus has led us on to know,
> The Helmsman lays it down as law
> That we must suffer, suffer into truth.
>
> (*Agamemnon*, lines 177–9)

The Greek of the concluding phrase is the proverbial *pathei mathos*. Lattimore's more literal if less memorable translation has 'wisdom / comes alone through suffering', with the conclusion of the verse rendered 'From the gods who sit in grandeur / grace comes somehow violent'. These lines are taken from the narrative immediately preceding the sacrifice of Iphigineia which sets the plot of the trilogy in motion, and immediately following her death we have the same insistence: 'Justice so moves that those only learn / who suffer' (lines 250–1).[19]

Nussbaum's commentary on the role of *pathei mathos* in the *Agamemnon* is illuminating:

> hard cases like these, if one allows oneself really to see and experience them, may bring progress along with their sorrow, a progress that comes from an increase in self-knowledge and knowledge of the world.[20]

She points out that Agamemnon, faced with appalling alternatives, at first responds with anger and grief but, once the decision is made, once he had 'slipped his neck through the yoke-strap of necessity', speaks and acts as if decision alone had resolved the conflict: 'For it is right and holy that I should desire with exceedingly impassioned passion the sacrifice staying the winds, the maiden's blood' (lines 214–7),[21] and in his action blinds himself to the human significance of what he is doing ' "Hoist her over the altar / like a yearling kid" ' (lines 231–2). The Chorus blame him not so much for carrying out the sacrifice as 'the change in thought and passion accompanying the killing'. Where, as she puts it, 'the gods themselves collide' we have an insistence on 'the supreme and binding authority, the divinity so to speak, of *each* ethical obligation', even though it is not possible to act in accordance with all of them. The proper response is to acknowledge there is no way out and suffer accordingly – 'not to stifle these responses out of misguided optimism': 'Let all go well!'. More generally,

> There is a kind of knowing that works by suffering because

suffering is the appropriate acknowledgement of the way human life, in these cases, is.[22]

This account of the significance of the collision of the gods fits well with the sense of deadlock Jones insists on in the trilogy, but Nussbaum considers only the *Agamemnon*. To see the actual operation of 'the grace that comes by violence' we need to look beyond it. When we meet Agamemnon in the opening play he is untouched by any such grace, in the full flush of victory without second thoughts, and easily provoked into displaying *hubris*. We remember that he had only had to describe his dilemma over Iphigeneia to himself to make his decision, and having done so to embrace it. But in *The Libation Bearers* Orestes has no such ease of decision. At the climax he wavers: 'What will I do, Pylades – dread to kill my mother?', and for the first and only time in the play his companion speaks:

What of the future? What of the Prophet God Apollo,
the Delphic voice, the faith and oaths we swear?
Let all men hate you rather than the gods.

(*The Libation Bearers*, lines 886–9)

Whether we read the Greek this way with Fagles or, with Lattimore, 'Count all men hateful to you rather than the gods', there is a contrast with his father for whom the crucial factor was the opinion of men ('Desert the fleets, fail the alliance?'; *Agamemnon*, line 213); it may be that some version of Dodds's conflict between guilt culture and shame culture[23] is also here being played out. There is an analogy with the *Eumenides* where the lots cast by humans are equal and a divine figure has to make the decision; here human judgement is deadlocked and an outside figure's invocation of the gods is required to break it.

Further, once Orestes has 'slipped his neck through the yoke-strap of necessity' he does not blot out the horror of what he has done. He is conscious he must answer to the justice of Zeus:

my witness when the day of judgment comes,
that I pursued this bloody death with justice,
mother's death.

(*The Libation Bearers*, lines 979–81)

He also wrestles with his own feelings in the light of the necessity laid upon him and faces the tragedy of his situation:

and she – I loved her once
and now I loathe, I have to loathe –
. . .
. . . I embrace you, you,
my victory, are my guilt, my curse, and still –

(lines 985–6, 1012–13)

or in Lattimore's version:

I grieve for the thing done, the death, and all our race.
I have won; but my victory is soiled, and has no pride.

The self-knowledge that this gives enables him to see his mother's Furies as they appear and flee to Apollo, the divinity in whose name he was acting; he has begun, we may say, to 'suffer into truth'.

The 'grace that comes by violence' (*charis biaios*; *Agamemnon*, line 182) we see finally operating in the closing play of the trilogy. The gods as represented by Apollo and the Erinyes have collided and Apollo's purifications proved inadequate. In his defence before Athena Orestes pleads human justification and divine sanction, as his father might have done and his mother did in that analogue of the trial scene in *The Libation Bearers* ('Destiny [*Moira*] had a hand in that, my child', line 897; see also her speeches in the *Agamemnon* following the murder, especially line 1692 [1658 Greek text] where – in a context strongly suggesting bad faith – the killing is attributed to Destiny or Fate [*Chreos*]). The crucial difference would appear to be Orestes' recognition both of his own responsibility and of the enormity of what he has – forced to choose in a context set by necessity – done, unlike his parents; Clytemnestra, one remembers, declares to the horrified Chorus: 'Rejoice if you can rejoice – I glory' (*Agamemnon*, line 1417). It is this that gives dramatic credibility to the concluding torchlight procession – the visual symbol of the progression from the darkness of revenge to the light of justice.

But is the credibility more than dramatic? At the level of rational argument as represented by Apollo – and as understood by the Enlightenment – Jones is clearly right; the trial solves nothing. At this level Athena's partiality is explicit: 'Orestes, I will cast my lot for you. / No mother gave me birth. I am / all for the male, in all things but marriage' (*The Eumenides*, lines 750–2). Further, the persuasion of the Furies looks at first sight like simple bribery, as if the ensuing celebration of Divine Justice was indeed the product of an executive decision in the service of efficient promotion of the general welfare – Rawls's criticism of classic utilitarianism.

But Athena is not Apollo, and her appeal to the Furies does, precisely, depend on 'the moral relations in which individuals stand' (to use Rawls's formulation). ' "Do great things, feel greatness, greatly honoured ... justly entitled, glorified forever" ' (lines 877, 899). They are greatly honoured because both they and the weight of their claims are recognised – in the first instance by Orestes himself. 'Watch out', says Clytemnestra, 'the hounds of a mother's curse will hunt you down'; 'But how to escape a father's if I fail?' responds Orestes (*The Libation Bearers*, lines 911–12); for Clytemnestra her husband's 'hounds' are of no account, but for Orestes it is far otherwise. It is this which makes it fitting that Orestes be freed; to paraphrase Cavell on Nora: specific right may not be claimable; yet the misery is such that, on the other side, wrong is not assertible; instead something must be shown, and this is what Aeschylus sets out to show: suffering into truth, the soul of Orestes – and by extension our conception of justice – as on an upward journey. Analogously, the Furies need time to assimilate Athena's offer – clearly represented by their repeating their initial rejection word for word and then relenting with little more than the repetition of the offer. And this internalisation of their own recognition is then marked by their being themselves made internal to the justice of the city: 'I enthrone these strong, implacable spirits here / and root them in our soil.' (*The Eumenides*, lines 940–1).

We have here a set of transformations which support Stanford's term, 'rite of passage', and return us to Wiggins's criteria for truth. The 'favourable circumstances' for convergence are provided by Orestes' integrity and hence capacity to 'suffer into truth', and the 'best explanation' of the conversion of the Erinyes is not bribery – which is incredible in itself and leaves the repeated speech unexplained – but recognition that universal justice requires both Apollonian reason and 'the formidable' – the 'psychological propensities' which lie behind blood-lust and purification alike. The play itself marks the possibility and significance for our sense of justice of our capacity for self-transcendence, at once countering Rawls's antiperfectionism and giving point to Castoriadis's perception of ancient Greece as instituting that form of reflective questioning of instituted tradition which has given rise to the self-conscious and self-transcending social project he terms 'political autonomy'.

Gulliver's Travels

Hubris is the proximate cause of Agamemnon's undoing, a blindness that appears to be a function of the repression of self-knowledge he accepted when he 'slipped his neck through the yoke-strap of necessity'. Analogously, it is human pride revealing lack of self-knowledge that is the underlying target of Swift's satire.

If treated with due caution, a useful distinction in considering modes of political imagining is that between the creative and the critical. Of course creative works are prone to criticise, implicitly or explicitly, the concepts or situations initially available or obtaining; and critical works may well serve some wider creative agenda; and no doubt to some works of political imagination the distinction is irrelevant. But the terms do gesture toward discernible emphases, such that the *Oresteia* is broadly creative and *Gulliver's Travels* critical.[24] Behind the *Travels*, no doubt, lies the balance of Aristotle's magisterial judgement: 'Man, when perfected, is the best of animals, but, when separated from law and justice, he is the worst of all',[25] but the tone of the satire is better represented by the King of Brobdingnag's emphasis on its negative aspect:

> I cannot but conclude the bulk of your natives, to be the most pernicious race of little odious vermin that Nature ever suffered to crawl upon the surface of the earth.[26]

The evidence on which His Majesty bases his conclusion is partly foreshadowed in the same Aristotelian passage: 'armed injustice is the more dangerous, and he is equipped at birth with arms, meant to be used by intelligence and virtue. which he may use for the worst ends'. But with Aristotle's next sentence we have moved from the second to the fourth book of the *Travels*: 'If he have not virtue, he is the most unholy and most savage of animals, and the most full of lust and gluttony' – in other words – a Yahoo. In Book 2 His Majesty does indeed soften the blow:

> I observe among you some lines of an institution, which in its original might have been tolerable, but these half-erased, and the rest wholly blurred and blotted by corruptions.[27]

(One remembers that within a generation of Aeschylus' celebration of the triumph of justice the dream had faded and the polity been subverted.) Further, in Book 4 Gulliver is not simply a Yahoo. There are models, that is, of justice and virtue to which Swift's satire would point us; but the mode is critical.

Gulliver himself is more a satiric device than a coherent fictitious character;[28] attempts to take seriously his inwardness in a manner analogous to my earlier discussion of Agamemnon and Orestes is a sure road to shipwreck – the account of the voyage to Lilliput is hardly the product of the half-crazed scribbler of the close of Book 4. The device is used to attack human pride in stages. In Lilliput the achievements of human society are treated with the distance afforded by the difference in size to bring out their absurdities, and a contrast drawn between (all too recognisable) present practice and their idealised 'original institutions'; thus, we are prepared for the similar contrast when the King of Brobdingnag pronounces his judgement of contemporary Europe. But satire is a powerful aid to complacency for those who feel themselves complicit with the satire, and on its own the first voyage serves to reinforce pride in what Peake terms 'the moral worth of the ordinary man'.[29] In Brobdingnag the limitations of such an outlook are revealed when confronted, again through the distancing effect of size, with a relatively primitive, but well-ordered and reasonably virtuous, society. Here Gulliver has only one defence that carries a degree of conviction, his appeal to the 'industry, art and sagacity' of his kind,[30] and of course it is this defence which Book 3 seeks to undermine – attempting to show the absurdity and worse of intellectual activity divorced from human benefit, and the relatively short and uncertain measure of its span. Peake summarises the matter well:

> What Swift is satirizing is pride, not intellect. The general theme of the whole book is that mere possession of social institutions, of the power to make moral judgements, of intellectual activity is no cause for pride since they can all be misused and corrupted. In the final voyage he makes the same attack on the last support of pride – man's possession of reason – especially as it is expressed in the definition of man as a rational animal.

Book 4 is philosophically the most interesting of the *Travels*. Here Swift 'invents a creature whose every characteristic was plainly rational, and another creature whose every characteristic was plainly irrational, in order to show how man compared with each.[31] The result, of course, is not flattering, but the theoretical interest lies in the conception of the rational embodied and its distance from the human. 'Houyhnhnm', we are told, means 'the Perfection of Nature' (we are reminded of Aristotle's claim),[32] and this is taken to exclude the erotic and irascible elements of man, which are the province of the Yahoos. It appears that a purely rational animal has great difficulty with saying 'the thing which was not. (For they have no word in their language to express lying or falsehood)' (p. 281; one notes by contrast that Gulliver's very asseveration of truthfulness [p. 341] embodies Sinon's treacherous oath to the Trojans); further, the notion of evil is entirely referential, drawn from 'the deformities of ill qualities of the Yahoos' (p. 323). These limitations prevent them from 'thoroughly understanding human nature' (pp. 345–6) for they cannot discriminate irrational forms of motivation in such a way as to identify the vice of pride – the primary study, of course, of the entire book. This makes for an effective peroration, for creatures governed by reason 'are no more proud of the good qualities they possess, than I should be for not wanting an arm or a leg' (p. 346); pride is unknown to them, thus, pride in being a rational animal in itself shows one not to be one – it is an 'absurd vice'. (As is remarked earlier, 'no person can disobey Reason, without giving up his claim to be a rational creature' [p. 328].) But the form of the peroration leaves one uneasy: 'I here entreat those who have any tincture of this absurd vice, that they will not presume to appear in my sight.' This sounds itself like the voice of pride, and the whole drive of the final chapter reinforces this impression. Gulliver's emulation of perfection blinds him to his own condition. He is not a Houyhnhnm; in this sense of 'perfection', human beings cannot achieve 'Perfection of Nature'.

But this sense of 'perfection' is problematic. It is the perfection of the rationality of the rational animal, but the perfection of reason turns out to be a hindrance to 'thorough understanding'; it represents, to use Castoriadis's terminology, the impossible aspiration to a 'symbolic network' without an 'imaginary capacity . . . the capacity to see in a thing what is not, to see it other than it is'.[33] Through the absurdity and near-madness into which Gulliver falls through trying to emulate an inhuman ideal Swift satirises human limitations – its subversive features make humour a particularly effective modality, a Trojan horse, for 'critical' works – but there is more than a hint that the ideal itself is flawed. If we are to have a model of rationality sufficiently relevant to our condition to subserve human justice it must incorporate the social imaginary (and perhaps the imaginary itself is not best conceived in terms of such simplicities as 'the thing which was not'); it is worth trying to envisage Ibsen's Nora in the land of the Houyhnhnms. The justice of the latter is static and abstract; it is reminiscent in many ways of Plato's *Republic* (as the Yahoos are of Hobbesian man in a state of nature) and, as in the *Republic*, there is no scope for a man to 'suffer into truth'.

It is not entirely clear why Gulliver is expelled, but there is a fear that he might subvert the Yahoos and there may be a hint that he might corrupt a master 'known frequently to converse with me';[34] if so, perhaps 'thorough understanding' is indeed possible to 'the Perfection of Nature' – but only through corrupting that perfection. We should be back with the myth of the Fall and the tree of the knowledge of good and evil – certain forms of knowledge are only possible through self-transformation. But it is only with a flawed model of reason that this transformation need be seen as a fall; on Cavell's account it is an upward journey – as it was for Aeschylus.

Four Quartets

> Although the *logos* is common to all, the many live as though their understanding were a private possession.

The Heraclitean epigraph which opens the *Quartets*[35] stands in stark contrast to Castoriadis's injunction 'Do not listen to Heraclitus'. It may turn out that the difference between them is not quite as at first appears, but the opposition can at best be softened – not eliminated.

If *The Waste Land* is predominantly critical, *Four Quartets* are essentially creative – but a creativity alive to criticism (including the satirical) and all too aware of the subversion of previous creativity. As in Aeschylus, there is an epistemological role for suffering, and as in Swift, the self-centredness represented by pride is a bar to self-knowledge and so, in turn, to wider understanding. The latter is represented by the *logos*, but its 'common' nature does not exclude an element of inwardness, and the 'private understanding' can be the communal fantasies Castoriadis also rejects ('personal authority, . . . mere opinion, incoherent arbitrariness'). The *Oresteia* can be seen as a movement from the comparative privacy of inter-communal blood-feud to the public face of the Areopagus, but in this sense the private is subsumed in the public; the two are not in the fundamental opposition the Erinyes at first fear – in Eliot's sense they are a part of the common *logos*. 'Difficulties of a States-man' brings out the complexity: the public face indeed represents 'mere opinion, incoherent arbitrariness' ('We demand a committee, a representative committee, a committee of investigation / RESIGN RESIGN RESIGN'); the *logos* common to all is to be found else-where ('Hidden in the stillness of noon, in the silent croaking night'). *Four Quartets* represent Eliot's attempt poetically to reorder his

'private' understanding of his own experience in the light of his perception of that universal *logos*, and thereby find that experience's
true meaning. The repetition of 'his' brings out Eliot's own recognition of the fact, insisted on by Castoriadis, that the supposed *logos*
is always mediated through an empirically situated (personal or
communal) standpoint; there is, that is, of necessity a double movement, for the nature of one's perception of any such universal norm
will itself be affected by one's own experience.

The desolating experience enacted in Eliot's earlier poetry, with
its wide cultural resonance, is still strongly present in the *Quartets*,
'Burnt Norton' ending with the lines: 'Ridiculous the waste sad
time / Stretching before and after.' But these lines are juxtaposed
with an evocation of what transcends that time: 'Quick now, here,
now, always –', and the dynamic of the *Quartets* is powered by the
tension between these two elements. In *The Waste Land*, too, such
moments of vision are to be found, but their capacity to transform
'the waste sad time' was deeply problematic and Eliot came to
believe that his grasp of their significance had been inadequate.
However, one's experiences are not static data, and the attempt to
return to them from a new perspective changes their nature. Eliot
sums up the situation in 'The Dry Salvages' (II):

> We had the experience but missed the meaning,
> And approach to the meaning restores the experience
> In a different form . . .

If the form of understanding sought conformed to standard scientific
models, dependent upon the testing of relatively stable data, the
sort of enquiry which Eliot's poetry represents would be void for
uncertainty. Plainly, such models are inappropriate. The aspiration
rather, in the words of 'Little Gidding' (III), is that such experience
may 'become renewed, transfigured, in another pattern'. The model
is remarkably close to that of Castoriadis's 'imaginary', 'the unceas-
ing and essentially *undetermined* (social-historical and psychical)
creation of figures/forms/images', but within the context of a norm
which breaks out of Castoriadis's vicious circle by transcending
the 'autonomous/heteronomous' opposition – in Tillich's terms it is
'theonomous'.[36] Heraclitus's *logos* is interpreted in terms of that
which transcends all *logoi*, and hence as much more like Cavell's
regulative ideal in the upward journey of the soul than the heteronomous imposition of a norm Castoriadis rejects.

'Burnt Norton', which came to be the first poem in the sequence,
fails to integrate public and private; the split consciousness of 'Dif-

ficulties of a Statesman' remains. Writing shortly before the Second World War, the poet rejected the common action of his fellow commuters as 'empty of meaning', and aspired to 'descend only / Into the world of perpetual solitude'. The result was, predictably, the split consciousness of the close of 'Burnt Norton'; the intense moment of personal immediacy is unable to transform the banality of our day-to-day social experience. But powerful voices in the poem had warned against the aspiration to solitude; we enter the 'place of disaffection' with 'Only through time time is conquered' ringing in our ears, yet the descent from it turns into an escape from 'time past and time future'; again, the *logos* of the epigraph is finally uncovered as 'The Word' with the warning that it 'Is most attacked by voices of temptation' in 'the desert', the place of solitude. Only transformation of the poet's consciousness, it is clear, can achieve a vision in which the *logos* is truly common to all – and this is the project of the subsequent sequence, a transformation only possible through engagement with the communal. Eliot embarked on the project with the coming of war, a crisis which promoted a sense of communal solidarity and a concern for what was of value – not merely a rejection of what was 'twittering' – among 'the gloomy hills of London' where his experience of the communal experience of fire-watching informs the final poem.

The approach of war had already deeply shaken Eliot:

> We could not match conviction with conviction.... Was our society, ... so confident of its unexamined premises, assembled round anything more permanent than a congeries of banks, insurance companies and industries, and had it any beliefs more essential than a belief in compound interest and the maintenance of dividends?[37]

Eliot found no comparable combination of vision and realism in the democracies of his day to match the totalitarian absolutisms of continental Europe; a society whose ultimate court of appeal was utilitarian was no match for the communal values of those who (in Castoriadis's terminology) 'recognized themselves' in the discourses of Mussolini, Hitler and Stalin. But a simple ignoring of communal claims in terms of some abstracted notion of 'justice', a heteronomous *logos*, would not do either. This perception is of a piece with his notorious embracing of 'Royalism' on becoming a British citizen a decade earlier, concurrently with his conversion to Christianity. Given the ultimate authority of God, the least inadequate political arrangements are those which recognise this; all principles and forms of government can be subverted (as Swift had insisted), but the archaic Royalist doctrines of the English seventeenth century at least provided the check that

> the king himself was a kind of symbol, and [the] assertion of divine right was a way of laying upon the king a double responsibility. It meant that the king had not merely a civil but a religious obligation toward his people.[38]

And of course a monarch accepting the doctrine knows that he, unlike principles or forms, ultimately faces the judgement of God for his stewardship. To use a more recent idiom, Eliot's 'Royalism' expressed the conviction that his society should not be dominated by the values of 'the military-industrial complex'.

'Little Gidding' was completed in 1942. Its 'broken king', coming by night 'Where prayer has been valid' and dying for his beliefs 'on the scaffold', is himself 'A symbol perfected in death' of a native political tradition which challenges contemporary banality. But of course the tradition remains archaic and Eliot knew it; this indeed was part of the point. The capital 'R' in the *Quartets* signifies the socio-political Rose (his other roses are the sensuous one of the opening and the spiritual one of the conclusion), and his poem is not

> ... an incantation
> To summon the spectre of a Rose.
> We cannot revive old factions
> We cannot restore old policies
> Or follow an antique drum.
> These men, and those who opposed them
> And those whom they opposed
> Accept the constitution of silence
> And are folded in a single party.
>
>   ('Little Gidding' III)

The Civil War period was one where recognition of responsibility under a transcendent *logos* was not the monopoly of a single faction. Eliot's 'use of memory' takes seriously the traditions of his adopted community, uniting old opponents 'in a single party' in virtue of their 'common genius', as a symbol of what it is to forget self in pursuit of a cause perceived as overriding the significance of one's own death. In this sense they were 'United in the strife which divided them', and in the dark days of wartime London the symbol is 'perfected' by those who die defeated but with integrity. But not any cause will do. The perception of the *logos* requisite to unmask delusion must be coherent, uniting all aspects of our (personal and communal) sensibility – all three 'roses' – and developed under circumstances favourable to one's own authenticity, which turn out to echo Aeschylus' *pathei mathos*:

> From wrong to wrong the exasperated spirit
> Proceeds, unless restored by that refining fire
> Where you must move in measure, like a dancer.
>
> ('Little Gidding' II)

The fire is purgatorial suffering, and we soon discover that, in terms of the poets present in the verse at this point, it is Dante's understanding of the purgatorial rather than Yeats's that is finally endorsed:

> The only hope, or else despair
>   Lies in the choice of pyre or pyre
>   To be redeemed from fire by fire.
>
> ('Little Gidding' IV)

Thus, we are prepared for the final parenthesis – the only way of overcoming that 'Waste Land' split between *logos* and common experience with which 'Burnt Norton' had ended:

> Quick now, here, now, always –
> A condition of complete simplicity
> (Costing not less than everything)
> . . .
> And the fire and the rose are one.
>
> ('Little Gidding' V)

This is no political blue-print, monarchist or otherwise, nor could it be given the enacted transcendence of the *logos*. It is a frame of reference by which to judge any political arrangements and to judge whether, in Swift's words, 'an institution, which in its original might have been tolerable' has been 'wholly blurred and blotted by corruptions'. On this account no communally based institution, and no perception of 'justice as fairness' or 'general welfare' can ever be final: 'We must be still and still moving / Into another intensity' ('East Coker' V); here at least Cavell, Castoriadis, Aeschylus and Eliot join hands.[39]

Endgame

If the direction Eliot descries can really be described, then Beckett's vision can be encompassed within Christianity. Within it, we could explain why we lack words, and have too many. . . . But can we really believe all this, or *must* these explanations be given in bad faith, blinding us to what we *do* believe? Beckett tests this because he is the contemporary writer complex and single enough to match with Eliot.[40]

With Beckett the 'waste sad time / Stretching before and after' is inescapable. At a theoretical level the doubt about what Eliot purports to descry is roundly declared by Arsene in *Watt*:

> What we know partakes in no small measure of the nature of what has so happily been called the unutterable or ineffable, so that any attempt to utter or eff it is doomed to fail, doomed, doomed to fail.[41]

We are here faced with the problem we found in Castoriadis and others; if the imaginary creates what the symbolic articulates as 'reality' and 'rationality' but is also interdependent with the symbolic, all claims to knowledge are nugatory, for the attempt to specify what will distinguish between knowledge and delusion is 'doomed to fail'.

In *Endgame* this failure is played out in a final 'refuge' (bomb-shelter, ark) where all outside is 'corpsed'. The play is written in the aftermath of the Second World War, following the Holocaust and the coming of the nuclear age, and is bleakly critical of all attempts to create meaning out of experience. As with Swift, humour is used subversively – for example, the hammer and three nails evoked by the proper names (in a place of a skull) both point to and undercut the Christian story, while Hamm's name reminds us of Ham, also from an ark, who was cursed – but the tonality is starker; we are beyond satire. Shards of meaning appear to disintegrate as one grasps them; the best commentary is perhaps Arsene's quasi-palindrome in Beckett's *Watt*: 'Do not come down the ladder, Ifor, I haf taken it away.'[42] We suffer indeed, but have no warrant for a conception of 'suffering into truth', let alone for an understanding of ourselves as 'rational animals':

HAMM: Clov!
CLOV: What is it?
HAMM: We're not beginning to . . . to . . . mean something?

CLOV: Mean something! You and I, mean something! Ah that's a good one!

HAMM: I wonder. Imagine if a rational being came back to earth, wouldn't he be liable to get ideas into his head if he observed us long enough. – 'Ah, good, now I see what it is, yes, now I understand what they're at!' – And without going so far as that, we ourselves ... we ourselves ... at certain moments ... To think perhaps it won't all have been for nothing![43]

There is indeed a community – the two parents, Hamm and Clov (and Clov claims to see a mysterious 'small boy' near the end, more being made of this in the French than the English version) – but this is not of itself sufficient to generate norms of justice or reason. 'Bottle him!' (that is, clamp down the lid on his father) Hamm brutally directs (p. 16), and this is of a piece with his ruthlessness:

> While there is life, the illusion of meaning may subsist. All that is living must be killed, exterminated without pity – the flea that Clov discovers, the rat in the kitchen, the strange 'child' outside.[44]

Endgame appears to be one stage beyond the nihilism of the denial of meaning, for nihilism is itself a well-known part of a 'grand narrative' and Beckett distrusts such narratives; as Cavell puts it, 'The problem seems to be that there is no way of *knowing* that there is no answer. . . . (An unconnected telephone cannot be left unanswered)';[45] all that is left is brute force.

To this it may be objected that the play itself operates through meanings, and that it is incoherent for the symbolic to be used to question the symbolic. It is a paradox of which Beckett is well aware, and Adorno's commentaries are helpful. On the one side:

> Through its own organized meaninglessness, the plot must approach that which transpired in the truth content of dramaturgy generally. . . . The interpretation of *Endgame* therefore cannot chase the chimera of expressing its meaning with the help of philosophical mediation. Understanding it can mean nothing other than understanding its incomprehensibility, or concretely reconstructing its meaning structure – that it has none.[46]

And on the other,

> Beckett's plays are absurd not for their absence of meaning – if

they had no meaning they would be irrelevant rather than absurd – but because they put meaning on the agenda.[47]

Bernstein puts the two elements together:

'Look at the earth . . . Since it's calling to you.' And so, too, is Beckett's play. The calling is, to be sure, a call to meaning, but as such, as it appears and calls it is equally the play's resistance to meaning. The call is meaning being put on the agenda; the resistance is the meaning we are trying to leave behind. The play works if these two meanings can be separated and their difference sustained.[48]

But can they? In Cavell's terminology, can the direction Beckett descries really be described, any more than in the case of Eliot? How are we to judge the 'test' when Beckett is 'matched witn Eliot', 'critic' with 'creator' in the sphere of meaning? These questions are nor rhetorical, but they are complex and cannot be tackled here. What I have been concerned to bring out is what is at stake. Serious political imagining, whether in the creative or critical modes, cannot be divorced from its ethical and metaphysical context, which bears on self, community, benefit and rationality itself. From the perspective of *Endgame* we can be sure of nothing but blind force as represented by Hamm's ruthlessness; justice, one might say, cannot be shown to be anything but orders backed by force – 'Bottle him!'; the force may not, of course, be simply physical (Hamm is physically helpless against Clov), it may be the force of persuasion – millions of Germans, we remember, ' "recognized themselves" in Hitler's discourse'. But we remain in the sphere of persuasion as criticised by Plato in the *Gorgias*, with no reliable dialectic to set against it.

The alternatives we have considered point to the possibility of a truth here that is independent of judgement, not by the imposition of a heteronomous of rational 'law' – such as 'justice as fairness' specified in a 'radically disembodied' context – but through taking seriously our embeddedness in communities and the aspiration to transcend that embeddedness without neglecting it. The possibility turns, at least in part, on the satisfactory specification of what count as 'favourable circumstances'. for discernment of that truth. Stanford's 'rite of passage from savagery to civilization' has a disconcerting suggestion here: we must 'suffer into truth'. It is a far cry from most contemporary political theorising, but it can hardly be dismissed as a cultural relic of 'savagery'; it remains pertinent to Swift,

Eliot and Beckett. If rational choice depends, at least in part, on self-knowledge, and justice is a function of rationality in choice, then it may not be absurd to look again at the thoroughly Aristotelian contention that the capacity to understand justice is not purely theoretical but depends on the state of the self who would understand.

Aristotle, of course, is not usually thought of as a proponent of *pathei mathos*,[49] but then it is almost as difficult to imagine his *phronimos* as the trilogy represents Orestes as (to move from Aeschylus to Eliot) suffering in the garden of Gethsemane. And in the refuge of *Endgame*?

PART III

To this whole line of thought it may be objected that the liberal ideal of justice as fairness need not be heteronomous, that the 'communitarian' criticism can be met on its own terms, for Rawls's recent *Political Liberalism*[50] reconceives his theory of justice as that of political liberalism in a democratic society – relative, that is, to specific sets of communities. The reconception, however, is somewhat Pyrrhic, for Rawls's original fine brash hypothesis, promising to give a definitive answer of universal relevance to the ancient Platonic question 'What is Justice', is thereby substantially weakened and relativised by its proponent.[51]

The heart of his theory, nevertheless, is unchanged and it remains the case that for Rawls political justice requires that citizens should not try to build their own moral ideals into the basic institutions of their societies, though political justice is itself a proper aspiration of one's moral nature alongside others. The key questions, of course, are why we should suppose that what Hampshire has termed 'the political domain of overlapping consensus and the private domain of protected moral diversity'[52] are ultimately separable and, if they are not, what should happen when these aspirations conflict – when the gods collide. Rawls, one might say, in such circumstances sides with Zeus:

> Under reasonably favourable conditions that make democracy possible, political values normally outweigh whatever non-political values conflict with them.[53]

The justification is that public reason by definition aims at overlapping consensus, and its requirements are integral to democratic citizenship; political justice, one might say, has been rewritten as democratic justice, and when we come to such issues as abortion the appeal to consensus begins to look suspiciously like the tyranny of the majority thinly disguised as appeal to 'the ideal of public reason'. But this ideal is itself problematic. As Hampshire trenchantly enquires:

> Why should an overlapping consensus among 'reasonable' persons about basic liberal values be either required or expected?[54]

This is only plausible if desires and emotions are seen as wholly distinct from reason, but this curiously archaic piece of faculty psychology seems a somewhat rusty sword to rely on. Alternatively, one might argue, as Hampshire does, that Rawlsian political justice is a procedural, not substantive matter; that we all have our values, some of them incompatible, and civilisation requires a method for dealing with conflicts between them; one can recognise that an immoral result has been justly arrived at and live with the result rather than defy it because of the neutrality, impartiality, consistency, in a word 'fairness', of the procedure – while one seeks to change the consensus. Athene's intervention when the votes are evenly balanced could be seen as providing a decision procedure only when consensus is unobtainable; where there is a majority vote one of the colliding gods submits. But one may wonder whether procedure and substance are wholly separable here (short of a radical form of relativism which may not itself be part of the consensus); some putatively immoral results so skew the situation as to debar the losing party from attempting to right the consensus (e.g., execution – not least that of Orestes) or subject to massive injustice those outside the decision-making process (e.g., the embarking on an unjust war). My suggestion is that, at least from Aeschylus onwards, there are alternative models of justice available that relate procedure to substance and integrate our passional lives into our conception of reason. And this is as relevant to Rawls Mark II as to Rawls Mark I.

On these alternative models not only are the political and private domains not ultimately separable, but within the 'private' the inward and the outward interpenetrate, and Wiggins's 'favourable conditions' for the discernment of truth may be only specifiable in first-person terms; in such cases the investigation of the connection between certain forms of inwardness and the putative favourability of the conditions so obtained may lead directly into issues of philosophical psychology. One is reminded of Scheler's analysis of the way that certain forms of suffering can lead to forms of 'purification' which involve 'ever increasing *clarification* of the center of our existence for our consciousness'.[55]

But for any such account to be sustainable one needs not only an adequate philosophical psychology, but also sophisticated conceptions of rationality and truth. Reason must not be so related to our passional nature as to make the truth it seeks dependent on judgement, whether of individuals or of communities (even when those communities are denominated 'democratic'), nor yet so detached from the particularities of our experience as to make that truth in principle unobtainable; it must be both independent of judgement and socially contextualised – at least when we are concerned with such matters as justice. The desiderata are relatively easy to state; the difficulty lies in meeting them. This chapter has taken up Wiggins's suggestion of articulating the 'marks' of truth – where the concept itself is specified (more or less) in the standard Tarskian manner; the contextualisation is given by the notion of convergence under favourable circumstances, and the independence by the demand that the best explanation of convergence requires the actual truth of the beliefs converged upon (or some variant of this requirement). But this of course puts pressure on the notions of 'best explanation' and 'favourable circumstances'. The 'creative' literary texts instanced suggest interpretations which are, I suspect, no part of Wiggins's programme but which, if accepted, point a way through the deadlock between 'community' and 'Enlightenment' ideals sketched in the first part of the chapter. If they are rejected without analogues being found to replace them, or if all variants of Wiggins's *via media* between moral realism and anti-realism and between (in a sense) correspondence and coherence conceptions of truth collapse then, so far as justice is concerned, the critical mode of political imagining has the last word and Beckett's *Endgame* may represent the only honest alternative – meaning and truth here are humanly inescapable aspirations but forever resisted by reality, forever mocked by the quite probably non-existent gods:

HAMM: We're not beginning to . . . to . . . mean something?
CLOV: Mean something! You and I, mean something! Ah that's a good one!

But, as Hamm also says: 'I wonder'.

My suggestion that we should reconsider *pathei mathos* is no doubt wildly unfashionable, but it may be more relevant to contemporary Bosnia than Rawsian liberalism. Given the length of the shadow the Enlightenment casts on our culture, it might indeed be useful to drop the now weakened term 'Justice' as a translation of the Aeschylean *Dikê* and replace it with something like the Hebrew '*Shalom*', which incorporates elements of justice, peace and wholeness integrating the personal and political levels. The relegation of such concepts to the fringes of all but religious contemporary discourse may perhaps indicate something of the problems of adequately coming to terms with human depth in secularised cultures – but that would be another story.

NOTES

1 John Rawls, 'Justice as Fairness' *The Philosophical Review*, 1958, vol. LXVII, 2, pp. 184, 192, 187; emphasis in original.
2 Rawls, *A Theory of Justice*, Oxford, Oxford University Press, 1973, pp. 11–12.
3 Rawls, *A Theory of Justice*, p. 560; Michael Sandel, *Liberalism and the Limits of Justice*, Cambridge, Cambridge University Press, 1982, pp. 21, 416, 127.
4 Charles Taylor, *Sources of the Self: The Making of the Modern Identity* Cambridge, Cambridge University Press, 1989, p. 521; see also Alasdair MacIntyre, *After Virtue*, London, Duckworth, 1981 and *Whose Justice? Which Rationality?*, London, Duckworth, 1988. For an outline of the debate see Stephen Mulhall and Adam Swift, *Liberals and Communitarians*, Oxford, Blackwell, 1992.
5 Stanley Cavell, *Conditions Handsome and Unhandsome: The Constitution of Emersonian Perfectionism*, Chicago and London, University of Chicago Press, 1990, p. 2.
6 Rawls, *A Theory of Justice*, p. 533.
7 Cavell, 'The Conversation of Justice: Rawls and the Drama of Consent', in his *Conditions Handsome and Unhandsome*, pp. 109, 112.
8 Cornelius Castoriadis, *The Imaginary Institution of Society*, trans. K Blamey, Cambridge, Polity Press, 1987, pp. 4, 5; see also p. 68; emphasis in original.
9 Castoriadis, *The Imaginary Institution of Society*, pp. 117, 127, 132–5.
10 Castoriadis, *Philosophy, Politics, Autonomy*, ed. and trans. D. A. Curtis, Oxford, Oxford University Press, 1991, pp. 81–123.
11 Castoriadis, *The Imaginary Institution of Society*, p. 3.
12 David Wiggins, *Needs, Values, Truth: Essays in the Philosophy of Value*, Oxford, Blackwell, 1987, p. 147.
13 Bernard Harrison, *Inconvenient Fictions: Literature and the Limits of Theory*, New Haven, CT and London, Yale University Press, 1991, p. 7. It is not necessary, however, to privilege the critical over the creative modes of literary imagining in the way this formulation might be seen as implying; see my review in *Philosophy*, 1993, vol. 68, 263, pp. 105–7.
14 W. B. Stanford, 'Introductory Essay: The Serpent and the Eagle' to *Aeschylus: Oresteia*, trans. Robert Fagles, ed. Robert Fagles and W. B. Stanford, London, Wildwood, 1976, p. 9; Hugh Lloyd-Jones, *The Justice of Zeus*, Berkeley, Los Angeles and London, University of California

Press, 1971, p. 94; John Jones, *On Aristotle and Greek Tragedy*, London, Chatto & Windus, 1962, pp. 111–13; emphasis in original.

15 Jones, *On Aristotle and Greek Tragedy*, p. 112; Stanford, 'The Serpent and the Eagle', p. 11.

16 Unless otherwise specified, quotations from and line references to the *Oresteia* are taken from Robert Fagles's translation cited above.

17 Lloyd-Jones, *The Justice of Zeus*, p. 94.

18 Line 461 in the Oxford Classical Texts edition (*Aeschyli: Septem Quae Supersunt Tragoedias*, ed. Denys Page, Oxford, Clarendon Press, 1972).

19 *Aeschylus I: Oresteia*, trans. Richard Lattimore, Chicago and London, University of Chicago Press, 1953.

20 Martha Nussbaum, 'Aeschylus and Practical Conflict' in her *The Fragility of Goodness: Luck and Ethics in Greek Tragedy and Philosophy*, Cambridge, Cambridge University Press, 1986, p. 45.

21 Nussbaum's translations in *The Fragility of Goodness*, pp. 35 and 36.

22 Nussbaum, *The Fragility of Goodness*, 49–50; 45.

23 E. R. Dodds, *The Greeks and the Irrational*, Berkeley, CA, Los Angeles and London, University of California Press, 1951, especially Chapters 1 & 2. But see also Douglas Cairns, *Aidos: The Psychology and Ethics of Honour and Shame in Ancient Greek Literature*, Oxford, Clarendon Press, 1993, especially the Introduction, where it is persuasively argued that Dodds's antithesis between shame and guilt cultures is highly problematic; at best it is 'one of degree rather than of kind. . . . Any attempt to maintain a revised antithesis between shame- and guilt-cultures would have to be based on a more sophisticated phenomenological analysis of shame and guilt than was carried out by the proponents of the original antithesis' (pp. 44–5).

24 With respect to Eliot, while the main emphasis of *The Waste Land* is critical (albeit with significant creative elements) that of *Four Quartets* is creative (though in part through criticism, including self-criticism). Common to all the literary texts discussed in Section II are the characteristic features termed by Harrison (*Inconvenient Fictions*, p. 60) 'disturbance and renovation' of our vision of reality, often through the disturbance and renovation of language itself; but renovation is more prominent in Aeschylus and Eliot than in Swift and Beckett.

25 Aristotle, *Politica*, in *The Works of Aristotle: Volume X*, ed. W. D. Ross, trans. B. Jowett, Oxford, Clarendon Press, 1921, 1253a.

26 Jonathan Swift, *Gulliver's Travels*, Harmondsworth, Penguin, 1967, p. 173.

27 Swift, *Gulliver's Travels*, p. 172.

28 See Charles Peake, 'The Coherence of *Gulliver's Travels*', in C. J. Rawson (ed.), *Swift*, London, Sphere, 1971, pp. 171–4.

29 Peake, 'The Coherence of *Gulliver's Travels*', p. 178.

30 Swift, *Gulliver's Travels*, p. 167.

31 Peake, 'The Coherence of *Gulliver's Travels*', pp. 181–2.

32 Swift, *Gulliver's Travels*, p. 281.

33 Castoriadis, *The Imaginary Institution of Society*, p. 127.

34 Swift, *Gulliver's Travels*, pp. 328, 327.

35 T. S. Eliot, *Four Quartets*, London, Faber and Faber, 1959. For quotations

from and allusions to Eliot's poetry other than *Four Quartets* see his *Collected Poems: 1909–1962*, London, Faber & Faber, 1974.

36 Paul Tillich, *Systematic Theology: Volume One*, Digswell Place, Welwyn, Nisbet, 1953, pp. 92–6.

37 Eliot, *The Idea of a Christian Society*, London, Faber & Faber, 1939, p. 64.

38 Eliot, 'John Bramhall', in his *Selected Essays*, London, Faber & Faber, 1951, p. 360.

39 The similarities and contrasts with Yeats, so powerfully present in 'Little Gidding' but also significant earlier in the *Quartets*, are illuminating at the political as at other levels. That projection ('tutelary deity' perhaps) of his community, Irish nationalism, is a force from the early poetry, but in the mature work there is an effort to transcend without disowning 'The fury and the mire of human veins' – in the imagery of 'Byzantium' to move from dolphin to golden bird (W. B. Yeats, *The Collected Poems*, London, Macmillan, 1961). But ultimately this self-transcending aspiration is overwhelmed by consciousness of mortality and by the time of 'The Black Tower' nothing grounds human integrity but sheer will – the determination that 'Those banners come not out'; reports of other possibilities are those of 'a lying hound', for 'There in the tomb the dark grows blacker, / ... Old bones upon the mountain shake'. The *Quartets'* diagnosis of this failure is that the Yeatsian vision of transcendence is merely 'enchantment' ('East Coker' II) for it fails to meet the 'condition of complete simplicity' of 'Little Gidding', leaving the images of 'Byzantium' indeed 'unpurged'. 'Love of a country' needs to be 'transfigured', but Eliot's emblem for the possibility of this transfiguration is 'a broken king'; the king of 'The Black Tower' is merely 'forgotten'.

40 Cavell, 'Ending the Waiting Game: A Reading of Beckett's *Endgame*', in his *Must We Mean What We Say?*, Cambridge, Cambridge University Press, 1976, p. 162; emphasis in original.

41 Samuel Beckett, *Watt*, London, Calder & Boyars, 1970, p. 61.

42 Beckett, *Watt*, p. 42.

43 Beckett, *Endgame*, London, Faber & Faber, 1964, pp. 26–7; stage directions omitted.

44 Richard Coe, *Beckett*, Edinburgh and London, Oliver & Boyd, 1968, p. 98.

45 Cavell, 'Ending the Waiting Game', p. 146.

46 Theodor Adorno, 'Trying to Understand *Endgame*', trans. Michael Jones, *New German Critique*, 1982, vol. 26, p. 120.

47 Adorno, *Aesthetic Theory*, trans. C. Lenhardt, London, Routledge & Kegan Paul, 1984, p. 220.

48 Jay Bernstein, 'Philosophy's Refuge: Adorno in Beckett', in David Wood (ed.), *Philosophers' Poets*, London and New York, Routledge, 1990, p. 186.

49 However Fragment 15 (Fr. 45 in Rose's Berlin edition) suggests that in Aristotle's *On Philosophy*, while *pathos* may properly be contrasted with *mathos* (Synesius), there are occasions when *pathos* may be the proper means to the illumination of *nous* (Michael Psellus). (Aristotle, *Fragmenta Selecta*, ed. W. D. Ross, Oxford, Clarendon Press, 1955, p. 84.)

50 John Rawls, *Political Liberalism*, Columbia, NY, Columbia University Press, 1993.
51 The Rawlsian retreat has far-reaching implications. In Aeschylus the projection of one's community imaged in the tutelary deity may have universal significance if that deity has Athene-like qualities, and the associated aspiration to the self-transcendence of community values has been a significant strand in Western political culture ever since. At the present day it is reflected in the way the internationally oriented foundation documents of the United Nations affirm values articulated in the 'liberal democratic' constitutions of some of the member nations; some forms of nationalism, it appears to be implied, are so capable of self-transcendence that they potentially project values of universal authority. If this is false then such affirmations indeed represent a form of 'neo-colonialism', as is often alleged, or other kinds of power play – for all nationalisms are in this respect equivalent. The way is open for the Yeatsian disillusion sketched in note 39 where values are grounded in community will (plus, no doubt, the contemporary equivalents of the maxim gun). The relativistic problems of communitarianism re-emerge.
52 Stuart Hampshire, 'Liberalism: The New Twist', *The New York Review of Books*, August 12, 1993, vol. XL, 14, p. 44.
53 Rawls, *Political Liberalism*, p. 146; see also pp. 156, 207–9.
54 Hampshire, 'Liberalism: The New Twist', p. 45.
55 Max Scheler, *Formalism in Ethics and Non-Formal Ethics of Values*, trans. M. S. Frings and R. L. Funk, Evanston, IL, Northwestern University Press, 1973, p. 348, emphasis in original.

6 Literature and moral choice

Anthony Arblaster

A significant part of the moral education of children consists in the passing on of general precepts: it is wrong to steal, you must never tell lies, and so on. What then puzzles children is not that adults do not necessarily behave according to these precepts (that there is a gulf between ideals and reality is one of the earliest lessons of human experience); what puzzles them is that adults apparently think it *right* sometimes to break the very rules they tell children to follow.

'Goodbye, Jane: thank you so much for a really lovely lunch. We all enjoyed it.' Then, not five minutes later, in the car going home: 'Wasn't that a really awful lunch! The chicken was almost inedible, and I really loathe their home-made wine.' Any child can work out that both statements cannot be true, and may soon conclude that there are occasions when lying is not only permissible but more or less mandatory. Unfortunately, a child's idea of which occasions these are may not coincide with the conventional adult view.

Is it possible to formulate general rules of morality which can guide us through the decisions and dilemmas of everyday life? One view of morality is that it does essentially consist of general rules of conduct which, if only it were possible to formulate them with sufficient precision, would provide us with the guidance we need in our efforts to live good lives. Many, perhaps most, religions aim to provide their followers with such rules. But this view of morality is also associated with Kant, and his maxim that 'I ought never to act except in such a way that I can also will that my maxim should become a universal law.'[1]

It is interesting to find this approach endorsed, from a very different angle by Jean-Paul Sartre, in *Existentialism and Humanism*:

To choose between this or that is at the same time to affirm the value of that which is chosen; for we are unable ever to choose the worse. What we choose is always the better; and nothing can be better for us unless it is better for all.[2]

Sartre seems to be saying that we cannot knowingly choose evil rather than good – a challenging proposition, the implications of which I shall not explore here. But he is also suggesting that if we are prepared to defend our choice in moral terms, as the better course or the right course, we are, by implication, saying that this is the better or right one for everyone in those circumstances. Some moral philosophers would argue that that is what is implied in the very use of terms like 'right' and 'good'.

Sartre is concerned to bring out the significance of the choices which we have no option but to make all the time: 'what is not possible is not to choose. I can always choose, but I must know that if I do not choose, that is still a choice.'[3] Choice is unavoidable, and so, therefore, is responsibility. In asserting that existence precedes essence, Sartre is denying the concept of human nature, or even of some particular nature or character with which we are endowed or with which we are born, that determines our actions or 'behaviour', and so relieves us of responsibility for them or it. We make ourselves, asserts Sartre. We create our characters through our actions and choices: 'Man is nothing else but that which he makes of himself.'[4]

It is only fair to point out that this bracing but burdensome philosophy of personal responsibility was formulated by Sartre before he became involved with Marxism and with Freudian psychology, both of which draw attention to the limits within which individuals can exercise their freedom of choice. Nevertheless, the essential existential emphasis on the inescapability of choice and responsibility does correspond to a central experience of moral life: the moment of hard choice, the agonising but inescapable dilemma in which we have to do one thing rather than another, and the awareness of having to make a choice is unavoidable, however predictable that choice may look in retrospect. These moments often constitute the focus and the pivot of works of fiction or drama, and literature, it seems to me, is peculiarly well-equipped to explore and illuminate such dilemmas.

Although Sartre places great stress on the universal moral significance of the decisions we make as individuals, he does not at all believe that there are general moral rules which can supply us with ready-made reliable guidance in making those decisions. On the contrary, he is at pains to show how useless such general maxims or rules are when someone is confronted by an actual, detailed moral dilemma. Such maxims do not, in other words, relieve us of the necessity of working out for ourselves what is the right thing to do in any specific situation. The example Sartre gives, in this lecture of 1945, is surely a very telling one. During the war which had just ended, a pupil of Sartre's, living in Nazi-occupied France, faced the following dilemma. He was living alone with his mother, who was deeply distressed both by the death of her elder son in the war and the collaborationist tendencies of her husband. Her one consolation was her younger son. But he, while realising this, was anxious to avenge his brother's death and join the Free French Forces then based in Britain. What was he to do?

> He also realized that, concretely and in fact, every action he performed on his mother's behalf would be sure of effect in the sense of aiding her to live, whereas anything he did in order to go and fight would be an ambiguous action which might vanish like water into sand and serve no purpose.[5]

Sartre argues that established moral codes provide no guidance in such a situation:

> Which is the more useful aim, the general one of fighting in and for the whole community, or the precise aim of helping one particular person to live? Who can give an answer to that *a priori*? No one. Nor is it given in any ethical scripture.[6]

No rule, no general maxim, can be sufficiently precise and detailed to relieve us of the obligation and necessity of making our own moral choice in any particular situation.

Yet all institutions, perhaps all social life, function in part on the basis of rules, customs, norms which are specifically intended to relieve us of the responsibility of constant choice and decision-making. If a student gets a mark of 60 she gets a 2.1 grade, if 59 or 58 it's a 2.2 – or whatever. But this rule is not applied inflexibly. Other academic or personal or medical factors may lead us to raise the 59 to 60, or count it as a 2.1 mark, or whatever. Even when there is a rule, we still have to decide whether and how to operate that rule. The station master will normally close the platform gate a minute before the train is due to leave, but in an emergency or under exceptional circumstances he or she will relax this rule – at least they will if they have any sense or imagination; and if they do not, that is also a decision for which they are responsible: to enforce a rule when enforcement may have dreadful consequences.

The rubric contained in most notes of guidance for examiners, to the effect that in the end the examiners must award the degree that they think is fair or right, is acknowledgement that no set of rules, together with all its provisos, caveats and exceptions, is complex enough to cover all the permutations of reality itself. They always make up a procrustean bed into which life itself must be squeezed – sometimes necessarily or justifiably. But it is central to existentialist morality to remind us of the uniqueness and complexity of existence, and its real priority over any schemes, theories, rules or meta-narratives which we may construct in order to control it or make sense of it.

It is one function of literature, and in particular of fiction and drama, to do the same, and Sartre was surely speaking as a novelist and playwright as well as a philosopher when he gave this lecture. In what follows I want first to focus on one very sharp and powerful example of a moral dilemma explored in a recent work of fiction, Brian Moore's novel, *Lies of Silence*, first published in 1990.[7] I shall then try to broaden the discussion and connect this text with others dealing with similar themes.

Michael Dillon is in his mid-30s, we infer, and is manager of a large hotel in Belfast. Born in Northern Ireland to Catholic parents, he is unhappily married to Moira, who is also Catholic in background and comes from the Falls Road. For nearly a year he has been having a clandestine affair with a younger woman, Andrea Baxter, and now he is on the brink (or thinks he is) of making the break with Moira and starting afresh with Andrea. But Moira is a deeply unhappy and insecure woman who, although she too is miserable in the marriage, is nevertheless dependent upon Michael, and will find it hard to manage without him. This is apparent not only to us, the readers, but also to her husband, who hesitates to make the break with her.

At this moment their lives are invaded by the IRA. Michael and Moira are held at gunpoint in their house at night. A bomb is placed in the boot of his car, and he is ordered to drive in his normal way to the hotel in the morning and park the car in the hotel car park. The plan is to kill a leading Protestant clergyman who is due to address a breakfast meeting in the hotel. It goes without saying that the bomb will certainly randomly kill and injure other people in and around the hotel at the same time. A coachload of French tourists is also staying there. While he drives his car to the hotel, followed by the IRA, Moira is being held hostage at their house, and if he makes any attempt to prevent the bombing, they have promised that she will be killed.

Unlike us, quietly reading the novel, or perhaps discussing it, he has very little time to decide what to do, and his dilemma is as fearful as can be imagined. If he tries to save the lives of the people in the hotel of which he is the manager, his wife will be killed. If he saves her life, it can only be by allowing the bomb to go off, and apart from the IRA he is the only person who knows that it is there, outside the hotel diningroom.

It is an imagined and constructed dilemma, but it is an entirely credible one. The practice of hostage-taking is now so common that situations in which the lives of two different groups of innocent persons are placed at risk in competition with each other, are quite familiar. So is the practice of making threats against someone's family if that someone does not 'co-operate' with the threateners. In the event as narrated, Dillon does not hesitate once he has left his car. He phones the emergency services and the hotel is evacuated in time to avoid death or injury to those inside.

As it happens his wife is not killed either. And so, as a policeman says, all's well that ends well? Of course it is not. Dillon is unavoidably aware of the significance of the decision he has made, and so is Moira, who, without knowing of his relationship with Andrea at this stage, takes his decision as irrefutable proof of his indifference towards her. When she later discovers their relationship, that inevitably confirms her interpretation of his behaviour. His 'courage' in thwarting the assassination attempt could also have been personally convenient to him in its consequences.

In their joint confrontation with the IRA in their own house it is Moira, not Michael, who is openly defiant. She makes an attempt to escape while going to the toilet, and makes no secret of her contempt for the masked youths and their behaviour. Having survived, she decides to go public with her defiance and tell the whole story to the media. She does what people inside and outside the novel say ought to be done. She 'stands up to the terrorists, the men of violence'. She also has her 15 minutes of fame.

But this in its turn has consequences. Dillon receives a phone call from the IRA warning him about the likely consequences of speaking out. He moves to London with Andrea to take over another hotel in the American-owned chain. The police in Belfast make some arrests, and he is asked to come back and identify one of those arrested, whose face he glimpsed during the nocturnal hold-up. Since he has broken with Moira and with Belfast, and is hoping to start a new life in London with Andrea, he is unwilling to be drawn back into the Irish quagmire with its manifest dangers. A Catholic priest, evidently close to the IRA, comes to London to beg him not to help the police: the young man to be identified is his nephew. Dillon is angered by the dishonest and unctuous terms in which this plea is made, and refuses. Within hours he is shot dead at his new home in north London. This ending is sudden, brief and shocking – exactly as it would be, and therefore fictionally should be, I think.

Moore is not given to elaborate authorial commentary, and events move too fast for his characters to have much leisure for reflection and introspection. One reviewer complained that 'the moral complications need to be extracted by the reader: they are largely unexplored by Moore'.[8] This seems to me to miss the point. The moral dilemmas need no underlining, and Moore is concerned with how his characters deal with them.

Dillon's first appalling choice is followed by other, less urgent but comparably difficult and life-endangering decisions. Moira's decision to publicise what happened to them places them both in danger, while Dillon's refusal to respond to the priest's pleas (with their undertones of threat) leads directly and swiftly to his death. In each case, the consequences of the alternative courses of action open to them are clearly perceived by the characters, while at the same time their highly ambiguous and even possibly disreputable motives for acting in certain ways are made plain to us, while being much less clearly apprehended by the characters themselves. Two familiar versions of morality, one of which stresses the consequences of actions, while the other focuses on the need for good motives, are here brought together, being intertwined, not merely juxtaposed, in the way that they typically are in actual experience.

Moore's portrait of Moira is subtle and perceptive. She is consistently cold and distant towards Michael after the episode in which he put her life at risk. She never gives him the opportunity to talk to her about it, and her decision to go public about it is taken without consulting him. Although she is evidently a person of some courage, it also looks as if this decision is an act of revenge against her husband. So her motives for defying the IRA are probably extremely mixed, just as it is impossible not to wonder whether Michael Dillon would have acted so decisively to save the hotel residents if the hostage had been Andrea not Moira – a point which Moira puts directly to him once she has found out about the relationship.

Michael Dillon's lack of courage under normal circumstances is crucial to his behaviour throughout. He has no wish for the full story of the bomb-planting episode to be made public. He refuses to go on TV with his wife. He accepts the proposed transfer to London with alacrity, both because it facilitates the break with Moira and because he wishes to get away from the danger of IRA retaliation and from the whole risky and sordid imbroglio of Northern Ireland. When the police ask him to return to Belfast he is deeply reluctant to do so. Urged on by Andrea, he is desperate to put the whole affair and place behind him and make a new life in London. Moore depicts quite movingly the few days of comparative happiness, always underlaid by unease, which he and Andrea enjoy together when they first arrive in London. It is the evasive, morally corrupt arguments of the priest which tilt him towards helping the police, so that for the second time in the story he takes a brave and dangerous decision.

Both decisions are impulsive. They are not the outcome of cool deliberation. Ironically, in the second, fatal case he *has* spent some time thinking and talking about what to do, but the outcome of this debate is that he is apparently resolved not to help the police, but to put his personal happiness and safety first. This is even recon-firmed after he has met the priest. Andrea persuades him, without much difficulty, to tell the police that he will not return to Belfast to testify. But he knows what this means in terms of his own self-esteem and integrity:

> The time had come. There had been no war in his life. He would never be called up as a soldier and put to the test of bravery in battle. He would never be asked to perform an act of heroism as a member of a resistance group. He had, instead, been put to the test by accident, a test he had every right to refuse. And yet as he unlatched the gate and went up to the frontdoor of the house he knew that the moment the phone rang and he answered it, the moment he told them he was afraid, he would lose for ever something precious, something he had always taken for granted, some secret sense of his own worth.

He never gets to have that phone conversation, and so we never know how he would actually have responded to the police request. But that paragraph suggests that he could very well have taken the brave and dangerous path. Rational arguments about happiness and effectiveness, about consequences – not simply for oneself – might well yield to this strange deep sense we nearly all have of what we cannot do without violating the very core of our being, without destroying whatever we may have in the way of integrity.

Dillon's final predicament and his response are not so different from those of John Proctor in Arthur Miller's play *The Crucible*. Imprisoned and accused of witchcraft along with his pregnant wife and his friends, a clergyman urges his wife to persuade him to save himself by making a false confession:

> It is a mistaken law that leads you to sacrifice. Life, woman, life is God's most precious gift; no principle, however glorious, may justify the taking of it. I beg you, woman, prevail upon your husband to confess. Let him give his lie. Quail not before God's judgement in this, for it may well be God damns a liar less than he that throws his life away for pride.[9]

Proctor himself sees the force of this. 'I want my life', he says. Besides, having betrayed his wife by sleeping with Abigail Williams he has lost his sense of his own worth: 'I cannot mount the gibbet like a saint. It is a fraud. I am not that man.' And so he makes his confession.

But the process demands too much of him. He cannot bring himself to go a step further and name names (the implicit comparison with the anti-communist witchhunt of the early 1950s, when the play was written and Miller himself was summoned to appear before the House UnAmerican Affairs Committee, is clear and deliberate). He can hardly bring himself to sign the confession. Then when it is proposed to nail the document to the church door, he rebels: 'You will not use me! . . . I am John Proctor. You will not use me! It is no part of salvation that you should use me!' He cannot bear to lose his 'name': 'How may I live without my name? I have given you my soul: leave me my name!' And so, like Joan of Arc in Shaw's play of 30 years earlier, he tears up his confession and goes out to his execution.

Proctor, as a farmer in the religion-saturated society of seventeenth-century Massachusetts, is endowed by Miller with a much stronger moral sense than Moore's late-twentieth-century hotel manager. Proctor was always less likely to compromise his integrity. Nevertheless, he faces the same choice, between life won by compromise and, on the other hand, integrity and, in his case, the certainty rather than just the risk, of death. And he too is willing, at one level, to make the necessary compromise, to accept rational consequentialist arguments, to do what might seem a small wrong action for the sake of a greater future happiness.

It is entirely plausible that with Dillon we should be left in some uncertainty as to what course he would finally have chosen; whereas John Proctor makes, at the last moment, a defiant, heroic choice. But in both cases there is the same pattern: of a willingness to follow the path of common sense and rational self-interest until, suddenly, something is said or asked which demands too much of them in terms of compromise, or self-abasement or self-deception, and the moral self rises up in revolt: 'Here I stand. I can do no other.'

I do not at all want to suggest that this is a universal pattern of behaviour. On the contrary: it looks as if there are people for whom there are no limits to what they are prepared to tolerate or even to do if that is the price of their own survival, especially if the excuse of obedience to some higher authority is available. This willingness to grovel, and even to betray friends in response to the demands of the state and the dominant ideology, was much in evidence in the behaviour of former communists and leftists before the McCarthyist inquisition of the early 1950s. It was one of the spectacles which prompted Miller to write his play.

On the other hand, though, there is the contemporary phenomenon, very convincingly represented in Michael Dillon, of the 'ordinary', uncommitted person who nevertheless at a certain point of crisis feels that their integrity or self-respect is at stake, and so takes a stand. Another, and even more striking example, is the central figure in Thomas Keneally's novel or 'faction', *Schindler's Ark*, now brought to a far wider audience in Steven Spielberg's film, *Schindler's List*.

Oskar Schindler was, of course, a real person, and the story that Keneally and Spielberg have told is in all essentials a true one. Schindler was an apparently unremarkable opportunistic businessman and member of the Nazi Party who, in the wake of the Nazi invasion and occupation of Poland in 1939, moved in to take advantage of the money-making opportunities afforded by this expansion of the German Reich.

His success depended on his maintaining friendly contacts with leading members of the party and SS in Poland, and on supplying them with luxuries otherwise unobtainable under wartime conditions. There was nothing in his record which would suggest someone who would risk his own life to protect Jews against deportation to the extermination camps. Yet this was the course on which he embarked as an employer. He systematically employed Jews in his factories, and managed by all kinds of means, both risky and devious, to prevent their removal. He even rescued a group of women and children from Auschwitz itself.

Schindler was responsible for saving about 1,200 Jews from the Holocaust: a handful, in numerical terms, but he did it in effect single-handed, and his achievement is rightly honoured and remembered in Israel, where he is buried. After the war he stayed in West Germany, but fell on hard times, moved for a while to Argentina, returned to Germany and lived out his life in relative obscurity. His fellow countrymen and women were not on the whole much interested in his story.

The extraordinary thing about Schindler is his apparent ordinariness. He had no history of political or religious commitment, let alone of opposition to Nazism. It is far from clear what prompted him to take the stand and the risks he did. Perhaps he would have had difficulty in explaining it himself. But I would suggest that Schindler's stand is another example of someone who, despite his normal routine willingness to go along with what the state and authority do and demand, discovers in himself a limit to what he can tolerate, accept and co-operate with. A sense of outrage comes into play. And that, surely, represents the core of our moral being – if we have such a core.

What the sources of this sticking point, this point of resistance and commitment, may be is another matter. But it is of the utmost importance that we do learn what elements in upbringing, education and social experience help to create such a moral core, since without it there really are no limits to the moral and human (or, rather, inhuman) atrocities which people, and especially perhaps men, will commit under adverse conditions. If you contrast Oskar Schindler with Eichmann, or with Lieutenant Calley of My Lai, or with some of those involved in the war crimes in Bosnia the moral gap is plain. All perhaps unremarkable people outside the time of moral testing and crisis, but when that comes upon them, some, a few, turn out to be life-savers, while others become murderers and torturers, or the agents and accomplices of mass murder. In sheltered England it is relatively rare to be confronted with such momentous moral choices, but it has been common enough across much of the globe in the twentieth century, and writers like Moore, Miller and Keneally are right to grasp that it is in such testing circumstances that a person discovers who he or she really is, what matters to her, what she is really committed to. 'My unconscious method is to find the moment of crisis', Brian Moore has said. Certainly that is the case with *Lies of Silence*.

This novel also casts light, as I briefly indicated earlier, on the two versions of morality which may be labelled 'consequentialist' and 'motivational'. Was Dillon right to risk his wife's life to save the people in the hotel? If we have a general obligation to save lives of others, we also have particular obligations to relatives and friends which may sometimes weigh more heavily with us than a general obligation. This is not because our friends and relatives are objectively more important and valuable than anyone else, but simply because they *are* our friends and relatives, and going specially out of our way to support, help and protect them is what love and friendship mean. It would be a bold person who would condemn Dillon outright if he had decided to save his wife's life instead. Yet Moira herself comes to believe in the moral integrity of what Michael did. And it is not difficult to justify his actual decision in normal consequentialist terms. Many random deaths and injuries were avoided.

So perhaps he did the right thing – or the less dreadful thing. But did he do it for the right reason?

The last temptation is the greatest treason:
To do the right deed for the wrong reason.[10]

Eliot's couplet is the quintessence of motivational morality, and no doubt if you're keen, like Eliot's Becket, to be a saint, it is important to get your motives right, although the *ambition* to be a saint is surely a self-contradictory enterprise! It does seem likely that Dillon's readiness to risk Moira's life reflects, at some level, both his lack of love for her, and the fact that her disappearance from the scene would be personally convenient in some ways. In forming an opinion of Dillon as a moral being this is certainly relevant. If his action was prompted partly or primarily by self-interested motives, then our admiration or respect for him is much reduced. This is where a consideration of motives is relevant and necessary.

But it does not follow that because his motives were mixed, or even disreputable, that he did the wrong thing. There are plenty of circumstances under which the right deed remains the right deed even it if is done for the wrong reason – as Eliot's lines perhaps inadvertently imply. Someone who rescues a child running into a busy road may do so for vainglorious or self-interested reasons which, if they come to light, will certainly affect our opinion of him or her; but it will not alter our judgement that he or she did the right thing. The great virtue of consequentialism is that it is outward-looking, concerned with the effects of our actions upon others. A concern with motives is inherently introspective and tends towards narcissism (as with Eliot's Becket) and, at worst, paralysis of the will. This is well-illustrated by the case of Bernard Sands, the central figure in Angus Wilson's novel, *Hemlock and After*, another searching fictional exploration of the difficulties of the moral life.

There are, of course, situations in which motive and action are inseparable, where the nature and value of the action depend absolutely upon it being done for the right reason, with the right motive. A child, an old person, anyone who craves affection, will not be made happy by someone who looks after them merely out of a sense of duty, although that may well be better than total neglect. But this is the opposite of Kant's view: that the *only* morally worthy motive is the sense of duty or obligation.[11] There are occasions when that is the appropriate motive; but there are many others when it is not. In many circumstances a sense of duty is not an adequate substitute for sympathy or solidarity, for affection or love.

Novelists naturally tend to be interested in the exploration of motive, and the normal focus of the novel upon particular individuals may lead to a corresponding lack of interest in the consequences of action when they affect persons not central to the design of the fiction. It is a merit of *Lies of Silence* that this is not so. The hotel guests threatened with death and injury are real to Michael Dillon, and to us. And, allowing for the possible ambiguity of his motives, we might well think it a virtue in him that he feels concern and responsibility for these people who are not close to or even known to him.

I would suggest, too, that if one did not know from other sources of the consequentialist and motivational approaches to morality, it would be possible for a sufficiently thoughtful and analytical reader of *Lies of Silence* and *The Crucible*, or of *Murder in the Cathedral* and *Hemlock and After* – or perhaps *Hamlet* alone would be enough – to formulate this distinction. It seems to be grasped, in a wonderfully specific and three-dimensional way, by novelists and dramatists with an ease and naturalness which put most moral philosophers to shame – with their dry schematic formulae and their reluctance to use complex, real-life examples (Sartre is a conspicuous exception to these generalisations).

We witness also in these fictions something which takes us beyond these rather simplified antitheses, and which is in some ways of even greater importance. We see people put to the test by situations and demands which are extreme, yet by no means uncommon. The pressures of these conjunctures exposes whether or not at the heart of their being there is a moral void, an absence of any fundamental principles or convictions which are held so deeply that they are integral to their sense of identity, their definition of themselves; or whether some sense of morality, of what is permissible and what is not, however deeply buried under layers of flexibility, indifference, self-interest and accommodation to 'reality' will, under exceptional pressure, assert itself and force them, often most unwillingly, to acts of courage and integrity.

These acts are not always easily justified in terms either of likely good consequences or of pure motives. They may indeed seem like futile moral gestures or hopeless acts of defiance even to those who undertake them, let alone the prudent, worldly-wise ones who would never dare to commit them. But they are the good deeds which in a naughty world restore our faith in human decency and courage. Oskar Schindler's project must have seemed foolhardy even to himself. He was imprisoned more than once. No one would or could have blamed him if he had failed, if the SS had rounded up the Jews in his factories and marched them off to the cattle trucks and the death camps. That he did not fail, that he saved over a thousand Jews and survived himself, tells us something very important about what can be done under the most terrible circumstances imaginable – something we might prefer not to know. But even if he had failed completely, he would rightly be honoured, along with all the other active opponents of Nazism, for his refusal to collaborate with absolute evil. For without that capacity to refuse, to resist, to take a stand, however useless it may seem in the immediate context, there is no light to lighten our darkness, and every kind of atrocity becomes possible.

As was suggested earlier, consequentialism has much to be said for it. A failure or refusal to do what needs or ought to be done because we are worried about the purity of our own motives is really a kind of moral conceit or self-indulgence. Nor, on the other hand, is the person of inflexible principle exempt from a consideration of consequences either. We lie politely about the awful lunch because that is one of a good many situations in which telling the truth would have far more damaging consequences, however strongly we endorse a general principle of honesty and truth-telling. Given that Schindler wanted to save the Jews he employed, he then had to decide how best to do this, and that involved all kinds of nauseating compromises. He had to keep on friendly terms with criminals and monsters, and do endless favours for them. He had to keep silent about arbitary cruelty and murder. And much much more. The end abundantly justified the means, as it so often does.

But consequentialism also has its limits and its dangers, the greatest of which is probably short-termism, the failure to look beyond the immediate balance of advantages and disadvantages. It is not difficult, for example, to construct hypothetical situations in which torture, even the torture of a child, could be justified in terms of its beneficial consequences. In the same way the mass bombing of German cities at the end of the Second World War, or the use of atomic weapons against Japan a few months later, have both been defended in terms of having shortened the war and saved more lives than were lost by the actions themselves.

But one consequence that consequentialism often neglects is the effect of setting a precedent. Once torture is justified by reference to its supposedly beneficial consequences, it will be used again and again, for a host of different causes, all of which are thought to provide adequate justification by their adherents. When, during the Spanish Civil War, German planes bombed and machine-gunned the Basque town of Guernica and its inhabitants, there was an international outcry. But it set a precedent, and in the Second World War and in many wars since the bombing of civilian 'targets' has become a routine aspect of aerial warfare.

What I am saying could be construed simply as an argument for a more complex and extensive consequentialism. But there is more to it than that. There are occasions when it is impossible to be sure that our action will have any good consequences, and when, on the other hand, we can be sure that it will have terrible consequences for ourselves and those nearest to us. That is John Proctor's situation. As a Protestant Christian in a Protestant community, he might be expected to justify his stand by reference to his religion, and probably a real-life John Proctor would have done so. But Miller, perhaps anachronistically, shows him as concerned with his 'name', his dignity and self-respect. This might verge on vanity or egoism, but as presented it is plainly a stand against bullying and hysteria. And the essence of morality is this readiness to take a stand, however hopeless and useless it may seem to be.

This goes beyond consequentialism, but it does not finally contradict it, I think. For what is certain is that evil is only defeated if people are prepared to make a stand against it. The witch-hunts of the seventeenth century did not die out of their own accord. Nor did the anti-communist persecution of the 1950s. Only persistent criticism, ridicule and opposition did that. And in these cases as in so many others those who opposed must often have felt that they were fighting a hopeless battle against overwhelming odds. Some battles are hopeless; others are not. But that is a judgement that can often only be made after the event. It is often morally necessary to fight battles which are lost as well as ones which are won.

Finally, I return to the points with which I began – Sartre's points about the burden of choice and the inadequacy of general rules to guide us when confronted with specific, complex moral decisions. The choices faced by Moore's fictional character, and by Miller's, as well as by Sartre's pupil, are all difficult ones, in that they are choices between conflicting obligations and loyalties, and as such they are typical of moral dilemmas in general. Sartre's contention is that nothing can relieve us of the burden of choice in such situations.

Traditionally, religions were designed to relieve the individual of this onus of choice. Suicide is wrong, divorce is wrong, abortion is wrong, alcohol is wrong: the blanket prohibitions upheld by traditional Catholicism, or fundamentalist Protestantism or fundamentalist Islam, are all intended to simplify life and decision-making for the individual, relieving him or her of the anxieties of choice and the weight of responsibility. 'I was only obeying God's laws.'

But increasingly in the modern, post-Reformation epoch, people have not been content, or have not found it easy or natural, to follow such rules unquestioningly. Fiction, drama and other arts explore this dilemma. Graham Greene, in those of his novels most preoccupied with Catholic themes, focuses precisely on the conflict between individual experience and impulse and the rules of the Church; especially in *The Heart of the Matter*, where he suggests that even suicide, a mortal sin according to Catholic dogma, may not be beyond God's forgiveness, which transcends the strict rules of the Church.

The novel, and post-Renaissance drama, were from the start individualist forms in that they focus on individuals and the choices they have to make; and they reflect a society, Western society, in which the old clear guiding rules of conduct are being steadily eroded, leaving individuals with the unfamiliar burden of having to make their own decisions about life-patterns, morals, marriage and much else. (Burke's defiant praise and defence of habit, custom and prejudice is a late attempt to stem this tide of individualistic erosion.) Many people still find this load of responsibility too heavy to carry on their own. They cling, with increasingly desperate inflexibility, to the old religious rules of conduct; or else they gratefully transfer responsibility to some secular authority, usually the state. 'I was only obeying orders' is probably the commonest modern excuse for committing evil and not accepting personal responsibility for it. But there is still an element of choice. Orders can be defied, or disregarded or disobeyed. Oskar Schindler showed us that it is possible to do good even in the most hostile circumstances. One virtue of literature is that it continues to set before us examples of defiance, of independence and the acceptance of responsibility – a responsibility which cannot now be evaded, because acceptance of the authority of a church or a god, let alone any secular authority, is, for the inhabitants of modern societies (as opposed to traditional ones) also an act of choice for which the individual is responsible. About responsibility Sartre and the existentialists were surely right.

NOTES

1 Immanuel Kant, *Groundwork of the Metaphysic of Morals*, in H. J. Paton (ed.), *The Moral Law*, London, Hutchinson, 1948, p. 67.
2 Jean-Paul Sartre, *Existentialism and Humanism*, trans. Philip Mairet, London, Methuen 1948 p. 29.
3 *Ibid.*, p. 48.
4 *Ibid.*, p. 28.
5 *Ibid.*, p. 35.
6 *Ibid.*, p. 36.
7 Brian Moore, *Lies of Silence*, London, Bloomsbury, 1990. I have given no page references, since the book is now also published in paperback. The passage quoted later comes from the final pages of the novel.
8 Mark Lawson in The *Independent*, April 21, 1990.
9 Arthur Miller, *The Crucible*, Act 4, in *Collected Plays*, London, Cresset Press, 1958. Again I am giving no page references. All quotations from *The Crucible* are from Act 4.
10 T. S. Eliot, *Murder in the Cathedral*, London, Faber & Faber, 1935. Becket's words are spoken at the end of Part 1 of the play.
11 Kant, *op. cit.*, pp. 63–4.

7 The aloofness of liberal politics[1]

Can imaginative literature furnish a private space?

Paul Seabright

Liberal political theories famously require society to offer individuals a space in which to live out their own fulfilment according to their own conceptions of the good. What can fill this space? Not anything intrinsically and necessarily political, or else politics has invaded the space it was supposed to respect. Once immediate threats to that space have been lifted – violence halted, hunger and physical discomfort alleviated, preventable disease eradicated; once individuals have access to some of the basic building blocks of a life, any life (literacy, numeracy, health, some social skills) – then, on any recognisably liberal view, the task of politics is substantially done. The outer world stands aloof. What remains?

It is a question to which the most natural answers are metaphorical. One could liken liberal politics to gardening. To make a garden and all its various physical, aesthetic and spiritual pleasures possible, there needs to be a staking out of territory, a clearing of weeds, a prevention of encroachment; this is the 'negative liberty' of the garden, to use Berlin's phrase.[2] There must also be a provision of soil and its nutrients, access to both sunshine and shade, a supply of water; these are the necessary conditions of its 'positive liberty'. There will be much argument and dispute between gardeners in a community about how and how much to assure these liberties, and both the activities required to do so and the dispute about them will occupy a significant part of each gardener's time. But, though necessary, they are not sufficient. One may have all these things and produce a straggle, a wilderness or a desert. A gardener will bring something else to the task: taste, skill judgement – qualities unrelated to, though possibly partially nourished by, the activities involved in assuring the liberties. It is the exercise of these qualities, the metaphor suggests, that makes all the hard work involved in assuring the liberties worthwhile. How can we characterise these qualities, and (more importantly) where can the gardener turn for guidance, inspiration and a sense of shared endeavour?

In classical political theory the metaphor for the private space was not the garden but the hearth. And the kind of private space it denoted was very different from the liberal conception. In traditional agrarian societies the labour required to ensure the basic necessities of life was performed at or near home. The hearth therefore presented the locus of toil and hardship, the ultimate end and purpose of which was to enable citizens to step outside the home and excel themselves in the public sphere. Hannah Arendt in *The Human Condition* discusses how

> excellence itself, *arete* as the Greeks, *virtus* as the Romans would have called it, has always been assigned to the public realm where one could excel, could distinguish oneself from all others. Every activity performed in public can attain an excellence never matched in private; for excellence by definition, the presence of others is always required, and this presence needs the formality of the public, constituted by one's peers, it cannot be the casual, familiar presence of one's equals or inferiors.[3]

Incidentally, warfare (since it evidently took place outside the home) was consequently one of the areas in which excellence could be displayed, and was not generally regarded as the evil it clearly came to represent for liberal societies. Arendt claims that the division of labour turned production into a public activity ('the rise of housekeeping, its activities, problems and organizational devices – from the shadowy interior of the household into the light of the public sphere', so that 'the activities connected with sheer survival are permitted to appear in public'); this in turn left space for 'a sphere of intimacy . . . whose peculiar manifoldness and variety were certainly unknown to any period prior to the modern age'. Although she does not cite Benjamin Constant in this connection, there is clearly a reflection here of his famous distinction between the Liberty of the Ancients and the Liberty of the Moderns,[4] the former indicating the liberty of the Greek citizen to participate in public affairs and the latter the right of citizens to a private space in which to practise their religion and carry on their own affairs.

Critics of Arendt have argued that the activity of the household was not as universally devalued as she claims.[5] And in other civilisations than the Greek and Roman, the private sphere was certainly capable of being treated on a more equal footing. For example, classical Tamil poetry celebrated equally the fulfilments of the 'akam' (hearth or interior) and 'puram' (town or exterior), without privileging one over the other.[6] But it is fair to say that the idea of the private space as a project, indeed as *the* project that makes the effort in creating and defending it worthwhile, is a much more modern idea.

The metaphor of the garden has not been widely employed in political writing in the liberal tradition. One notable exception is in Voltaire's *Candide*, where the Turkish gardener of the concluding chapter presents a picture of untroubled fulfilment away from the quarrelsome and dangerous currents of politics ('il faut cultiver notre jardin', says Candide). Even here, though, the satire is savage: Martin says approvingly that 'to work without thinking is the only way to make life tolerable'.[7] Furthermore, Jack Goody has argued that the cultivation of flowers for ornamental purposes depended on a culture of luxury that was itself the product of social stratification and consequently the target of criticism by social reformers as well as a source of guilt and unease.[8] In these circumstances it is unsurprising that the metaphor of the garden may have seemed too compromised by its associations of *ancien régime* conspicuous consumption to have appealed to liberal writers. The garden has indeed been used as a metaphor for fulfilment, but typically by writers of a less reformist bent: Montaigne, for example, says 'I would like death to find me planting my cabbages, but caring little for her, and even less for the state of my imperfect garden.'[9] The metaphor of planting was used, more ambivalently, by Hayek to explain the tendency of liberals to become more closely involved in understanding (and, by a subtle shift, planning) human society:

> The attitude of the liberal towards society is like that of a gardener who tends a plant and in order to create the conditions most favourable to its growth must know as much as possible about its structures and the way it functions.[10]

Nevertheless, the garden as metaphor for the private space is an encouraging one (though perhaps particularly within the culture of the British Isles),[11] if only because it is clear what kind of activity might be fulfilling within the private space. Most of us can recognise and appreciate a lovingly tended garden even if we cannot produce one ourselves. But the idea of a private space ('space' is itself a metaphor, not a neutral description) is much more ambivalent. Compare two visions of a world that has removed most of the material threats to that space:

1 Cities do not contrast sharply with the countryside, but form part of a spectrum of living possibilities which intersperse buildings and parkland. Citizens spend a part of their time working in the production of goods and services, in offices and factories that they seek to decorate and make pleasant with the same care they expend on their homes. They pass a part of the remaining time in the activities of citizenship – serving on their community council, doing military service, visiting the elderly and the sick who have no relatives. The remainder of their time they pass with their friends, children, lovers, parents. They undertake projects: building, exploration, music-making, travel, the theatre and the arts. They use some of the resources guaranteed by the public space: libraries, sports grounds, national parks, theatres. They add resources of their own: to build churches and mosques, make sculpture and hold concerts, sail around the world. They talk, argue, sing, murmur and shout, sometimes to persuade others that their own projects are more worthwhile, sometimes to celebrate the value of these projects with the like-minded. It is a publicly complacent world, but one in which complacency is no vice; privately it involves hope, determination, disappointment, anger and fulfilment as the individual activities ebb and flow.

2 The citizen leaves home to do work. The work is somewhat unpleasant, and she would do less of it if she could; but if she did, it would diminish her command of the goods she needs to furnish her private space. As she works she is buoyed up by the thought of what all this is for. As she leaves her workplace, payslip in hand, she hurries home via the shopping centre, there to choose with a wonderful sense of freedom from a bewildering array of physical goods, some edible, some not. She lingers a little; she can afford to, since the labour-saving machinery she buys saves her at least as much time as she spends in contemplating its purchase. There is a hint of anxiety about where she will find the space for all this – the price of housing rises inexorably compared to the price of goods, and most people's domestic interiors seem a lot more cluttered than she can remember when she was young. But when she gets home to her family there will be a pleasant time in which the goodies are unwrapped, the preparations are made, the more edible items consumed. And before they have to think too hard about what to do next, it will

be time to sleep. The only time she contemplates with some concern is the weekend – how will they occupy themselves? At least, she reflects with relief, if all else fails they can spend Saturday shopping.

There is much in this contrast between two visions of the relation between inner and outer worlds that is exaggerated by the rhetoric in which it is expressed. For one thing, even in the first vision there is going to be work that is at times unpleasant or at least dull, and the hope that a training in Kierkegaardian reverence or in Zen can always come to the rescue of those who have to do such work is at best optimistic. For another, 'shopping' is just a derogatory description of a number of activities of judgement and selection that would be a necessary and admirable part of any of the worthwhile projects in a fulfilled life. Most of the later novels of Henry James (especially *The Ambassadors* and *The Golden Bowl*) are devoted to celebrating such activities; indeed, one might say that such works differ in subject matter from the modern shopping-and-fucking novels on airport bookstalls chiefly in that the shopping is as delicately understated as the fucking.

Nevertheless, the point of the contrast is clear. The private space left by liberal politics can become a void. The physical goods we need to stake it out, far from furnishing it with grace and light, can stand clumsily like metal objects in parkland in which children no longer want to play. If it is the business of politics to ensure that this does not happen, the space ceases to be (at least in the original sense) a private one. And if it is not the business of politics, whose business is it?

A possible, though not very convincing answer is that it is nobody's business. Liberal politics is not only liberal but radically individualist. It is up to individuals (or at best families) to work out their own destines in their own way, without any of the resources of a collective social life. Were it not for the fact that liberal theory has been repeatedly attacked from both left and right for giving such an answer (Michael Sandel's attack on Rawls in *Liberalism and the Limits of Justice* is a relatively recent exemplar of a tradition that includes Burke, Carlyle, Hegel and others too numerous to mention),[12] it would be tempting to suggest that this answer is an obvious misunderstanding of what liberal theory could possibly intend. Only if the political and the social are coterminous[13] could a private space aloof from politics be deprived of the privileges and duties of community. And to suppose that everything social is political, to suppose that what has been going on in, say, the Arab–Israeli peace talks is to be understood as no different from what is going on in a heated discussion of literary style in a Parisian café, or an evangelical bible-study class in Bradford (to call it all 'conversation', as Richard Rorty might do) is to miss the point in several ways. Most importantly, it misses the point that both the group in the café and the bible-readers are more or less voluntary associations; the peace process in the Middle East is an attempt to referee differences between groups each of whom would be profoundly pleased if the other did not exist. The peace talks need therefore to seek minimum conditions for co-existence; there is no point in asking for peace and love since they will be lucky just to get peace. The other two groups can be as ambitious about their association as they please.

A more promising answer, then, could be that there are many communities whose business it *might* be how we furnish our private space, but that it is not the business of liberal politics to decide whose business it actually *is*. Liberal politics is about ensuring that there is space to furnish. Whether we wish to call such space 'private' is less important than to note that it will be in an important sense non-political. This view may or may not be coherent, and it is not my task in this chapter to defend it, though it will be clear that I find the spirit of the argument sufficiently attractive to make some aspects of it worth examining.[14] My task is more limited: even if, for the purposes of argument, we can accept that a liberal political process should not be in the business of arbitrating between the claims of different communities to offer guidance on the furniture of our private spaces, one can nevertheless ask whether the culture of a liberal politics is especially favourable to the claims of some communities rather than others. This is consistent with the view that politics itself does not provide the guidance, since some communities reject the premises of liberal politics, while others adapt their activities well to the kinds of space a liberal politics can offer.

I want to ask this question specifically about modern imaginative literature (poetry, drama and prose fiction) in the shape this has taken from about the sixteenth century. The question has two parts. First, can the activity of reading or writing imaginative literature be viewed as paradigmatic of the kind of project that would furnish a private space sufficiently well to have made it worthwhile creating the space in the first place? Second, can imaginative literature provide guidance as to the furnishing of a private space with *other* projects and activities? My answers will be oblique and partial (I don't in any case know what full and direct answers would look like). In particular, I shall claim that while the answer to both questions could be and at times has been 'yes', the fact that a great deal of modern literature has sought explicitly to erode or undermine the distinction between politics and private space means that it furnishes such space at best uncomfortably. This does not make the distinction untenable, just uncomfortable, but perhaps comfort in these matters cannot or should not be our goal.

The idea that the reading or writing of imaginative literature could itself constitute part of the furniture of a private space was an integral feature of European Romanticism. It was particularly central to the thought of the German Romantics, whose cultivation of '*Innerlichkeit*' raised the notion of a private sphere to almost sacred heights. Its influence is still visible in a number of more modern theories of the personality, such as (for example) the Kleinian aesthetics of Adrian Stokes, for whom the creation of artistic objects represents a kind of never-ending healing process[15] for the inwardly riven and alienated personality. In keeping with its psychoanalytical origins, this theory takes the sick to mean everyone:[16] the very fact that a personality is never fully healed is what makes the creation of such objects a completely absorbing quest.[17]

Reflecting on its German origins tends, however, to undermine fairly rapidly the idea that *Innerlichkeit* or anything like it might provide a general answer to the problem of the furniture of a liberal private space. The issue is not whether it can furnish a private space – clearly it can – but whether the kind of private space to which it is most suited is one to which liberal politics should aspire. It may have been no accident that the cult of *Innerlichkeit* developed among a middle class deprived of political participation in an absolutist state.[18] This diagnosis is scarcely new: it was indeed used in a florid form by the German sociologist Max Scheler in 1916 to resist the allied claim to the moral high ground because of the allied countries' (somewhat) more democratic politics; Scheler claimed that Germany's more authoritarian politics were a necessary condition of its greater spiritual heritage.[19] Of course, the fact that the cult of *Innerlichkeit* happened to develop in these circumstances is not incompatible with the view that it is nevertheless just what the doctor ordered for the liberal spirit. But its history is disturbing for a number of reasons. One is that if even a weak version of Scheler's thesis is true – if, that is, *Innerlichkeit* both developed and is most at home in an atmosphere of political repression – then the very end for which liberalism has striven to stake out these private spaces has undermined the preconceptions of liberalism itself. Of course, late-eighteenth-century Germany was not a tyranny – the middle classes more or less had human rights, if not political rights – but the private and unwordly focus of most published literature was due to a considerable extent to the impossibility of publishing anything else.

This is not to deny an intimate connection between the conditions that made *Innerlichkeit* possible and at least some of the components of a liberal politics: the search for spiritual liberty of the German middle classes was undoubtedly given added determination by the memory of the terrible carnage of the Thirty Years War, for example. This same experience had also given the impetus to the currents in political theory we recognise as liberal (as James Tully has convincingly argued in opposition to the C.B. Macpherson view of 'possessive individualism'), as well as to the international analogue of interpersonal liberalism, namely, the Westphalian doctrine of non-interference in the so-called internal affairs of sovereign states.[20] But political developments in Germany showed that the nature and extent of private space necessary for the development of a rich inner life were considerably more restricted than that to which the contemporaneously developing liberal theory would aspire.

A second reason why this history is disturbing is that it suggests *Innerlichkeit*, even if achievable by some, might well be distributed very unequally.[21] This in turn is for two reasons. First, if an economically comfortable but politically emasculated class provided the best breeding ground for such literature as *The Sorrows of Young Werther*, presumably this implies that those who are either economically uncomfortable or politically emancipated can expect comparatively impoverished inner lives. The presence of the former might perhaps be considered an unfortunate and temporary feature of society before technology makes possible the conquest of hardship, but the presence of the latter can hardly be so regarded. Indeed, there is something faintly ludicrous about the idea of politics as requiring from its practitioners a selfless sacrifice of the capacity for inner life in order to procure that good for others.[22] However much commentators may deplore the effect of the media's trivialisation of modern political life upon its practitioners, it is hard to think that it could be a part of any liberal theory to suppose that politics *ought* to be like that.

Second, the idea of *Innerlichkeit* as in a sense the birthright of any educated person has always coexisted uneasily with another central Romantic idea, that of the individual genius. If an inner life is a universal birthright then geniuses have essentially the same capacities as anyone else, only more so. If, on the other hand, the genius is a human being apart, and if what such people possess (whatever it is) is what is really valuable about the inner life, then a private space for the educated non-genius seems hardly much of a goal worth striving for. If a private ownership economy happens to require an educated middle class capable of purchasing the books written by geniuses in order for the geniuses to be able to live, so much the worse for a private ownership economy, it might be thought: the Stalinist solution of separate academies for chess-players and the like seems a more efficient way to nourish society's supply of geniuses. Interestingly, Marx himself seems to have thought the problem should be solved by the alternative means of rejecting the Romantic conception of the genius. Under communism there would no longer be specialised artists, or indeed any specialists at all: people would be able to 'hunt in the morning, fish in the afternoon, rear cattle in the evening, criticize after dinner'.[23]

Of course, European Romanticism produced other notions of the inner life than the German version. Neither French nor English Romanticism was as insistent on the purity of the divorce between inner aestheticism and outer events; indeed, many Romantic artists were famously politically radical – and more importantly, thought their radicalism to be intrinsically connected to their art. However, both were to accept rather cheerfully the idea that genius was something quite unlike the sensibility of the ordinary educated person, and implicitly that it was genius rather than sensibility that really mattered. But that could hardly provide the vision of a liberal private space generally available to all: the most dedicated *fin-de-siècle* aesthete would have difficulty coming to terms with the idea of a future society freed from the toils of production, whose members would simply retire to their cork-lined rooms to suffer and write. Indeed, for many Romantics throughout Europe it was intrinsic to the vivid inner life that it should be incompatible with living a 'normal' – that is to say, either a worldly or an absorbingly domestic – life. Andrew Boyle in his biography captures vividly the tension between Goethe's sense of his own artistic calling and the appeal of marriage and family, which he felt very strongly but for most of his life forced himself to reject. The idea resurfaced throughout the next two centuries, finding notably expression in Cyril Connolly's inclusion among the *Enemies of Promise* of 'the pram in the hall'.

But it is an idea that would have been incomprehensible to the ancients, and even to such early modern authors as Montaigne.

As is well known, the Romantic idea of the vivid inner life was soon to be undermined by modernism. For our purposes there are two main aspects to this undermining that are important. The first is economic. Emptiness is a condition that arises above all in the midst of plenty. As Martin puts it in Voltaire's *Candide*, man was born to live either in convulsions of anxiety or in the lethargy of boredom.[24] Emma Bovary's ennui is something that a worker in a Victorian factory would have had neither time nor energy for (the fact that her financial problems are part of what precipitates the novel's tragic climax doesn't invalidate this judgement, for her financial difficulties are caused precisely by her buying recklessly things she does not need, but wants no less desperately for all that). The nausea of the existentialists is nausea at a world that is at least comfortably furnished. A French novel of the 1960s, Georges Perec's *Les Choses*, is an attempt to capture some of that puzzling hair's-breadth distance between enchantment and ennui, between connoisseurship and consumerism, between the ingenuity of appreciation and strategies of desperate boredom ('the pleasure of paying dearly for something is a pleasure for which one pays dearly'). Now of course ennui may be (and on the evidence of the quantity of writing devoted to it, must be) an artistically interesting subject; but that hardly makes it a morally uplifting goal. It may be better, all in all, to be Madame Bovary than to be Monsieur, but her inner life is a predicament, not a project.

Not surprisingly, writings in politics and economics have almost entirely ignored ennui, presuming that it is a luxury to be considered, if at all, once the more evidently pressing problems of deprivation have been overcome.[25] A striking exception is Tibor Scitovsky's *The Joyless Economy*, which draws on the distinction made by experimental psychologists between comfort and stimulation, and argues that modern production of goods and services has been overwhelmingly concerned with the former rather than the latter. One reason is that stimulation is not something it is easy to achieve passively; it requires a kind of active participation and seeking out by the subject, the capacity for which in turn depends on exactly the kind of training and education that modern private ownership economies are bad at providing, and that modern command economies have (or had) a vested interest in suppressing. Scitovsky's analysis is a fairly optimistic one (for all its deadly analysis of modern American consumer society), since it treats the necessary education as a kind of public good, and the underprovision of public goods by the private sector is a problem that, once recognised, has a chance of being more or less alleviated. But a common theme among modern literary critics has been the *intrinsic* dullness of the literature produced by rich and stable societies (John Carey was recently quoted as explaining the comparative vigour of Indian writing in English by saying that 'there is a little truth in the idea that English life is dull, so our literature is a little dull').[26] Furthermore, in discussion of the state of literature in Eastern Europe since the fall of communism there has often been an elegiac tone, as if to say that life in the future, instead of being about great issues such as freedom and repression, will be about choosing between increasingly sophisticated brands of washing machine, and what kind of literature can you make out of that? (This theme has been somewhat muted since the outbreak of civil war in the former Yugoslavia and Soviet Union.) There is a reflection here of the roots of modern liberal theory. Possessive individualism undoubtedly seemed most attractive in the century after the Thirty Years War; you need to have enjoyed your private space for some time before you can feel confident enough to despise it.

Modernism also undermined the Romantic notion of the inner life in a second, more subtle and more intrinsically literary way. A certain undermining of the subject's conception of itself is not just an unfortunate by-product of a literary sensibility, but (on a modernist and even more on a postmodernist view) part of what it means to be a literary sensibility in the first place. Now it is true that this does not in any direct way invalidate the claim that literary activity may be suitable for filling the private liberal space: one might reasonably claim that a modernist concern with self-redefinition is just the kind of luxury which a liberal political theory should aspire to make available to all its citizens, the more so since the results of this redefinition will be likely to be multifarious and pluralist. But that reading and writing literature should hold any kind of privileged position among the activities that might lead to such redefinition looks an altogether more dubious proposition; modernism is about questioning such judgements of hierarchy, not about reinforcing them. If, on the other hand, one defines 'literature' to mean not novels, plays and poems but any kind of communication that provokes self-reflection in the subject, one has come very close to merely restating in elaborate terms the basic liberal claim: subjects should be free to furnish their private space as they will. This is unexceptionable (given the liberal starting point of the argument), but hardly very illuminating.

So, to recapitulate, the idea that reading and writing literature *as an activity* might substantially furnish the liberal private space has thrown up quite a few difficulties. These might be summarised as follows: first, the kind of sensibility that responds in an appropriately 'private' and non-political way to novels and poems is not necessarily the product of political arrangements that liberals would find attractive; second, it may be distributed much more sparsely and more unequally than a liberal would find acceptable; third, it may deteriorate into depression and ennui once the struggle to carve out and protect a comfortable private space has been substantially achieved; and finally, the tendency of modern literature has been towards a questioning and undermining of all settled views about the foundations of the stable personality, including any views that would ascribe to reading and writing literature a particularly favoured status.

What, then, of the second possible role for imaginative literature in the liberal space – not as itself part of the furniture, but as a source of guidance and inspiration about the means of furnishing that space with other and different projects? One must be careful not to construe 'guidance' too narrowly here, otherwise the description will apply, if at all, to only the most boringly didactic of literature (*Tom Brown's Schooldays*, perhaps). Imaginative literature has often had a self-consciously uplifting or didactic component[27] but it has never been just the continuation of the sermon by other means.[28] Nevertheless, in a more generous sense of the term it is certainly possible to imagine a wide variety of kinds of imaginative literature serving to share conceptions of a private space, to allow readers to explore alternative spaces and to grant depth and timbre to their own private space with the resonance of the private spaces of others. Surrealist or Dadaist poetry can deepen such resonance; so can the deliberate exploration of moral dilemmas (in *The Crucible* or *Huckleberry Finn*, for example), even if there is nothing else that such works can plausibly be said to have in common. Indeed, such a conception would fit well with a certain modernist view of literature and the self: paradoxically, the self is constituted by a certain awareness of alternative possible selves; and literature, which can move playfully around and away from the actual, is particularly well placed to bring these possibilities home to the reader. Henry James put the point well in his Preface to the New York edition of *The Ambassadors*, the first great novel of the modern century:

> ... for development, for expression of its maximum, my glimmering story was, at the earliest stage, to have nipped the thread of connexion with the possibilities of the actual reported speaker. *He* remains but the happiest of accidents; his actualities, all too definite, precluded any range of possibilities; it had only been his charming office to project upon that wide field of the artist's vision – which hangs there over in place like the white sheet suspended for the figures of a child's magic lantern – a more fantastic and a more moveable shadow.

If one can make sense in principle of the idea that literature can serve to explore alternative spaces, one must nevertheless ask more questions about the nature of these spaces. First of all, what kinds of project or activity could fill those spaces, and will imaginative literature do them justice? At the simplest level, literature and especially poetry may help us to reassess our relationship to physical space. Hannah Arendt in *The Human Condition* talks of the way in which

> what the public realm considers irrelevant can have such an extraordinary and infectious charm that a whole people may adopt it as their way of life, without for that reason changing its essentially private character. Modern enchantment with 'small things', though preached by early twentieth century poetry in almost all European tongues, has found its classical presentation in the *petit bonheur* of the French people. Since the decay of their once great and glorious public realm, the French have become masters in the art of being happy among 'small things', within the space of their own four walls, between chest and bed, table and chair, dog and cat and flowerpot, extending to these things a care and tenderness which, in a world where rapid industrialisation often kills off the things of yesterday to produce today's objects, may even appear to be the world's last, purely humane corner. (p. 52)

One need not share Arendt's upbeat assessment of French sensibility to agree that poetry may itself help to weave this physical enchantment.[29] Here is Anna Akhmatova:

> The lime-trees by the open door
> Breathe sweet and rich,
> Forgotten on the table
> A glove and riding switch.

A yellow disk of lamplight,
A rustling near at hand.
(But why did you leave me?
I do not understand.)

How beautiful the world is
In the morning, cool and clear!
Be patient now, be good, my heart,
The dawn will soon be here.

And oh! you must be weary,
So low you beat, and slow,
The soul is immortal –
Someone told me so.[30]

One of the beauties of this poem is its hint that the same rather precious physical enchantment that consoles the grieving spirit may be the very source of whatever claustrophobia has prompted the beloved to leave. As these lines show, even reassessments with respect to physical space soon expand into reassessments in psychological space. There are all kinds of candidate psychological projects – the Christian-inspired project of building one's moral character, the psychoanalytic project of coming to terms with one's neurosis, the erotic project of finding a mate (or mates) – that are demanding enough to absorb an individual's private energies and that have provided matter for countless works of poetry, drama or fiction (one might cite respectively Jane Austen's *Emma*, Philip Roth's *Portnoy's Complaint* and virtually any novel by Barbara Cartland as instances of works preoccupied by the projects described above).[31] However, although there are certain things such as these that imaginative literature does well, there are others which (at least historically) it has handled much less well. David Lodge has said somewhere that 'literature is mostly about having sex and hardly at all about having children; real life is mostly the other way round.' Certainly, it would be hard to imagine any persuasive account of the various ways in which a liberal private space could be filled that did not accord an extremely important part to the activity of raising children. Yet it is striking that, while there are countless works of literature dealing with erotic love, few deal centrally and persuasively with parental love (viewed from the perspective of the parent, that is),[32] even though this can be as compulsive, absorbing and desperate as erotic love. (For instance, the theme of losing one's lover to somebody else fills many novels, while very few indeed deal with the theme of losing one's children to somebody else).[33]

Now this omission may partly reflect a narrowly patriarchal bias in much existing imaginative literature; certainly, both feminist criticism and feminist fiction have sought to broaden the emotional range that can be brought within the conventions of the genre. But it may also reflect psychological as well as literary truths. Other people's erotic loves may simply be more interesting to us than other people's parental loves (one may come to love other people's children, but people's emotions of love for their children tend to strike others as faintly embarrassing rather than interesting – let alone exciting). And the interest of literature may partially echo this feature of psychology. Whatever the truth of the matter, at least this example will suggest that literature as a source of imagined alternatives will be limited and partial in its scope; it is not, and could not be, the *Encyclopaedia Britannica* of the private space.

A second crucial question about the space in which imaginative literature works is how private it really is. By this I mean not whether it is private in some radically subjective, Cartesian sense – clearly it is not, for even the most private of the German Romantics would have thought literature was a means by which soul called to soul – but rather whether it can sensibly be freed from the kind of interdependence with the political which, I suggested at the beginning, defined the liberal notion of a private space. The end of liberal politics, I suggested, is that politics should stand aloof. If it did so, would imaginative literature be deprived of all that gave it its spark? More precisely, are the criteria that determine how one reacts to the imagined spaces to which literature gives us access criteria that can coherently be evaluated in other than political terms?

There is a whole critical literature starting from a non-liberal perspective that would give a negative answer to this question; it is not my purpose to consider these arguments here, except to remark that one could accept this literature's analysis of certain authors and works (Lukàcs on Walter Scott, for example)[34] without thereby being bound to accept the substantive claim that all literature is intrinsically in some sense political. However, what is more awkward for the view that imaginative literature can offer guidance in the furnishing of a private space is the fact that a great deal of literature itself has, superficially at least, sought to undermine the private/public distinction upon which this ambition depends. This is not simply because many writers have written at points or in circumstances in which political events intruded so forcefully on their lives that they could not ignore them: Akhmatova, for example, lived in dramatic times of political upheaval the consciousness of which informs all of her work, but this does not prevent it from reflecting also a sense that she would dearly have loved to live in times that allowed her a private space. Rather it is that much imaginative literature mocks or erodes even such barriers as individuals manage to erect, mocks them with explicitly literary devices.

Take, for example, William Gerhardie's novel *Futility*, set at the time of the Russian Revolution but in its immediate setting echoing many of the nineteenth century's works of drawing-room drama. Its characters make history in spite of themselves; they dance and go to parties and marry and separate according to a logic that is not apolitical but, as the irony reminds us, positively and sulkily anti-political:

> Nikolai Vasilievich was very bitter. He had regarded the war almost as a deliberate attempt of providence to complicate his already very complicated domestic situation, and considering that providence had had the satisfaction of achieving its pernicious end, it seemed he could not understand the necessity of a revolution.[35]

The detachment of the characters from events around them is used to comic ends. One chapter begins:

> Who can convey at all adequately that sense of utter hopelessness that clings to a Siberian winter night? Wherever else is there to be found that brooding, thrilling sense of frozen space, of snow and ice lost in inky darkness, that gruesome sense of never-ending night, and black despair and loneliness untold, immeasurable? Add to this the knowledge of a civil war fumbling in the snow, of people ill-fed, ill-clothed and apathetic, lying on the frozen ground, cold and wretched and diseased. A snowstorm is blowing furiously; the wooden house groans and yells in the night; the tin roof squeals in agony, fearful lest it be cast to the winds; and the storm now howls like a beast, now sobs like a child, now dies away, gathering for another outburst.
>
> The house was lit and warm and comfortable. It was the Admiral's house. But the Admiral was away, and in his absence I had conceived it possible to give a dinner-party. (p. 138)

What is interesting about this is that the writer is not, say, Brecht, a 'committed' writer scornfully mocking the pretensions of the bourgeoisie who seek refuge in the salon as their society disintegrates around them. He is a writer who enters fully into the aspirations of his characters to a private realm; the novel is about a family and its disintegration, about a hesitant love affair and *its* disintegration, and the novel ends, faithfully to its characters, without ever showing much interest in or reporting the outcome of the Revolution that is going on around them. The point is more subtle: their very apolitical aspirations are, in these circumstances, a political stance, and the attempt to keep them private is a political decision. It is less a moral than a conceptual point: their attempt to be private is not reprehensible, just absurd. It parallels neatly Gerhardie's mockery of one of the minor characters, Uncle Kostia, who is considered brilliant by his family in spite of, or even because of, his unwillingness ever to express any of his ineffable brilliance. The scene in which the central character presses Uncle Kostia (on a train journey) to divulge his thoughts is a comic masterpiece, of which this is a brief extract:

> 'Today I have been thinking. It will seem nothing to you if I tell you; it will seem nothing to me if I tell it; but, believe me, it was something infinitely beautiful just when I thought of it – without the labour of exertion.'
> 'What was it, Uncle Kostia?' I inquired.
> 'It was vague,' he said evasively.
> 'Oh, come, Uncle Kostia?'
> 'How can I tell? I know too much'.
> I was aware of the unpleasant shrinking of ideas when set down on paper. So I persisted.
> 'Come on, Uncle Kostia! Out with it!'
> 'Well,' said Uncle Kostia, and his face became that of a mystic. 'I thought, for instance – I wonder if you will understand me? – I thought: *Where* are we all going?'
> 'Hm,' I said significantly.
> 'I thought: *Why* are we all moving?'. (p. 118; emphasis in original).

Here again Gerhardie makes a point about privacy and its contradictions – a clearly literary point. Likewise his mockery of the family's apolitical stance is done using literary tools: accepting, as it were, the distinction his characters are seeking to uphold, and watching it collapse under its own weight.

The argument I am making here needs to be stated quite carefully. It would be fallacious – and trite – to argue that, because some novels, or even many novels, happen to have mocked their characters' pretensions to an apolitical private space, this conception is incoherent. I do not want to claim that the conception is incoherent, and even it if were, the fact of its being mocked in literature would not show it to be so. Nor do I want to claim that what is in evidence in works of literature written in the shadow of 'great events' must somehow be present embryonically in works of literature written in less stressful times. Instead, the argument is a kind of *reductio ad absurdum* of a certain way of conceiving the public/private distinction, rather than a refutation of any possibility of such a distinction.

The way of conceiving this distinction that I am referring to is one which assumes that once the liberal private space has been staked out, the human capacities that are exercised in tending it are quite different from and unrelated to the human capacities that served to stake it out in the first place. That is, once health, economic prosperity and physical security are assured, the scene is set for the characters to grow, fight, love and die according to imperatives that have nothing to do with those that drive their 'political' lives. *Futility* undermines this view. The reason is not that (as a Marxist view of a Chekhov play might imply) characters who grow, fight, love and die are just expressing the political attitudes of the landed gentry whose private space is continually propped up, as it were, by the exploitation of a producing class. One could, after all, reasonably ask how the characters in Chekhov would behave if their economic security were guaranteed by machinery in a world of plenty; some but not all of the drama would change its character, and those aspects that did not (say, a relationship of rivalry in love, or a depression brought on my ennui) could be said to be independent of this aspect of their political context (namely, the underlying production relations). Instead, what the irony in *Futility* forces us to confront is that certain attitudes which in the apparently static isolation of a Chekhovian landed estate (or a country parsonage of Jane Austen's day) might appear to be without political content, become in easily imagined circumstances a move in an essentially political game (one of the comic aspects of Nikolai Vassilievich's attitude to the Revolution is that he thinks the Revolution is intruding unwarrantedly into his private affairs; his attitude and that of others like him is, however, one of the components of the revolutionary situation itself). These attitudes may be moral and psychological, like those of Nikolai Vassilievich, or more strictly literary (like the bathos used by Gerhardie in the second extract above, where an apparently apolitical literary device makes a surprisingly political point). And because it is the business of literature to imagine alternative spaces, then the role of literature will be to infuse situations where the private space is in fact independent of the outer political world with an awareness of alternative situations where it might not be.

As I have already suggested, this does not imply that a common-sense distinction between public and private[36] would not be perfectly tenable, in the imagined circumstances of a liberal society that assured security, health and prosperity to its members. What it does imply is that imaginative literature would be continually blurring and eroding this distinction, by reminding its members of imaginable alternative circumstances in which politics invaded what they had become used to thinking of as their private realm. But this in turn need not be taken to mean that, though imaginative literature is compatible with the idea of a liberal private space, it offers little positive support for the liberal vision. There are two respects in which a more positive conclusion can be drawn.

The first is due to the essentially playful character of much imaginative literature. It is central to the literary imagination, not just that it presents us with alternatives, but that it does so in a more non-chalant way than, for example, a moral philosopher carefully setting out a thought experiment. It unsettles us by blurring alternative worlds into each other, rather than fortifying us by precisely distinguishing them. Plato was understandably disturbed by such playfulness, and since he did not conceive of a private space distinguished in the way we have discussed here from the world of politics, he thought the only solution was that any would-be artists in his Republic should be politely but firmly asked to leave. Plato has had a bad press for this,[37] but he was right about one thing: playfulness is not a desirable quality in certain kinds of political decision. That the weak should be protected from violation is not a matter about which a just society should engage in any equivocation, even pretended equivocation. For judges, the police and even tax inspectors to behave in a Kafkaesque fashion is something to be kept strictly in the realms of fantasy. Playfulness is, in that sense, not a desirable public quality. Since it is clearly a desirable quality somehow, the answer must be that it is a desirable private quality, and imaginative literature has reason therefore to be grateful for the existence of a liberal dichotomy to give it space in which to play.

The second more positive conclusion is that it does not necessarily weaken the exercise of moral, psychological or artistic capacities to reflect that in different circumstances they might need to be exercised in very different ways. Virtues such as courage and decency are necessary every day even in stable and prosperous societies; it does not undermine them but if anything strengthens them to reflect that, if stability and prosperity break down, they will face different and more dramatic challenges. The fact that some of the most brutal Nazis were capable of sincere appreciation of Mozart and Goethe, and that – notoriously – the Nazi regime found much support among the decent and the courageous, shows perhaps that *Innerlichkeit* had become too inner and had failed to imagine real and important alternatives,[38] not that the virtues it celebrated were other than virtues. Less dramatically, it need not impoverish and may positively enrich the legacy of a liberal society to its members for them to be aware, through the imagined spaces that literature can create for them, of the invasions of the person against which they seek its protection. Liberal gardeners may take a more profound pleasure in their lawns and flowerbeds if they do not forget entirely the jungle they have kept at bay.

NOTES

1 For their thoughtful comments and suggestions, I should like to thank Andrea Baumeister, Isabelle Daudy, Philippe Daudy, Geoffrey Hawthorn, Angela Hobbs, John Horton, Emma Rothschild, Lucy Sargisson, Amartya Sen and Martin Warner, as well as participants in the conference discussion and in a seminar at the Centre for Philosophy and Literature, University of Warwick.

2 Isaiah Berlin, 'Two Concepts of Liberty', in *Four Essays on Liberty*, Oxford, Oxford University Press, 1969.

3 Hannah Arendt, *The Human Condition*, Chicago, University of Chicago Press, 1958, pp. 48–9.

4 Benjamin Constant, 'De la liberté des Anciens comparée à celle des Modernes', in Constant: *De La Liberté chez les Modernes* (ed. Gauchet), Paris, Livre de Poche, 1980.

5 Arlene W. Saxonhouse, 'Classical Greek Conceptions of Public and Private', in S. I. Benn and G. F. Gaus (eds), *Public and Private in Social Life*, London, Croom Helm, 1983, argues that after the Peloponnesian War the fragility of domestic values and the stupidity of warfare came to be more generally acknowledged (as in Euripides' *Trojan Women*) than in Homer, and that even Aristotle 'recognises that the city survives only as long as the particular private world of the family does' (p. 381). William James Booth, *Households: On The Moral Architecture of the Economy*, Ithaca, Cornell University Press, 1993 suggests that autarky and leisure are for the Greeks 'the principal goods of the household to which its productive activities are subordinated' (p. 8). He also disagrees with Arendt's claims that 'the economy has until the modern period remained invisible' (p. 6), and her overlooking of the fact that slaveowners could work in the fields side by side with their slaves (p. 23).

6 See A. K. Ramanujan (ed.), *Poems of Love and War*, Chicago, Chicago University Press, 1988, especially the fine Afterword by the editor.

7 'Travailler sans raisonner . . .' c'est le seul moyen de rendre la vie supportable'; Voltaire, *Candide*, Paris, Livre de Poche, 1983, p. 125).

8 Jack Goody, *The Culture of Flowers*, Cambridge, Cambridge University Press, 1993. However, Chandra Mukerji has suggested that French formal gardening in the seventeenth century was both a signal of and a vehicle for the social ambitions of a more commercial and capitalist class, albeit one that sought acceptance by the court (Chandra Mukerji, 'Reading and writing with nature: a materialist approach to French formal gardens', in John Brewer and Roy Porter (eds), *Consumption and the World of Goods*, London, Routledge, 1993).

9 'Je veux . . . que la mort me treuve plantant mes chous, mais nonchalant d'elle, et encore plus de mon jardin imparfait'; Montaigne, 'Que Philosopher, C'est Apprendre à Mourir', *Essais*, Paris, Flammarion, 1969, vol. 1, pp. 134–5.

10 Hayek, *The Road to Serfdom*, London, Routledge and Kegan Paul, 1976, p. 14.

11 Mukerji, op. cit., suggests that French and Italian gardens symbolise a much more 'public' set of ambitions than those embodied in the great age of English landscape gardening.

12 Sandel views the essential contradiction of liberalism as being between the insistence of deontology that 'we view ourselves as independent selves, independent in the sense that our identity is never tied to our aims and attachments', and the fact, which may be epistemological or phenomenological (it is not clear which) that 'we cannot regard ourselves as independent in this way without great cost to those loyalties and convictions whose moral force consists partly in the fact that living by them is inseparable from understanding ourselves as the particular persons we are' (Michael Sandel, *Liberalism and the Limits of Justice*, Cambridge, Cambridge University Press, p. 179). One of the difficulties with Sandel's argument is that he never establishes that liberalism as such entails the former claim; this would in any case be hard to do since the claim is not evidently a coherent one.

13 Hannah Arendt discusses the way in which Aristotle's term *zoon politikon* was translated into Latin as early as Seneca by *animal socialis*, and comments that 'more than any elaborate theory, this unconscious substitution of the social for the political betrays the extent to which the original Greek understanding of politics has been lost' (*The Human Condition*, p. 23).

14 A valuable discussion of many of the issues involved is the volume edited by S. I. Benn and G. F. Gaus *Public and Private in Social Life*, op. cit.

15 There are, of course, more exclusively literary accounts of why the task of creating literary objects has no end, usually based upon the inadequacy of any actual literary expression to the sentiment it is seeking to express or the effect it is intending to create (as Flaubert put it in *Madame Bovary*, 'la parole humaine est comme un chaudron fêlé ou nous battons des mélodies à faire danser les ours, quand on voudrait attendrir les étoiles' – the human word is like a cracked cauldron on

which we beat out tunes for bears to dance to, when we long to touch the very stars).

16 As Jules Romains' character Doctor Knock puts it: 'Les gens bien portants sont des malades qui s'ignorent' – the healthy are just the sick who lack self-knowledge (Jules Romain, *Knock*, Paris, Gallimard, 1924, p. 31).

17 Adrian Stokes *The Invitation in Art*, London, Tavistock Press, 1965. Stokes was particularly concerned with the effect of urbanisation on the capacity of the personality to perform this healing process. He complains (p. 30) that 'in the old days, art was a means of organising the incantatory element that had been felt in the length of land or in the restless sea. Today art is entirely outmoded in the choice of such phenomena by the scintillating lack of limitation of urban things in general', and later describes modern collages as 'beseeching a piece of environment arranged as art for the meaning that our streets refuse to us' (p. 47). But it is clear that what he called the 'enveloping mechanisms and disconnecting noise of limitless cities' (p. 30) threaten the private space in similar if less dramatic ways to the effects of war and intrusion of a more direct physical kind; it is in this sense that his philosophy of art, which he describes as 'humanist', deserves also to be called liberal. Certainly its psychoanalytic underpinnings would fit quite closely the description of romanticism that Nietzsche castigated in *The Gay Science*: ministering to a spirit that 'suffers from poverty of life, who seeks in art and knowledge either rest, peace, a smooth sea, delivery from himself, or intoxication, paroxysm, stupefaction, madness', with a creativity that comes (as he put it) from hunger rather than superfluity (Friedrich Nietzsche, *The Gay Science*, New York, Random House, 1974, section 370).

18 See Boyle, *Goethe*, Oxford, Clarendon Press, vol. 1., *passim* but especially pp. 137–40.

19 He put forward a 'tragic law of human nature' relating inversely the spiritual liberty and the political liberty of a nation. In Germany, he claimed, 'the magnificent feel for spiritual liberty, spiritual breadth and for disconnectedness of the state from the most intimate personality sphere' went hand in hand with 'frequently all-too-willing subordination to state authority'; whereas in England the 'emphasis on political liberty' had a negative counterpart in a 'relative parochialism, intellectual narrowness, lack of feeling for the liberty of the highly original individual intellect, and in a for us Germans inconceivable ... conventionality, (Max Sheler, 'Der Geist und die ideellen Grundlagen der Demokratien der grosser Nationen', *Gesammelte Werke*, vol. 6, Bern, Francke 1963; cited in Albert Hirschman, *The Rhetoric of Reaction*, Cambridge, Massachussetts, Harvard University Press, 1991).

20 For 'possessive individualism' see C. B. Macpherson, *The Political Theory of Possessive Individualism*, Oxford, Clarendon Press, 1962; James Tully: *A Discourse on Property: John Locke and his adversaries*, Cambridge, Cambridge University Press, 1980; Tully, *An Approach to Political Philosophy: Locke in contexts*, Cambridge, Cambridge University Press, 1993. It is part of Tully's argument that 'the specific groups of people in England (and France) who Locke believed had their rights

and property violated, and so had the right to resist, were not capitalist landowners but oppressed religious minorities' (1993, p. 3), though he stresses that Locke's theory was not just Anglo-French in its focus, but a response to a series of pan-European problems, notably 'the religious and civil wars of the sixteenth and seventeenth centuries' (ibid., p. 9). Geoffrey Hawthorn (in 'How to Ask For Good Government', *IDS Bulletin*, 1992) and Hawthorn and Paul Seabright (in 'Where Westphalia Fails: conditionally and the multilateral financial institutions', in Adrian Leftwich (ed.), *Democracy and Development*, London, Polity Press, forthcoming) discuss the non-interference doctrine in relation to the modern imposition of political conditions on sovereign loans by international donors.

21 It is true that liberalism is not necessarily tied to a belief in equality (and on some interpretations of 'equality' the two are actually incompatible). Nevertheless, a general theory that what is valuable for human beings (and what should in consequence be the goal of political striving) is the nature of the private space they occupy will lose much of its attractiveness if it evaluates the quality of the private space according to criteria that few human beings would have much chance of satisfying.

22 It is significant that in earlier writing about privacy the emphasis is on the physical danger of politics and the public life: the Turkish gardener in *Candide* holds that 'those who get involved in public affairs sometimes perish miserably, and deserve to; I never try to find out what's happening in Constantinople; I'm content to send the fruit from my garden to market there' (p. 124). By the twentieth century (especially in German writing), the risks of politics are aesthetic and spiritual, like those embodied in the character of Permanent Secretary Tuzzi in Robert Musil's *The Man Without Qualities*: 'aside from a period of honeymoon caresses, Permanent Secretary Tuzzi had always been a utilitarian and a rationalist who never lost his equilibrium' (English translation, London, Picador, 1979, vol. 1, p. 119).

23 Karl Marx, *The German Ideology*, in Marx and Friedrich Engels *Collected Works*, New York, International Publishers, 1975, p. 47. Amartya Sen has pointed out that it is important to distinguish attitudes to genius and talent from views about the specialisation of labour. Adam Smith accepted the division of labour but was hostile to the notion of genius; Marx, suggests Sen, was critical of the consequences of the division of labour but seemed less hostile to the notions of genius and special talent (personal communication). If this interpretation is correct it implies that what Marx disputed was the Romantic idea that the essence of the arts was the cultivation of the individual genius, rather than the very existence of such genius.

24 'L'homme etait né pour vivre dans les convulsions de l'inquiétude, ou dans la léthargie de l'ennui' (*Candide*, p. 122).

25 One might have expected the literature on the so-called 'Limits to Growth' (D. Meadows et al., *The Limits To Growth*, Earthscan Publications 1972, 1992; Fred Hirsch: *Social Limits to Growth*, 1976) to consider more explicitly the question of what economic growth is *for*. But this literature almost entirely takes the goal – human welfare – for granted and argues instead that measured economic growth is a less and

less effective means to achieve this goal, because of hidden environmental costs, either pollution and depletion of natural resources (Meadows) or congestion (Hirsch).

26 *The Sunday Times*, 21 March, 1993.

27 Particularly so in the oral tradition where the speaker may furnish a kind of commentary on the action (a tradition very much alive, for example, in popular retellings – even in written form – of the Indian epics the *Mahabharatha* and *Ramayana*). Nevertheless, the fact that the action is thought to require a commentary is a sign that the recounting of the action is not solely didactic in spirit.

28 S. L. Goldberg argues in *Agents and Lives: Moral thinking in literature*, Cambridge, Cambridge University Press, 1993, that 'literature represents a kind of moral thinking in its own right – a kind necessary to our moral understanding, and which moral philosophy has spoken of, but cannot supply'. The reason for this, he claims (p. xv), is that 'literature does its moral thinking in the particulars it imagines ... in a double way. On the one side, [it] does consider people much as moral codes and moral philosophy do, as voluntary agents, each of whom is like any other ... But at the same time, literature also considers people as lives: as ... individual unique modes of human life – whose particular qualities and trajectory in time are, in quite crucial ways, not like others', not by any means entirely a matter of voluntary actions, and yet no less morally important for that.' The fact that Goldberg uses the term 'moral' rather more broadly than some might do is not important; he is, however, rather restrictive in supposing that all literature is centrally about 'people' and 'lives' (how is this true of Rimbaud's poem 'Voyelles', for example?). If one rephrased his argument by saying that it was about imagining alternative spaces, though, it would still make his central point while being sympathetic to the point of view expressed here.

29 Reading or writing poetry could even, as an activity, be particularly suited to this enchantment. A slim volume of poetry would go very well on the bedside table in the room of Hannah Arendt's vision. In spite of the misgivings I have expressed in the earlier section, literature as activity (rather than just as guidance) may suit some private spaces very well.

30 Translation by Reginald Mainwaring Hewitt in a privately published memorial volume to him edited by V. de S. Pinto.

31 At the risk of repetition I should stress that these works need not be read as manuals on how the reader should conduct such a project, merely as explorations of such a project in action.

32 There are a number of works dealing with parental love of adult children (*King Lear*, most notably, as also some novels of Balzac that were consciously influenced by that play, particularly *Le Pere Goriot*). With adult children the boundaries between parental and erotic loves may (especially for the audience) be particularly uncertain. I hope it is clear at this point that it is not studies of the parent–child relationship whose absence I am remarking, for there have been a great number of those; it is that relationship viewed specifically from the point of view of the parent.

33 However, my attention was recently drawn to Ruth Rendell's novel *A*

Dark Adapted Eye via a very fine television adaptation; in this novel a woman is driven to madness and murder by fear of losing her child to someone else.

34 Georg Lukàcs, *The Historical Novel*, Harmondsworth, Penguin Books, 1962, especially Chapter 2.

35 William Gerhardie, *Futility*, London, Robin Clark, 1990, p. 68.

36 One would not need to believe that this distinction was marked by a sharp dividing-line, either. One may be unable to tell exactly where green becomes blue on a spectrum without thinking that green and blue are the same colour.

37 See Iris Murdoch, *The Fire and the Sun*, Oxford, Clarendon Press, 1976.

38 Ervin Staub, *The Roots of Evil: the origins of genocide and other group violence*, Cambridge, Cambridge University Press, 1989, discusses 'the bystander effect', and in particular the way in which taking the initiative in small instances of group action (for example, at a road accident) may develop habits both in the agent and in any spectators that make it easier to act against more serious waves of group violence.

8 'Breathes there the man, with soul so dead . . .'

Reflections on patriotic poetry and liberal principles[1]

Margaret Canovan

Poetry may seem an odd place to look for illumination on matters of political theory. Although most of the great political thinkers of the past were also great writers who consciously used literary and rhetorical techniques to make their views persuasive and memorable, generally speaking they did not break into verse. The poems with which I shall be concerned in this chapter are not themselves examples of political theory, but I shall argue that political thinkers would be wise to consider the implications of the sentiments they express.

The relevance of another kind of literature to moral and political thinking has been recently and controversially argued by Richard Rorty, who suggests in *Contingency, Irony and Solidarity* that liberals should look to novels rather than political philosophy for support. According to Rorty, the philosophical project of finding a secure metaphysical basis for liberal democratic institutions and aspirations cannot be defended against sceptical and historicist attacks. Instead of being cast into despair by this discovery, however, we should acknowledge that the liberal ideal of human solidarity is 'a goal to be achieved . . . not by inquiry but by imagination, the imaginative ability to see strange people as fellow sufferers. Solidarity is not discovered by reflection but created', and those who help to create it and extend its bounds are the novelists who widen the meaning of 'us' by intensifying our sensitivity to suffering and forcing us to understand and identify with those we would previously have regarded as other.[2]

Although Rorty abjures the search for philosophical underpinning for liberal principles and acknowledges their historical contingency, his political aim evidently remains the traditionally ambitious liberal goal of solidarity with all human beings. In what follows, I would like to bracket that ambition and return to it after considering the creation of solidarity on a smaller scale. The first part of this chapter illustrates the way in which patriotic poetry mobilises fellow feeling and harnesses it to causes and collectivities that transcend the individual and his (almost invariably it is 'his') personal interests and relationships.

PART I

> Breathes there the man, with soul so dead,
> Who never to himself hath said,
> This is my own, my native land!
> . . .
> If such there breathe, go, mark him well;
> . . .
> The wretch, concentred all in self,
> Living, shall forfeit fair renown,
> And, doubly dying, shall go down
> To the vile dust, from whence he sprung,
> Unwept, unhonour'd, and unsung.[3]

Scott goes on in the next stanza to give voice to a specifically Scottish patriotism, but in the lines just quoted he is speaking generally about a love of country that expresses itself in remarkably similar terms in the poetry of many different nations. Within this celebrated effusion are concentrated all the main themes of patriotic verse. There is, first, the contrast between generous love of country and narrow selfishness. The unpatriotic man, a 'wretch, concentred all in self', sounds like the asocial liberal individual recently caricatured in communitarian political thought. In resisting the call to fight and die for his country, this selfish man evades his obligations. What is particularly worthy of note, however, is that in doing so he is himself the loser. For sooner or later he will die, and by missing the chance to share in his country's glory and to live on in the collective memory of the nation he is in fact 'doubly dying': he has failed to take the opportunity offered him to overcome death. It is with this transcendence of individual mortality in the life of the nation that we shall be chiefly concerned.

Patriotic poetry is not exclusively concerned with death and glory – one thinks, for example, of Browning's idyllic vision of England in 'Home Thoughts from Abroad' – but the prominence of these themes is scarcely surprising, for it is a form of literature that has commonly been evoked by war or armed struggle of some kind. Often it takes the form of a call to arms, either to an impending battle or to an imagined or recollected one, as with the words Burns puts into the mouth of Robert Bruce before Bannockburn:

> Scots, wha hae wi' Wallace bled
> Scots, wham Bruce has aften led
> Welcome to your gory bed,
> Or to victory![4]

Welcoming soldiers to blood and death is not as utterly bizarre as it may seem, for one of the emotions such words evoke is the sheer exhilaration of combat and danger, that 'impulse of delight' that drove Yeats' Irish airman to volunteer during the First World War. For him, however, it was a 'lonely impulse':

> Nor law, nor duty bade me fight,
> Nor public men, nor cheering crowds,[5]

That sort of aesthetic choice of danger is a world away from patriotism, which is essentially concerned with the transcendence of individualism, merging the self and its vital interests into a larger whole. The language of patriotism is the quasi-religious language of dedication and sacrifice:

> I vow to thee, my country – all earthly things above –
> Entire and whole and perfect, the service of my love,
> The love that asks no questions: the love that stands the test,
> That lays upon the altar the dearest and the best:
> The love that never falters, the love that pays the price,
> The love that makes undaunted the final sacrifice.[6]

Those lines, written during the First World War, express a kind of idealism that was widely shared in 1914 among the young men who rushed to volunteer. It received a rude shock as they discovered how very far from 'dulce' or 'decorum' dying for their country in the trenches actually was.[7] Hence the immense amount of bitterly anti-patriotic poetry written during and after that war. It would be a mistake to suppose, however, that the language of dedication and sacrifice for one's country could be uttered only by those who didn't know what war is actually like. One of the most memorable of patriotic poems is Victor Hugo's 'Nos morts', written after visits to the battlefields of the Franco-Prussian War. Up to the very last line this reads like something by Wilfred Owen or another of the anti-war poets, giving a horribly graphic description of dead bodies on a battlefield, mangled and mutilated, preyed on by carrion-birds and insects, hideous, squalid and totally without grandeur or dignity. Having confronted the realities of warfare, however, Hugo ends the poem in a totally unexpected way with one simple final line:

O morts pour mon pays, je suis votre envieux.[8]

What could possibly be enviable about this sacrifice? The answer, I think, is solidarity: the expansion of life and death into a shared existence that transcends mortal individuality, but that is larger and more permanent than the evanescent 'we' of immediate loved ones, having a collective existence more imposing and more secure: one's nation, a powerful amalgam of land, polity and people. Patriotism may be about sacrifice, but the message of patriotic poets is that the sacrifice of individual interests is rewarded with a share in the pride and glory of a much larger entity, with the sanctification of one's existence by the sacred mission of the nation, and above all with the overcoming of death in the nation's collective life. Let us look more closely at these rewards of patriotism.

To begin with, the patriot enjoys pride in the glories of his nation. Boasting, of a kind that would be merely ludicrous if indulged in by an individual, is one of the staples of patriotic poetry: boasting about one's country's landscape, its riches, its culture, its valour, its women, its wine, anything that human beings are capable of taking pride in:

Deutsche Frauen, deutsche Treue,
deutscher Wein und deutscher Sang.[9]

In the nature of things, the valour and victories of the country's soldiers take pride of place, but poets invariably manage to drape the flag over other aspects of national life. Here, for example, is Thomas Tickell boasting, during the reign of Queen Anne, that England's women are more beautiful than those of France or Spain:

Soft beauty is the gallant soldier's due
For you they conquer, and they bleed for you.
In vain proud Gaul with boastful Spain conspires
When English valour English beauty fires:
The nations dread your eyes, and kings despair
Of chiefs so brave, till they have nymphs so fair.[10]

Notice that France is 'proud' and Spain 'boastful': we English do no more than state the plain unvarnished truth. For the self-satisfaction is invariably justified by a sense of national mission. Long before Kipling urged his countrymen to 'take up the White Man's burden',[11] the sense of manifest destiny was being strongly expressed by British poets.

> Britain like Heaven protects a thankless world
> For her own glory, nor expects reward.[12]

Thomas Tickell spelled out quite clearly the terms of Britain's mission of dominance:

> Her guiltless glory just Britannia draws
> From pure religion and impartial laws
> . . .
> Her labours are to plead the' Almighty's cause
> Her pride to teach the' untamed Barbarian laws.
> Who conquers, wins by brutal strength the prize,
> But 'tis a godlike work to civilize.[13]

We should not suppose that this complacent sense of being God's chosen people was confined to English or British[14] poets. On the contrary, it is characteristic of patriotism from Poland to Ireland, from Germany to the United States of America, from Russia to the Tyrol. Sometimes what is expressed in verse is the reflective acknowledgement of a gift enjoyed, as in James Russell Lowell's Harvard 'Commemoration Ode' of 1865:

> We sit here in the Promised Land
> That flows with Freedom's honey and milk[15]

In less fortunate circumstances we find a call to a holy crusade for national liberation. A poem from the German war against Napoleon in 1813, Theodor Korner's 'Aufruf' makes clear that this is no ordinary war, but something sanctified:

> Es ist kein Krieg, von dem die Kronen wissen;
> Es ist ein Kreuzzug, 's ist ein heil'ger Krieg![16]

Although the use of religious language can no doubt to some extent be put down to unthinking appropriation of a convenient vocabulary, it is important to recognise that what we have here is in a sense a religious phenomenon, a concern with eternal life: eternal life achieved through participation in the life of a nation that transcends individual existence. Patriotic poetry not only promotes solidarity among the multitude of living individuals to whom it is addressed: more important, it links them to the past of their glorious ancestors and promises them a future in the nation's memory.[17] Individuals, as the poets remind us, are deeply rooted in their country:

> Was ich bin und was ich habe,
> dank ich dir, mein Vaterland.[18]

Consequently, they owe a debt to those who created and defended the country and passed it on to the present generation. One of the most common themes of patriotic poetry is the summons to the present generation to show themselves worthy of their ancestors:

> Men of England! Who inherit
> Rights that cost your sires their blood![19]

In fact, in Thomas Campbell's 'Ye Mariners of England' the ancestors are invoked to aid the struggle as if they were actually present at the battle:

> The spirits of your fathers
> Shall start from every wave![20]

Perhaps they are there to frighten the enemy, but even more to stiffen the resolve of the present generation of warriors, partly by shaming them into valour but also by assuring them that death can be overcome, that they can continue a transfigured existence in the immortal memory of their country.

No one has expressed this most crucial aspect of patriotism more eloquently than Yeats in *Cathleen Ni Houlihan*. As the mysterious Old Woman who symbolises Ireland says,

> It is a hard service they take that help me. . . .
> They that have red cheeks will have pale cheeks for my sake,
> and for all that, they will think they are well paid.
> > They shall be remembered for ever,
> > They shall be alive for ever,
> > They shall be speaking for ever,
> > The people shall hear them for ever.[21]

Yeats was of course very far from being a straightforward, simplistic patriot, and he was to suffer misgivings about the effects of his heady words:

> Did that play of mine send out
> Certain men the English shot?[22]

But after the Easter Rising of 1916, it was quite clear to him that whatever he personally might think of those concerned, or of the wisdom of their actions, his office as a poet was to celebrate (and in doing so to help create) their eternal memory:

> I write it out in a verse –
> MacDonagh and MacBride
> And Connolly and Pearse
> Now and in time to be
> Wherever green is worn
> Are changed, changed utterly:
> A terrible beauty is born.[23]

PART II

> 'Tsar Lazar, thou Prince of noble lineage,
> What wilt thou now choose to be thy kingdom?
> . . .
> If thou should'st now choose an earthly kingdom,
> Knights may girdle swords and saddle horses,
> Tighten saddle-girths and ride to battle –
> You will charge the Turks and crush their army!
> But if thou prefer a heav'nly kingdom,
> Build thyself a church upon Kossovo,
> . . .
> For thine army shall most surely perish,
> And thou too, shalt perish with thine army.'
> . . .
> And the Turks o'erwhelmed Lazar the Glorious,
> And the Tsar fell on the field of battle;
> And with him did perish all his army,
> Seven and seventy thousand chosen warriors.
>
> All was done with honour, all was holy,
> God's will was fulfilled upon Kossovo.[24]

For centuries after the battle of Kossovo in 1389 the Serbian guslars preserved the memory of another sacrifice, another willed defeat out of which a terrible beauty was born. But the recent history of the Serb nation that crystallised around that tradition is likely to confirm our suspicion that the terror of patriotism is more apparent than its beauty. The doctrine, preached by the nineteenth-century Italian nationalist Giuseppe Mazzini, that there is a natural progression from love of one's country to love of humanity, may now seem unforgiveably naive. Patriotism can undoubtedly lift individuals out of their narrow lives and selfish interests, inspiring solidarity, sacrifice and heroism. The trouble is that the solidarity it evokes is not merely limited but positively antagonistic; nor just a devotion to something less than humanity, but an emotion specifically directed against one's country's enemies. Immemorially, Serbian patriotism was directed against Muslims; Irish patriotism against England; the strident eighteenth-century patriotism that created a British nation out of the United Kingdom was directed against France;[25] patriotism in general is characteristically adversarial and concerned with the opposition between Us and Them. One of its typical features, indeed, is preoccupation with actual physical boundaries. Some countries are more fortunate in this respect than others:

> Britannia needs no bulwarks,
> No towers along the steep;
> Her march is o'er the mountain waves,
> Her home is on the deep.[26]

Particularly calculated to arouse patriotic feeling is a border that may seem geographically 'natural', but that is easily breached. In the early days of German nationalism, when Germans felt threatened by French conquest rather than vice versa, their patriots betrayed an obsession with the Rhine:

> Zum Rhein, zum Rhein, zum deutschen Rhein,
> wer will des Stromes Hüter sein?[27]

However, this particular border dispute is ancient history. Despite the recent resurgence of nationalistic sentiments in both countries, it seems safe to predict that France and Germany will not in the foreseeable future come to blows and that the Rhine will not need to be watched for boarding parties from either country. Similarly, we can feel reasonably confident that disputes between Britain and France over fishing rights or lamb imports will not now become a *casus belli*. Why then should we pay attention to poetry that chronicles feelings so out of tune with contemporary commitments? Both the intensity and the narrowness of patriotism rouse justified suspicions. On the one hand, calls for individuals to sacrifice themselves for the nation remind us of all the oppressive collectivisms of our time, while on the other hand the limited and confrontational solidarity fostered by patriotism runs against the grain of modern political thought, which is mainly concerned with ideals that cross national frontiers and extend in principle to all humanity.

Confronted with patriotic poetry, we are likely to feel, with Rorty, that the proper function of literature is to stretch these narrow solidarities rather than to intensify them, 'to expand our sense of "us" as far as we can'.[28] In place of visceral loyalties to our own people, we can and should cultivate an imaginative sympathy with people in general. In what follows, I shall argue, nevertheless, that whatever their moral misgivings, theorists of politics need to pay more serious attention to patriotic sentiment.

The main reason for this is that the nations in whose name patriotic sentiments may be invoked are much more complex phenomena than we usually recognise. A simple contrast between imaginative and unimaginative solidarities will not do, for the nations invoked by our patriotic poets are not in fact primordial kinship groups; they are entities that exist only because sympathies have already been imaginatively stretched far beyond the range that is instinctive or historically normal. When we recognise a fellow-national as one of 'us', or cheer 'our' national side in the World Cup, we are participating in a community that is, as Benedict Anderson has wisely said, an 'imagined community',[29] with most of whose members we would have no more in common than with the rest of the human race, were it not for the crucial role of imagination. The rhetoric of nationhood, and particularly of patriotic poetry, is concerned to assimilate national solidarity to kinship and to make its loyalties and obligations seem natural and inevitable. But this is the art that conceals art, hiding from us the fictive quality in national solidarity.

One of the most interesting features of nations (and the one that causes most confusion) is indeed this fictive quality – the fact that they are communities which are highly contingent, but which function only in so far as they seem natural and inevitable. Whether or not any human groups can be said to be 'natural' is a question we can leave to the ethnologists: perhaps a few ethnic groups do have a kind of a claim to 'naturalness' in the sense that their members really are all close kin and that they form a distinctive and enduring genetic type,[30] but nations are certainly not natural communities in that or any other sense. Instead, they are historic communities that have come into existence, usually within the last few hundred years, typically through a highly contingent process of consolidation whereby distinct and often hostile groups or classes merged into a single entity.[31]

It is salutary to consider the long process of imaginative extension of solidarity that was required to produce what we now tend to think of as a narrow and insular British patriotism. Some of the stridently patriotic poetry quoted earlier must have contributed to that process, for it dates from the time when Britain was a new nation, in the century after the Act of Union with Scotland in 1707, greeted by Lewis Theobald,

> Hail, purple Union, lovely long-expected child![32]

England, the dominant partner in that marriage, already had behind it a long process of consolidation as a nation.[33] In the course of the Middle Ages Normans, Saxons and Danes had become English, and in the sixteenth century the Protestant Reformation allowed English national identity to crystallise around a sense of divine mission such that one bishop could write 'God is English', and call on his countrymen to thank God seven times a day that they had not been born Italians or Frenchmen or Germans.[34]

The eighteenth-century expansion of Englishness into Britishness, incorporating Scotland, may have been eased by the long-standing English habit of claiming the whole island of Britain as their own.[35] Shakespeare's John of Gaunt speaks, after all, of

> This royal throne of kings, this scepter'd isle
> . . .
> This precious stone set in the silver sea
> Which serves it in the office of a wall,
> Or as a moat defensive to a house,
> Against the envy of less happier lands;
> This blessed plot, this earth, this realm, this England,[36]

Nevertheless, as Linda Colley has shown, the emergence of the wider nationhood in the course of the eighteenth century was far from painless, and was made possible largely through almost continuous military confrontation with Catholic France.[37] The poets who helped to extend the range of patriotism were not always as frank about the dialectical relation between internal unity and external strife as Elijah Fenton in 1707:

> Io Britannia! fix'd on foreign wars,
> Guiltless of civil rage extend thy name:[38]

Almost three centuries after the Act of Union, British nationhood does now exist in the rough and ready sense that (at any rate on the mainland of Great Britain) the vast majority of British subjects readily recognise the polity as 'our' polity, and its people as 'our' people – if only by contrast with (for example) Frenchmen or Germans. To that extent, the national project of stretching instinctive loyalties has worked. It hardly needs pointing out, however, that even within so old-established a nation there are plenty of strains, particularly to do with the relationship between British and *English* identity. Spasmodic efforts have been made for the past two and a half centuries to induce the English to remember that they are British, with only partial success. An advertisement that appeared in the personal column of the London *Times* early in the First World War says it all:

> Englishmen! Please use 'Britain', 'British' and 'Briton', when the United Kingdom or the Empire is in question – at least during the war.[39]

But in spite of the bad feeling engendered along the Celtic fringes by English insensitivity or worse, in those times of crisis which (according to Carl Schmitt[40]) lay bare the distinction between friend and enemy that lies at the heart of politics, British nationhood did turn out to be a cause that masses of men were prepared to die for. If we compare the Scottish highlanders who died for Britain in great numbers in the First World War with their ancestors 200 years before, whose loyalties were strictly to their clan, we can see the expansion of solidarity that had taken place.

The purpose of this excursion into the mysteries of British nationhood is to underline a point that is simple but frequently overlooked. What modern universalists see as the deplorably partial and limited solidarity of most Britons (and other nationals) is actually the product of a remarkable feat of social synthesis and imaginative extension of sympathy.[41]

The reason why this is so hard to see is intrinsic to nationhood itself. Nations are not natural, but they cannot be transparently artificial either, since nationhood depends upon an optical illusion whereby we see the chance collection of people with whom we share state and territory as a kind of extended kin. The truth is that nations are very complex phenomena on which it is hard to get a firm conceptual grip. As Brian Barry observes, efforts are continually made to understand them either as states or as ethnic groups, when in fact they are neither.[42] On the one hand (in United Nations' terminology), all states are now supposed to count as 'nations', a fiction cruelly exposed by the break-up of Yugoslavia. On the other hand (according to the ideology of militant nationalism), the human race is supposed to be divided into primordial peoples possessing ethnic unity, a national territory and the potentiality for statehood – a belief equally refuted by the many attempts at 'national self-determination' that have broken down into political chaos and communal hostilities.

Anthony Smith remarks that 'there is an inherent instability in the very concept of the nation, which appears to be driven, as it were, back and forth between the two poles of *ethnie* and state which it seeks to subsume and transcend'.[43] Perhaps a more helpful way of dealing with this instability is to think of nationhood as a phenomenon of mediation. It is, I suggest, of the essence of nationhood to mediate between state and ethnicity, between the institutional order of the polity and the communal sphere of kinship. What emerges from this mediation is a particular kind of collectivity: a polity (actual or potential)[44] that is experienced by its members as if it were a community of kin.

For nationhood to exist, both aspects, the political and the communal, are essential, and both are modified by being mediated in this way. A nation is certainly a community of sorts, but it is an imagined community, not an actual clan or society. Furthermore, it is an imagined *political* community, not a religious or merely cultural one. On the other hand, although the nation is a political phenomenon it is much more than merely a political entity, for it is experienced as if it were a community of kin and assimilated in imagination to an extended family. Neither aspect can be dispensed with. Commentators on nationhood sometimes overlook or underemphasise the political element because of their anxiety not to confuse nations with states.[45] A more common mistake made by recent writers is to neglect the natal element in national community as a result of their understandable anxiety to avoid confusing nationhood with race.[46] Of course, no nation is an ethnic group in the genetic sense, and the immigration and exogamy fostered by modern communications ensure that genetic mixing will increase over the long term. Nevertheless, the sense of imagined kinship which nationhood evokes is not wholly fictitious. In the nature of things, it is very likely that some of my fellow-nationals really will be my kith and kin, and what is more important is that national political identity is passed on as an inheritance through the generations. Some sort of communal identity must always have been passed on from parents to children, but historically that identity has more often been a matter of genealogy, of religion or of locality rather than of political community. The salient point about nationhood is that political phenomena – states, their territories and their institutions – should have become so bound up with the inherited bonds of family that a political collectivity is experienced as a community of kin.[47]

The net effect of nation-formation has been to bind together polity, territory and kin in a way well described by Burke when he explained how, in England,

> it has been the uniform principle of our Constitution to claim and assert our liberties as an *entailed inheritance* derived to us from our forefathers, and to be transmitted to our posterity.... By a constitutional policy working after the pattern of Nature, we receive, we hold, we transmit our government and our privileges, in the same manner in which we enjoy and transmit our property and or lives ... In this choice of inheritance we have given to our frame of polity the image of a relation in blood: binding up the Constitution of our country with our dearest domestic ties.[48]

This is of course an exercise in myth-making, the effect of which is to make the polity seem natural and primordial. That cold and impersonal organisation, the state, is turned into *our* nation, to which all the atavistic loyalties of kinship can be harnessed. A generation after Burke, Macaulay put similar sentiments into the mouth of his ancient Roman hero, Horatius:

> To every man upon this earth
> Death cometh soon or late.
> And how can man die better
> Than facing fearful odds
> For the ashes of his fathers,
> And the temples of his Gods?[49]

Opponents of the nation and all its works, like Jonathan Rée, revile the fraudulent ideological hegemony that 'conspires to make us give our consent to state power by disguising it as an expression of our own feelings'.[50] But there is another side to the myth of nationhood, for it does make possible the expansion of 'us' and 'our' obligations and loyalties far beyond our natural ties to kin and friends, taking in our fellow countrymen and their shared interests and institutions. Whether or not this is, on balance, a moral gain may be a matter for debate. What is more certain is that it has important *political* implications, which are easily overlooked precisely because they are concealed by the illusion of naturalness that clouds nationhood.

Three political implications that are particularly important for the present discussion concern the power of nationhood, its mythical nature and its highly contingent quality. In the first place, a polity that is experienced as a family inheritance can mobilise remarkable political power. The fusion of the political and the familial creates an enduring 'we' that can form the basis of a strong and stable body politic and give the state unity and legitimacy. The nation makes it possible for the state that governs and taxes – that is, in fact, a coercive organisation – to do so in the name of the same collective 'people' who have to put up with these ministrations.[51] Indeed (though this is not a line of argument that can be pursued here), nationhood actually may be a necessary condition for the long-term success of both democratic politics and social welfare policies, since the first requires a widespread ability to recognise the victors in elections as *our* representatives,[52] and the second, similarly, is heavily dependent on the willingness of taxpayers to regard transfer payments as 'looking after our people'.[53] In other words, the mediating role played by nationhood in linking state with community and individual with collective may be a necessary, if neglected, condition for what we tend to think of as normal modern politics.

Second, where nationhood exists its apparently solid political structure is heavily dependent upon myth. The nation is in a sense modern and secular, referring to state and people here and now, but it is also immemorial, linking the present and the past, the mundane and the sacred. Patriotic poets remind us that as members of a nation, individuals are tied into a collective order that is at one and the same time an intimate community of birth and something grander and more demanding, a transcendent entity that comes down from the past and can call for sacrifices to take it into the future.[54]

Third (and this is where the myth can easily mislead us), nations look natural, but are in fact artificial and highly contingent. Nationhood is a matter of degree, not an all-or-nothing affair, but it is never natural and cannot be taken for granted. Where it does exist, its existence goes back at most only a few hundred years,[55] and in many parts of the world it does not exist. Western politicians, theorists and journalists, mistaking their own old-established nations for part of the order of nature, expect to find nations everywhere, able to provide the political unity that is necessary for stable democracy. Instead they are shocked to find in most cases either that nations do not exist at all, or else that (like the Croat, Serb and perhaps the Bosnian Muslim nation) they are in the process of emerging out of violent struggles. Not the least useful of the lessons to be drawn from patriotic poetry is that every nation, however peaceful and liberal now, has had a bloody birth.[56]

PART III

First drink a health, this solemn night,
A health to England, every guest;
That man's the best cosmopolite
Who loves his native country best.[57]

So far I have argued that the death-transcending loyalties evoked by patriotic poetry should not be seen as something atavistic or 'natural', since the imagined community of the nation rests upon a highly contingent extension of solidarity far beyond any natural bonds of kinship or friendship. Nations are neither natural nor ubiquitous, but where they do exist they are cloaked in a mythical 'naturalness' that gives them great power to mobilise populations for political purposes. In a sense, the stretching of 'us' to take in millions of unknown fellow-countrymen must be regarded as a considerable achievement. However, it is evident that this enlarged sympathy is a long way from the active concern for the rights of all humanity to which liberals aspire, and it is widely held that national loyalties actually get in the way of such universal solidarity. We therefore find ourselves returning to our starting point: can the limited loyalties evoked by patriotic poetry be reconciled with liberal aspirations?

Contemporary political thinkers who want to cherish communitarian solidarity without endorsing exclusiveness or chauvinism sometimes try to get round this problem by dissolving the complex unity of nationhood into its political and quasi-ethnic components and embracing the former while rejecting the latter. This move is usually articulated as a distinction between patriotism (which is good, even indispensable) and nationalism (which is deplorable). The language of patriotism comes down to us from the tradition of classical republicanism, and those who would like to revive that tradition today are rarely sympathetic to nations or nationalism. For Mary Dietz, who traces the use of the term in the politics of opposition in eighteenth-century Britain and America, 'patriotism' has an admirable history, associated with republican principles, 'love of liberty' and 'self-sacrifice for a common cause'.[58] 'Nationalism', by contrast, is a more modern term referring to an uncritical 'collective spirit rooted in a sense of national supremacy',[59] associated with warfare and conquest. John Schaar, defending patriotism, takes care to dissociate it from 'nationalism, patriotism's bloody brother'.[60] The precise content of the contrast is not usually spelled out, but seems to be along these lines:

1 Patriotism is a *critical* loyalty which demands that one's country should be true to its inherited principles. Consequently, patriots will often find themselves in opposition when their country's leaders are betraying that past. Nationalism, by contrast, is on this view an unthinking attachment to one's own side, and intolerant of any internal disagreement or criticism.

2 Patriots can combine loyalty with criticism because patriotism is a loyalty essentially to *principles* (such as those expressed in the American Declaration of Independence) This is contrasted with national loyalties, which are assumed to be ties of blood linking one to kith and kin and separating one from ethnic outsiders.

3 Consequently, although all supporters of patriotism recognise that it involves attachment to a specific, limited segment of mankind, patriotism is taken to be *universalist* in its attachment to principles, in contrast to exclusive national loyalties that lead their adherents to neglect or despise the rest of mankind.

4 Finally, the military posture of patriotism is said to be *defensive*, in contrast to the aggression supposed to be characteristic of nationalism and the nation-state.

John Schaar's essay putting 'The Case for Patriotism' is a particularly interesting example of this genre. Schaar, coming to the subject from the American left, wishes to distinguish his own attachment to his country from 'nationalism', by which he seems to mean bellicose attachment to the interests of the nation-state. The core of patriotism for him is 'love of one's homeplace . . . we become devoted to the people, places, and ways that nurture us'.[61] There is in this sentiment a strong element of natural piety. 'To be a patriot is to have a patrimony. . . . the gift of land, people, language, gods, memories and customs' which the patriot inherits, and which 'defines what he or she is'. Receiving with reverent gratitude what has been handed down to him, the patriot is 'determined to defend the legacy against enemies and pass it unspoiled to those who will come after'.[62]

Schaar acknowledges that the attachment to ancestral lands or immemmorial cities that is the stuff of classic patriotism is not available to a modern immigrant people like the Americans. Nevertheless, he suggests that there is a peculiarly American variety which he calls 'covenanted patriotism' and finds in the speeches of Abraham Lincoln. This is 'actively guided by and directed toward the mission established in the founding covenant', and is a matter of accepting one's inheritance from the Founders of the Republic and carrying on their work. He maintains that this sort of patriotism 'decisively transcends the parochial and primitive fraternities of blood and race, for it calls kin all who accept the authority of the covenant'.[63]

Like other attempts to distinguish between patriotism and nationalism, Schaar's at times caricatures the latter as ethnic loyalty and implies that the former can escape such primitive limitations. It is all the more interesting, therefore, that he should show a sensitivity to the familial side of political loyalty that recalls our earlier discussion of a nation as a polity experienced *as if* it were a community of kin. Although he denies that there is any ethnic element in Lincoln's patriotism and claims that it amounts to 'a strictly political definition of out nationhood', his deeply felt stress on the pieties of home and inheritance, and implicitly on the very specific duties to which those who inherit American citizenship are called, sounds extremely Burkean. Furthermore, he is aware that instinctive patriotism has a dark side, giving rise to 'fear and distrust of the stranger'.[64]

Nevertheless, Schaar tends to heap on to the shoulders of 'nationalism' the blame for that narrow and chauvinistic side of group loyalty, claiming that his and Lincoln's 'patriotism is compatible with the most generous humanism'.[65] How is this possible? Because (he explains) patriotism of this kind means loyalty to universal principles of liberty, equality and self-government. Covenanted patriotism 'assigns America a teaching mission among the nations, rather than a superiority over or a hostility toward them'.[66] Unfortunately, although Schaar takes pains to stress that this kind of patriotism does not involve an imperialistic urge to impose one's principles on others, that 'teaching mission' does rather give the game away, at any rate to those on the receiving end of the instruction. For, in spite of his claim that 'patriots do not comfortably support wars of expansion or wars of "principle"',[67] Schaar's attempt to reconcile modern universalism and ancient patriotism follows a familiar track. Over and over again, patriots of one sort or another have tried to overcome the limitations of their allegiance to one polity in particular by seeing it as the carrier of a universal message, a strategy which disguises the problem of limited loyalties without doing anything to solve it. Although Schaar seems to regard the American case as unique, it is actually very common, being directly descended, like other examples, from the *sanctified* patriotism that has sustained polities convinced of their status as God's chosen.[68]

One version of the kind of universalist 'patriotism' that gives its bearers a 'teaching mission among the nations' animated defenders of the British Empire from its earliest years. A descendant of the earlier conviction that Protestant England had a special divine calling, it can be observed undergoing a process of secularisation in the early eighteenth century. As we saw earlier in this chapter, long before John Stuart Mill defended his country's role in teaching 'barbarians' the benefits of freedom,[69] Thomas Tickell observed of Britain that it was 'Her pride to teach the untamed Barbarian laws'.[70]

We should not suppose that there is anything exclusively Anglo-Saxon about this kind of condescension. An even more dramatic transmutation of religious into political chosenness occurred among the 'patriots' of the French Revolution, for whom the land of Joan of Arc and the 'most Christian king' became the land of universal liberty, equality and fraternity. Looking back at those early French efforts to export the benefits of their revolution, we can see what tends to happen when the patriotism of a particular country is infused with universal principles. For it turned out that 'liberation' was difficult to distinguish from conquest, and that the collaborators with the invading French armies in the Netherlands and other 'liberated' countries – those who counted as 'patriots' in the eyes of the French – were often regarded as traitors by their own people.[71] (In France, as in the USA, crusading universalist patriotism has lasted a long time. Gerald Newman quotes an unconsciously chauvinistic French historian of the late nineteenth century who congratulated his fellow-countrymen on their precocious cosmopolitanism: 'It is we who taught the nations of Europe to detach themselves from a narrowly national ideal and to march resolutely towards a human ideal.'[72])

It is easy to mock any such patriotic 'teaching mission', and national pride disguised under the banner of humanity is particularly infuriating to those cast as pupils, whether it is Dutchmen being taught cosmopolitanism by the French, Indians taught 'tolerance' and 'fair play' by the British,[73] or assorted denizens of the Third World bombarded by American troops in the name of freedom and democracy. Britain, France and America have been the carriers of different versions of liberal universalism, and while (for example) the principles of the French Revolution may have seemed universally self-evident to those who propagated them across Europe, they were easily recognised by their opponents as 'French principles'. Similarly, the efforts first of Britain and more recently of America to spread what they believed to be the benefits of civilisation have, understandably, been received as imperialist hypocrisy.

The fusion of universalist communism with Russian chauvinism in the Soviet Union shows that no nation and no part of the political spectrum is immune to this temptation.[74]

In view of the ease with which supposedly universal principles turn into embellishments for national flags, we should perhaps be wary of these attempts to base patriotism upon them. It seems clear that where principles do play a large role in holding a political community together, they function not just as 'the true principles' but as '*our* principles', handed down to us by our forefathers. The limitations of loyalty to a particular political community cannot be transcended by interpreting that community as the mere carrier of principles which are the real focus of the patriot's loyalty. Patriotism demands loyalty to a particular community, and particular loyalty of that kind is bound at some point to conflict with the demands of universal principles. In Alasdair MacIntyre's provocative words, 'good soldiers may not be liberals'.[75] A stronger formulation comes from the conservative philosopher Roger Scruton, who takes pride (as conservatives often do) in his realism. Reflecting on the numerous political theorists who in various ways hanker after 'community' in the modern world, Scruton observes that 'none of them is prepared to accept the real price of community: which is sanctity, intolerance, exclusion, and a sense that life's meaning depends upon obedience, and also on vigilance against the enemy';[76] precisely the kind of sentiments to be found in patriotic poetry. Where, then, does this leave us?

PART IV

> Amid the foremost of the' embattled train
> Lo, the young hero hails the glowing fight;
> And, though fallen troops around him press the plain,
> Still fronts the foe, not brooks inglorious flight.
>
> His life – his fervid soul opposed to death,
> He dares the terrors of the field defy;
> Kindles each spirit with his panting breath,
> And bids his comrade-warriors nobly die!
>
> . . .
>
> Though mix'd with earth the perishable clay,
> His name shall live, while glory loves to tell,

'True to his country how he won the day,
How firm the hero stood, how calm he fell!'[77]

As a genre, patriotic poetry was invented in the ancient republics, by poets like Tyrtaeus (quoted above) in Sparta. The recent recovery by political theorists of the classical republican tradition has seen much celebration of communitarianism and participation at the expense of the atomistic liberalism of the modern West, but there has been a tendency to gloss over a feature of the tradition that is as uncongenial to most modern communitarians as it is to liberals. This is the fact that the freedom of the ancient citizen was inextricably linked with patriotism of the most belligent kind, and that the militaristic republics of Sparta and Rome provided the models of virtuous citizens as long as the tradition lasted.[78] At the tail end of that tradition, Rousseau (who had a taste for paradoxes) pressed home the implication that the price of free citizenship was loss of individuality at home and of humanity abroad,[79] but for a long time his successors seemed to have been released from this dilemma by progress, which seemed to promise that liberty (or at any rate 'modern' liberty, to use Constant's categories)[80] could be enjoyed at a cheaper rate and made compatible with individuality and universal commitments. The recent collapse of the modern assumption that history will solve all our problems for us confronts us with the old dilemma in a new form.

In this chapter I have used examples of patriotic poetry in order to raise questions about political identity and solidarity, and particularly about the relation between the limited national solidarities invoked by the poets and the universal humanitarian commitments associated with liberalism. I have argued that if there is a solution to these dilemmas, the road to it must lie through a better understanding of nationhood, and particularly of the similarities and differences between modern liberal nationhood and tighter solidarities, whether of ancient citizenship or of ethnic kinship. Nationhood as developed in Western Europe and its offshoots owes a great deal to both of these precedents and cannot be entirely dissociated from either. Nevertheless, it is a distinctive feature of modern nationhood (for liberals, *the* significant feature) that it has proved capable of expanding solidarity far beyond the bounds of locality and kin, and of containing plurality within a polity that can still be experienced as *ours*. The result is a political phenomenon which is extremely complex, and which (while the source of remarkable power) involves some delicate balances. For while it is not true that such nationhood requires either genetic homogeneity or moral consensus,[81] it must also be recognised that the sense of common inheritance is fundamental, and that *rapid* increases in ethnic and cultural plurality cannot avoid putting a strain on the mythical structure of kinship that supports national solidarity.[82] Looking back at instances of how apparently alien minorities have been accommodated within British nationhood can be both alarming and reassuring. During the 1930s the Scottish National Party was railing against the 'Green Terror' – Irish Catholic immigrants – in terms very similar to those used by Enoch Powell about a later generation of immigrants,[83] a reaction that seems almost incomprehensible now that Celtic supporters are just as 'Scottish' as Rangers fans.

In the heyday of the Enlightenment Project, the confrontation between universalism and nationalism was often seen as a battle between reason and myth.[84] Since liberals lost their faith in the grand narrative of progress, however, liberal universalism has itself come to be seen as a structure founded upon myths, and therefore ill-equipped to stand buffeting by the all-too-real storms of ethnic hatred. In an earlier paper, following the common practice of confusing nationhood with ethnicity and attributing to it the power of natural loyalties, I argued that precisely *because* of their philosophical deficiencies, liberal myths needed all the help they could get.[85] The situation looks very different, however, once we develop a more sophisticated understanding of the nature and history of nationhood, and realise, first, that nationhood is not the same thing as ethnicity; second, that nations have often been built through the subsumption of simple ethnicity into a more complex form of essentially political community; and third, that certain examples of that sort of national political community have provided the historical locus for the development of liberal universalism.[86] It turns out that neither the national nor the liberal side of the argument has a monopoly either of myth or of actuality. If liberalism does not inhabit the clear skies of reason, neither are nations plunged in the blood and soil of primeval reality. Both of them rely heavily on myths, whether the myth of humanity or the myth of the political community, and while it is true that the demands of nation and of humanity often conflict, it is also true that both may find themselves in alliance against particularistic communalism and conflicts based on ethnic, religious or racial hatred.

What follows from this, for Britain in particular? Clearly, not some crude attempt to shore up British national identity by repatriating immigrants, slamming the door on Europe and putting patriotic poetry at the heart of the national curriculum. But the implication surely is that political identities and loyalties are a matter of much greater importance and concern than has been generally acknowledged, and a topic that should not be abandoned to the right. In particular, we need to be clearer about the distinction between nationhood and ethnicity, and careful lest in weakening the former we may leave the field to mutually hostile intensifications of the latter. British nationhood is a complex and multi-layered form of identity that has managed to accommodate many ethnic groups in the past and can in all probability continue to do so. What we do need to bear in mind, however, is that where such accommodating national identities exist they are sustained by myths of inheritance and continuity that make the polity 'our' community and its inhabitants 'us',[87] and that those myths may be bound up with institutions that are ramshackle and vulnerable to criticism on other grounds.

As it happens, a great many of Britain's traditional institutions are looking shaky just at the moment when the question of relations with Europe is posing problems about national identity. The party system has ceased to deliver alternative governments, the electoral system is being seriously challenged, the monarchy (which could for so long be taken for granted as a symbol of national unity)[88] is discredited, and even the Church of England is splitting.[89] It may be that these developments offer the opportunity for long-overdue constitutional modernisation. If so, however, we would be wise to bear in mind the symbolic value of institutions as well as their more obvious utility. Britain as a constitutional republic (or a cluster of republics) within the EC *might* be a formula for the growth of a wider and more generous identity. However, experience suggests that large-scale political change (particularly in times of economic distress) is at least as likely to give rise to fragmentation and communalism. The alternative to the antiquated and embarrassing feelings celebrated by our patriotic poets may not be humanitarianism, but rather the narrowly communal sentiments expressed in a poem by Kipling, 'The Stranger'.

> The Stranger within my gates,
> He may be evil or good,
> But I cannot tell what powers control –
> What reasons sway his mood;
> Nor when the Gods of his far-off land
> Shall repossess his blood.
>
> The men of my own stock,
> Bitter bad they may be,

But, at least, they hear the things I hear,
And see the things I see;
And whatever I think of them and their likes
They think of the likes of me.[90]

NOTES

1 For helpful comments on a previous version of this chapter I am grateful to April Carter, Vincent Geoghegan, William Stafford and the participants in the 1993 Morrell conference at the University of York.
2 R. Rorty, *Contingency, Irony and Solidarity*, Cambridge, Cambridge University Press, 1989, pp. xvi, 189–98. Rorty's ideas are further discussed in Susan Mendus' chapter in this volume.
3 Walter Scott, 'The Lay of the Last Minstrel', Canto Sixth I, *The Poetical Works of Sir Walter Scott*, London, Macmillan & Co., 1935, p. 42.
4 Robert Burns, 'Robert Bruce's March to Bannockburn', *The New Oxford Book of English Verse*, ed. Helen Gardner, Oxford, Oxford University Press, 1972, p. 493.
5 W. B. Yeats, 'An Irish Airman Foresees his Death', *The Collected Poems of W. B. Yeats*, London, Macmillan, 1963, p. 152.
6 Cecil Spring-Rice, 'I Vow to Thee, My Country', *Poems of Today: First and Second Series*, London, published for the English Association by Sidgwick and Jackson, 1925, p. 207. The second verse is of course about 'another country', the kingdom of heaven, but it is striking that although the formal progression of the poem is from the earthly to the heavenly, the poet declares his commitment only to the former, and the latter is somewhat overshadowed by the intensity of his patriotism.
7 Wilfred Owen, 'Dulce et Decorum est', *Up the Line to Death: The War Poets 1914–1918*, ed. B. Gardner, London, Methuen, 1964, pp. 141–2.
8 Victor Hugo, 'Nos morts', *A Book of French Verse from Marot to Mallarme*, ed. L. E. Kastner, Cambridge: Cambridge University Press, 1936, p. 236.
9 Heinrich Hoffmann von Fallersleben, 'Lied der Deutschen', 1841, *Deutschland Deutschland: Politische Gedichte vom Vormärz bis zur Gegenwart*, ed. H. Lamprecht, Bremen, Carl Schunemann Verlag, 1969, p. 53.
10 Thomas Tickell, 'On the Prospect of Peace', *Poems of Thomas Tickell*, p. 132, *The British Poets* vol. XXVII, College House, C. Whittingham, 1822.
11 Rudyard Kipling, 'The White Man's Burden', *Rudyard Kipling's Verse*, definitive edition, London, Hodder & Stoughton, London, p. 323.
12 Anon, 'Blenheim', in 'A Collection of Poems by Several Hands, printed for R. Dodsley', 1748, vol. II, p. 22.
13 Tickell, 'On the Prospect of Peace', pp. 135–6.
14 On the ambiguities of 'English' and 'British', see below.
15 James Russell Lowell, 'Commemoration Ode', *The Complete Poetical Works of James Russell Lowell*, Boston, Houghton Mifflin, 1925, p. 345.
16 Theodor Korner, 'Aufruf', *Politische Lyrik: Deutsche Zeitgedichte des 19. und 20. Jahrhunderts*, ed. W. Gast, Stuttgart, Philipp Reclam Jun., 1973, p. 7.
17 Cf. A. D. Smith, *National Identity*, London, Penguin Books, 1991,

pp. 160–3; B. Anderson, *Imagined Communities: Reflections on the Origin and Spread of Nationalism*, London, Verso, 1983, pp. 18–19.

18 Hoffmann von Fallersleben, 'Mein Vaterland' (1840), *Deutschland Deutschland*, p. 57.

19 Thomas Campbell, 'Ye Mariners of England' (1822), *The Complete Poetical Works of Thomas Campbell*, ed. J. Logie Robertson, London, Henry Frowde, 1907, p. 203.

20 Campbell, 'Ye Mariners of England' (1822), *Poetical Works of Campbell*, p. 186.

21 W. B. Yeats, *Cathleen Ni Houlihan*, *The Collected Plays of W. B. Yeats*, London, Macmillan, 1952, p. 86.

22 Yeats, 'The Man and the Echo', *Collected Poems*, p. 393.

23 Yeats, 'Easter 1916', *Collected Poems*, p. 205.

24 *Kossovo: Heroic Songs of the Serbs*, trans. H. Rootham, Oxford, Blackwell, 1920, pp. 25–31.

25 L. Colley, *Britons: Forging the Nation 1707–1837*, New Haven, CT, Yale University Press, 1992, passim.

26 Campbell, 'Ye Mariners of England', *Poetical Works of Campbell*, p. 188.

27 Max Schneckenburger, 'Die Wacht am Rhein' (1840), *Deutschland Deutschland*, p. 35.

28 Rorty, *Contingency, Irony and Solidarity*, p. 196.

29 Anderson, *Imagined Communities*, p. 15.

30 For a range of views on this subject see D. Horowitz, *Ethnic Groups in Conflict*, Berkeley, CA, University of California Press, 1985; P. L. van den Berghe, *The Ethnic Phenomenon*, New York, Praeger, 1987; P. R. Brass, *Ethnicity and Nationalism: Theory and Comparison*, London, Sage, 1991; E. E. Roosens, *Creating Ethnicity: The Process of Ethnogenesis*, London, Sage, 1989.

31 E. Renan, 'What is a Nation?', in A. Zimmern (ed.), *Modern Political Doctrines*, London, Oxford University Press, 1939, 194–8; E. J. Hobsbawm, *Nations and Nationalism Since 1780*, Cambridge, Cambridge University Press, 1990, p. 14. Anthony Smith argues persuasively that where nations have come into existence, they have done so by crystallising around an earlier 'ethnic core' (A. D. Smith, *The Ethnic Origins of Nations*, Oxford, Basil Blackwell, 1986, passim).

32 Quoted in B. Dobree, 'The Theme of Patriotism in the Poetry of the Early Eighteenth Century', *Proceedings of the British Academy*, 1949, vol. xxxv, p. 49.

33 Perhaps as the archetypical nation, if Liah Greenfeld is right (L. Greenfeld, *Nationalism – Five Roads to Modernity*, Cambridge, MA, Harvard University Press, 1992, p. 6).

34 Greenfeld, *Nationalism*, p. 60. On English medieval nationalism see S. Reynolds, *Kingdoms and Communities in Western Europe 900–1300*, Oxford, Oxford University Press, 1984, p. 272; and C. C. O'Brien, *Godland: Reflections on Religion and Nationalism*, Cambridge, MA, Harvard University Press, 1987, p. 21. For an impressive study of the many-sidedness of English national identity in the time of Elizabeth, see R. Helgerson, *Forms of Nationhood: The Elizabethan Writing of England*, Chicago, University of Chicago Press, 1992.

35 Helgerson, *Forms of Nationhood*, p. 8.

36 *Richard II*, Act II, Scene 1.

37 Colley, *Britons*, p. 6.

38 E. Fenton, 'An Ode to the Sun, for the year 1707', *The Poems of Elijah Fenton*, p. 150, *The British Poets*, vol. XXIX, Chiswick, C. Whittingham, 1822.

39 Quoted in H. Cunningham, 'The Conservative Party and Patriotism', in R. Colls and P. Dodd (eds), *Englishness: Politics and Culture 1880–1920*, London, Croom Helm, 1986, p. 294. For a vigorous denial that there is such a thing as British nationhood (as opposed to the elusive and unanalysed Englishness that generally masquerades as such) see B. Crick, 'The English and the British', in B. Crick (ed.), *National Identities – The Constitution of the United Kingdom*, Oxford, Blackwell, 1991. While there is a great deal that is illuminating in Crick's comments, he seems to me to dismiss British nationhood too easily.

40 'War as the most extreme political means discloses the possibility which underlies every political idea, namely, the distinction of friend and enemy' (C. Schmitt, *The Concept of the Political*, ed. G. Schwab, New Brunswick, Rutgers University Press, 1976, p. 35).

41 It would be a great mistake to suppose that only the jingoistic feel this solidarity. The most striking testimony to national identity comes from those who deplore the activities of their ancestors, but nevertheless feel co-responsible with them. Christopher Hill says, for example, 'We have a great deal to be ashamed of in our history. We promoted and profited by the slave trade; we plundered India and Africa ...' (C. Hill, 'History and Patriotism', in R. Samuel (ed.), *Patriotism: The Making and Unmaking of British National Identity, vol. I, History and Politics*, London, Routledge, 1989, p. 3. By contrast, it would not make sense for Hill to be ashamed of (say) the Turkish massacre of the Armenians, or indeed of the Norman Conquest.

42 B. Barry, 'Self-Government Revisited', in D. Miller and L. Siedentop (eds), *The Nature of Political Theory*, Oxford, Oxford University Press, 1983, p. 138.

43 Smith, *Ethnic Origins*, p. 150.

44 'Potential polity' means that the collectivity concerned inhabits a territory that is a plausible candidate for statehood, and that it has acquired enough internal structure to be able to throw up representatives who can speak for the nation in the sense of undertaking commitments on its behalf.

45 e.g. H. Seton-Watson, *Nations and States*, London, Methuen, 1977, p. 1.

46 Even Anthony Smith, who stresses the ethnic element in the formation of nationhood, takes care to define ethnicity in cultural rather than genealogical terms (*Ethnic Origins*, pp. 15, 24). This has the effect of obscuring one of the most elementary features of nationhood, namely the fact that (as the word *natio* implies) nationhood is normally something we inherit by virtue of birth. Cf. R. Scruton, 'In Defence of the Nation', in Scruton, *The Philosopher on Dover Beach*, Manchester, Carcanet, 1990, p. 317.

47 Cf. Smith, *National Identity*, pp. 160–2. The question of how nationality is constructed is also considered by Paul Gilbert in his chapter in the present volume.

48 'Reflections on the Revolution in France', in B. W. Hill (ed.), *Edmund Burke on Government, Politics and Society*, Glasgow, Fontana, 1975, pp. 298–9; emphasis in original.

49 T. B. Macaulay, 'Horatius', V. XXVII, *Lays of Ancient Rome*, London, Longman, Brown, 1843.

50 J. Rée, 'Internationality', *Radical Philosophy*, 1992, vol. 60, p. 10.

51 Cf. D. Beetham, *The Legitimation of Power*, London, Macmillan, 1991, pp. 125, 127.

52 Cf. John Dunn: 'The possibility of representation stops at the boundary of the moral community' ('From Democracy to Representation: An Interpretation of a Ghanaian Election', in Dunn, *Political Obligation in its Historical Context*, Cambridge, Cambridge University Press, 1980, p. 154). The assumption that any given territory can be assumed to contain a 'people' (rather than several mutually hostile ethnic groups) has of course had very damaging effects in practice as well as in theory. For an eloquent diatribe against the evils of misapplied 'self-determination', see D. P. Moynihan, *Pandaemonium – Ethnicity in International Politics*, Oxford, Oxford University Press, 1993.

53 Some of the left have recently been willing to recognise that nationhood may be a necessary condition for socialist redistribution. Cf. D. Miller, 'The Ethical Significance of Nationality', *Ethics* 1988, vol. 98, p. 661; *Market, State and Community: Theoretical Foundations of Market Socialism*, Oxford, Oxford University Press, 1989, p. 238; Barry, 'Self-Government Revisited', p. 141.

54 Cf. Anderson, *Imagined Communities*, p. 19.

55 Just how old nations are is a hotly contested question. According to Hobsbawm (*Nations and Nationalism*, p. 14), 'The basic characteristic of the modern nation and everything connected with it is its modernity'. Ernest Gellner agrees. For an impressive view from the opposite extremity, see J. A. Armstrong, *Nations before Nationalism*, Chapel Hill, NC, University of North Carolina Press, 1982. Two courses can be steered through the middle of this controversy: Anthony Smith (*Ethnic Origins*) argues that modern national identity depends upon much older ethnicity; Liah Greenfeld (*Nationalism*) argues that different nations have come into existence at different times.

56 A distinction is sometimes drawn between two sorts of nations and nationalisms, 'civic' and 'ethnic' (Smith, *National Identity*, p. 11), often with the implication that the former, based on pre-existing monarchical states, are liberal whereas the latter, based on ethnic identity, are much less so (though Smith agrees that the two models are in practice found intermingled, p. 13).

57 Alfred Lord Tennyson, 'Hands All Round', *Poems of Tennyson 1830–1870*, London, Geoffrey Cumberlege, Oxford University Press, 1912, p. 454.

58 M. G. Dietz, 'Patriotism', in T. Ball, J. Farr and R. L. Hanson (eds), *Political Innovation and Conceptual Change*, Cambridge, Cambridge University Press, 1989, p. 187.

59 Dietz, 'Patriotism', p. 189.

60 J. H. Schaar, 'The Case for Patriotism', in Schaar, *Legitimacy in the Modern State*, New Brunswick, Transaction Books, 1981, p. 285.

61 Schaar, 'Case for Patriotism', p. 287.
62 Schaar, 'Case for Patriotism', p. 288.
63 Schaar, 'Case for Patriotism', p. 293. For sceptical comments on the notion that American identity has been essentially a matter of allegiance to political principles rather than of, e.g., ethnic ties, see R. M. Smith, 'The "American Creed" and American Identity: the Limits of Liberal Citizenship in the United States', *Western Political Quarterly*, 1988, vol. 41, pp. 225–51.
64 Schaar, 'Case for Patriotism', p. 297.
65 Schaar, 'Case for Patriotism', p. 293.
66 Schaar, 'Case for Patriotism', p. 293.
67 Schaar, 'Case for Patriotism', p. 302.
68 For a fascinating exploration of this topic see C. C. O'Brien, *Godland*, Cambridge, MA, Harvard University Press, 1987. See also M. Walzer, *Nation and Universe*, The Tanner Lectures on Human Values, Brasenose College, Oxford, 1989.
69 J. S. Mill, *Utilitarianism, Liberty, Representative Government*, London, J. M. Dent, 1910, pp. 73, 382.
70 Tickell, 'On the Prospect of Peace', pp. 135–6.
71 C. C. O'Brien, 'Nationalism and the French Revolution', in G. Best (ed.) *The Permanent Revolution: The French Revolution and its Legacy 1789–1989*, London, Fontana, 1988, pp. 38–43.
72 G. Newman, *The Rise of English Nationalism: A Cultural History 1740–1830*, London, Weidenfeld & Nicolson, 1987, p. 49.
73 For a contemporary reiteration of the idea that 'Britishness . . . means a sense of fair play . . . and a spirit of toleration', see J. Gray, *A Conservative Disposition: Individualism, the Free Market and the Common Life*, London, Centre for Policy Studies, 1991, p. 20. For a sharp reaction to recent attempts by British politicians (in the wake of the Rushdie affair) to instruct Muslim immigrants in British values of freedom and tolerance, see T. Asad, 'Multiculturalism and British Identity in the Wake of the Rushdie Affair', *Politics and Society*, 1990, vol. 18, pp. 455–80.
74 Cf. Lenin's essay 'On the National Pride of the Great Russians', quoted in Greenfeld, *Nationalism*, p. 270. For the earlier history of 'Holy Russia', see M. Cherniavsky, *Tsar and People: Studies in Russian Myths*, New Haven, CT, and London, Yale University Press, 1961.
75 A. MacIntyre, 'Is Patriotism a Virtue?', The E. H. Lindley Memorial Lecture, Lawrence, University of Kansas Department of Philosophy, 1984, p. 17.
76 'In Defence of the Nation', in R. Scruton, *The Philosopher on Dover Beach*, Manchester, Carcanet, 1990, p. 310.
77 Tyrtaeus, 'Elegy I', trans. the Rev. Richard Polwhele, *The British Poets*, vol. 92, p. 164.
78 See the description of Sparta in P. A. Rahe, *Republics Ancient and Modern: Classical Republicanism and the American Revolution*, Chapel Hill, NC, and London, University of North Carolina Press, 1992. Cf. A. Oldfield, *Citizenship and Community – Civic Republicanism and the Modern World*, London, Routledge, 1990.
79 J. J. Rousseau, *Emile*, trans. B. Foxley, London, Dent, 1911, p. 7.
80 B. Constant, 'The Liberty of the Ancients compared with that of the

Moderns', in B. Constant, *Political Writings*, trans. and ed. Biancamaria Fontana, Cambridge, Cambridge University Press, 1988, pp. 309–28.

81 *Pace* John Gray ('The Politics of Cultural Diversity', *The Salisbury Review* September 1988, p. 42), what nations inherit, share in and pass on is a *polity* with its practices, myths and symbols, rather than a set of moral beliefs.

82 For an interesting discussion of dilemmas of allegiance for Muslim immigrants in France during the Gulf War, see J. Leca, 'Welfare State, Cultural Pluralism and the Ethics of Nationality', *Political Studies*, 1991, vol. XXXIX, pp. 568–74.

83 A section entitled 'The Green Terror' in an SNP pamphlet from 1937 on 'Scotland's Dilemma' expresses sympathy with the fear that 'Scotsmen will be dispossessed of their own country by immigrants and their children', and goes on, 'The menage of Irish domination lies in the future. But it is certain that, unless measures are taken to arrest and control immigration and to put into the hands of the Scottish people the key to the racial destiny of their country, there will be inevitably a race-conflict of the most bitter kind.' Quoted in A. Marr, *The Battle for Scotland*, London, Penguin, 1992, p. 78.

84 Cf. E. Cassirer, *The Myth of the State*, London, Oxford University Press, 1946.

85 M. Canovan, 'On Being Economical with the Truth: Some Liberal Reflections', *Political Studies* 1990, vol. XXXVIII, pp. 5–19.

86 On liberalism as a national heritage see Greenfeld, *Nationalism*, passim; A. B Seligman, *The Idea of Civil Society*, New York, Free Press, 1992, pp. 147, 160; J. Rawls, 'Kantian Constructivism in Moral Theory', *Journal of Philosophy*, 1980, vol. 77, p. 519; Rorty, *Contingency, Irony and Solidarity*, pp. 61, 68; J. Gray, *Liberalisms: Essays in Political Philosophy*, London, Routledge, 1989, p. 240; *Post-Liberalism: Studies in Political Thought*, New York and London, Routledge, 1993, pp. 284, 328.

87 On the crucial importance of membership for political obligation see J. Horton, *Political Obligation*, Houndmills, Macmillan, 1992.

88 For a fascinating analysis of this neglected topic see T. Nairn, *The Enchanted Glass*, London, Radius, 1988.

89 Those who take for granted that the collapse of such anachronistic institutions could only be a blessing should read Tariq Modood's reflections on the uneasy relations between religious minorities and the liberal secularism dominant in Britain, and ponder his conclusion that a weak established church with traditions of tolerance may be a good deal more favourable to religious and racial harmony than the triumph of radical secularism. He also argues that a more explicit recognition of national identity in Britain would be all to the good: cultural minorities *need* clear national symbols (such as are provided by the flag and the Constitution in the USA), precisely because lack of such definitive symbols puts them under pressure to conform in any and all areas of life. (T. Modood, 'Ethno-Religious Minorities, Secularism and the British State', unpublished paper, 1993; T. Modood, *Not Easy Being British: Colour, Culture and Citizenship*, Stoke-on-Trent, Runnymede Trust and Trentham Books, 1992, pp. 85–6.

90 Kipling, 'The Stranger', *Rudyard Kipling's Verse*, p. 549.

9 The idea of a national literature

Paul Gilbert

PART I

The fundamental question of political philosophy is, one might suggest, 'What is a political community?' In a world of nation-states, where the claim to form a political community is justified by the claim to be a nation, one must then go on to ask. 'What is a nation?' The fundamental question of literary studies is, one might similarly propose, 'What is a literature?' What body of texts is it within which a particular work exists as a work of literature, and against which it is to be judged as such? In a world of nation-states, where literatures bear the names of nations, we must then go on to ask, 'What is a national literature?' and this is my question here.

That literatures bear the names of nations is not an accident. It is not just a reflection of the fact that nations and literatures both commonly bear the names of languages. The usage in which to speak of English literature, say, is to speak of all literature in English, is to be distinguished from the one I have in mind, in which English literature may by contrasted with American or, the example I shall largely draw upon, with Irish literature. Nor is it simply *locality* that is involved here, rather than nationhood. I do not deny that there may be a Yorkshire literature, for instance, but it is not in this sense only that we speak of Scottish or, still less, of Irish literature. There is an inescapably *political* context to the latter cases that is absent from the former. This is because, as Anthony Smith puts it, 'nationalism is a *form of culture* ... that has achieved a global resonance, and the nation is a type of identity whose meaning and priority is presupposed by this form of culture'.[1] National literatures are unintelligible apart from political nations.

National literatures are not necessarily, as the foregoing examples indicate, the literatures of nation-states. Though nations may often be identified through states, states are commonly justified as *national* polities, implying an independent criterion of nationhood in terms of which national literatures, or cultures generally, can be identified. Nor are national literatures necessarily *nationalist* literatures: their authors need not, that is to say, express the political aspirations of a nation; they need not, surely, *express* allegiance to it in any form. My question is, indeed, what an author does need to do to be a national author; what makes their literary work an instance of a national literature?

There are, broadly speaking, two principal kinds of answer to the question 'What is a nation?'[2] One, the realist answer, bases nationhood upon a common property of people independent of their will to associate together politically. The other, the voluntarist answer, bases it on their having that common will. Under realism people discover what nations there are and which they belong to by discovering what common properties mark out national groups and which they themselves possess. Different realist theories identify different sorts of property as playing this role. They may be natural properties, such as race is alleged to be, or social ones such as the possession of a common culture, viewing a culture as something that people find themselves in, not something which they choose or which results from their political choices.

The voluntarist answer might seem to make it hard to distinguish a national from nationalist literature: to be a member of a nation would be to have a shared political allegiance, to be a national author to express it in literature. Yet, just as I cannot normally make up my mind all on my own what nationality to be, so authors cannot, independently of their readers, make their work part of a national corpus. Thus, a further contrast appears. Under voluntarism, a national literature is chosen as such by the nation. Under realism, its national identity is independent of and prior to any political choice.

The importance of the contrast is this. The species of realism that we may call *cultural* nationalism holds that the common property of people which makes them a nation is participation in a common culture, of which a shared literature may be an important part. In order for the possession of a shared literature to be partly constitutive of a shared national identity realistically conceived, it must be the sort of thing that could help convince people they had that shared national identity and thus ought, perhaps, to have their own state, or in some other way associate together politically. But if a shared literature is simply the product of political association it can do nothing to justify it: its existence as a national literature is itself politically determined, not a reason for political choice. The importance of asking what is a national literature consists, then, in this: it helps to determine whether cultural nationalism, as a species of realism, is a plausible theory of nationhood, or, if it is not, in what ways nations might be identified culturally.

No doubt a great deal of idealisation is involved in this. Voluntarism is the official theory of the modern liberal democratic state, and it is the *state*, we may be inclined to think, which *constructs* a national literature, and uses it to patch up whatever holes in national identity are left by an imperfect national will. Trying to ride the realist horse simultaneously, however, the state presents its construct as a *fact* about the nation, rather than a reflection of state policy as to how the nation should be constituted. This alleged cultural fact is presented as something which should provide reasons for a national will to associate politically. But if a national will really *is* constitutive of nationhood then it does not need to be based on any belief in a national culture; while if a national culture is constitutive then it does not require the accompaniment of a national will.

'National literature; fact or construct?' defines my question further, however.[3] Are there any sensible generalisations one might formulate and test as to how national literatures are individuated – by discoverable facts about their instances or by processes of a different, and overtly political, kind? And, if the latter, could a literature belong to a nation because it reflects a voluntary association of its members, because it is, so to speak, *chosen* by them, rather than being imposed by a *soi disant* nation-state?

My aim will be to take a particular literature – Irish writing in English[4] – and ask how it might be delimited. No doubt here, as elsewhere, the boundaries are vague. But this does not mean that nothing sensible can be said about them, and in particular about how borderline cases might be treated. My plan will be to take one such case and see, by way of comparison and contrast, how our reasons for moving this way or that illuminate the identity of Irish literature and, by an optimistic extension, of national literatures in general.

PART II

Elizabeth Bowen was born in 1899 into a Protestant Anglo-Irish family, with an eighteenth-century seat, Bowen's Court in County Cork. She was educated in England and spent a good deal of her life there, though returning often to Bowen's Court, which she inherited in 1930, and which was eventually demolished after she was obliged to sell it 30 years later. She died in 1973. Bowen's novels, similarly, are often set in England, but in two, *The Last September* (London: Constable, 1929) and *A World of Love* (London: Cape, 1955), the action takes place principally in Irish homes just like Bowen's Court, about which she wrote a family history of the same name (London: Longman, 1942); Irish scenes and characters occur elsewhere in the novels and short stories. Was Elizabeth Bowen an *Irish* writer?

Interviewed in Dublin in 1942[5] she had no doubts:

> I regard myself as an Irish novelist. As long as I can remember I've been extremely conscious of being Irish – even when I was writing about very un-Irish things such as suburban life in Paris or the English seaside. All my life I've been going backwards and forwards between Ireland and England and the Continent, but that has never robbed me of the strong feeling of my nationality. I must say it's a highly disturbing emotion. It's not – I *must* emphasize – sentimentality.

Others have been less sure. 'The "Irishness" of Elizabeth Bowen may seem especially suspect', writes one.[6] With a startling compression of historical events he suggests that 'her claims to nationality might be said to have died in the revolution which made much of Ireland a republic independent of England, and presumptively too independent of the long history of the Anglo-Irish', before conceding that Bowen counts as an Irish writer because she was born in Ireland and continued to call herself Irish. Another critic[7] writes that Bowen is 'mainly an "outsider", closer to Oxford and London and the Bloomsbury group than to Ireland', although there is 'an Irish dimension in some of her work'. At least this distinguishes the question of Irish authorship from the Irish nationality of the author. Iris Murdoch, for example, was born in Dublin and, one understands, calls herself an Irish writer; but few could unhesitatingly agree, or even wish to bracket her nationally with Elizabeth Bowen.[8] One can scarcely imagine someone saying of Murdoch's writing, as Sean O'Faolain exclaimed of *The Last September*,[9] 'It's so entirely Irish, if that matters a damn.' But was O'Faolain right? Is Elizabeth Bowen's writing a part of Irish literature? And if it is, is it because it possesses a property that O'Faolain discerned, or just because O'Faolain and other Irish people acclaim it as such?

PART III

What kinds of property might hold or fail to hold of Elizabeth Bowen's writing in virtue of which she counts or fails to count as an Irish writer? We are not here seeking necessary and sufficient conditions of Irishness in the writing. That would be too much to expect: at most a realist might hope for a loose cluster of properties to be constitutive of national literary identity. We are, however, asking what kinds of property we understand as salient to determining it, and whether they spring from a taxonomy rooted in the facts; or whether, by contrast, they simply reflect our sense of what is claimed for a national literature, and how such claims can be upheld.

Language should, perhaps, stand at the head of any list of candidates for properties intrinsic to a work which bespeak its national identity. In many cases a distinct language corresponds to a national literature, as the partisans of a Gaelic revival hoped it would in Ireland. And even when the language of a people belongs to others too it may have features as distinctive in their literature as in the accents of their speech. Yet so far the connection between language and national identity will seem quite accidental. It gains significance only if it is seen as something of value. Here the speakers' sense of their language as *beautiful* is significant.[10] Eoin McNeill[11] said of Gaelic poetry that it was as 'distinct from ordinary language as the heavens are from the earth', giving rise to a vernacular that displayed 'a power of delicacy of diction certainly not excelled even by the educated classes in speaking English.' The suggestion of a *comparison* here is surely misplaced. Rather McNeill is registering a certain kind of *attachment* to the rhythms and idioms of Gaelic which reflects a judgement, not of taste, but, so to speak, of *comfort*. He feels comfortable with that language, at home in it, however well he knows the other. And he may – like Joyce's Stephen Dedalus – not feel fully at home in the other even if it is all he knows: in conversation with an Englishman, Stephen reflects that 'the language we are speaking is his before it is mine ... so familiar, and so foreign'.[12]

A language is a medium of social intercourse, and its forms are the forms of social exchange. The apparent *rightness* of a language is its appropriateness in this role or, since social relations are not characterisable independently of the language in which they are transacted, in the ceremoniousness of these relations.

When the landfolk of Galway converse with a stranger,
softly the men speak, more softly the women,
light words on their lips, and an accent that sings
in traditional cadences (once plucked by harpists
to cheer melancholic carousals of kings . . .

In these anthologised lines[13] the memory of social relations in a part of Ireland is derived from a romanticised Gaelic past. The language, English as I suppose it to be here, is placed in, and viewed as expressive of, a particular history through which these social relations persist.

There are two related tests here, then, for the candidate for Irish letters. One is a sympathetic ear for English as it is used in Ireland. For it could scarcely be supposed that an author contributed to a national literature if they lacked the capacity to use, as it were, the national tongue. The other is a sense of the language as a medium for social relationships – as, to borrow a pertinent phrase of Yeats, 'a house where all's accustomed, ceremonious'.[14]

Frank O'Connor was thinking of the former test when he said of Somerville and Ross that 'with Joyce's *Dubliners, The RM* is the most closely observed of all Irish story books, but, whereas Joyce observes with cruel detachment, the authors of *The RM* observe with love and glee'.[15] Consider, then, Slipper's well-known account of a riding fall:

'The blood was dhruv out through his nose and ears' continued Slipper, with a voice that indicated the cream of the narration, 'and you'd hear his bones crackin on the ground. You'd have pitied the poor boy'

'Good heavens!' said Leigh Kelway, sitting up straight in his chair.

'Was he hurt Slipper?' asked Flurry casually.

'Hurt, is it?' echoed Slipper in high scorn, 'killed on the spot!' He paused to relish the effect of the *dénouement* . . . [16]

The ear may be accurate, but it is an ear, surely for a *foreign* tongue remote from the arch reflections of the authorial commentary. It is through the English of 'the educated classes' alone that *serious* relationships are possible. The 'cruelty' of Joyce, by comparison, is that of one who has a sharp sense of what relationships are expressed within such an idiom and who detaches himself from them despairingly. In contrast to both might stand such passages from Synge as this:

It's little you'll think my love's a poacher's, or an earl's itself, when you'll feel my two hands stretched around you, and I squeezing kisses on your puckered lips, till I'd feel a kind of pity for the Lord God is all ages sitting lonesome in His golden chair.[17]

What shocked audiences of *The Playboy of the Western World* was surely the very beauty of the language and the corresponding sensuous intensity of the relationship which it mediates.

How, on these two tests, does Elizabeth Bowen score? Bowen treats us to few of those encounters with 'the Irish properly so-called'[18] characteristic of Anglo-Irish fiction. Here is one from *The Last September*.[19]

'You remember Mr. Montmorency'
'Sure indeed I do!' exclaimed Michael, and shook hands with Mr. Montmorency again with great particularity.
'And very well I remember your father. You are looking grand, sir, fine and stout: I known you all these years and I declare I never seen you looking stouter. And welcome back to Danielstown, Mr. Montmorency, welcome back sir!' (pp. 64–5)

At first sight this may seem a patronising view of a rustic Irish welcome to the gentry. But in its context it heightens the underlying tension of the situation. Michael Connor's son, Peter, is a Republican on the run from the English in the War of Independence, Danielstown's owners Sir Richard and Lady Naylor are concerned for him at the same time as they entertain English officers, and it is, one is led to suspect, as a result of his eventual arrest and a consequent misunderstanding of their role that Danielstown is burned.

The first wave of a silence that was to be ultimate flowed back, confident, to the steps. Above the steps, the door stood open hospitably upon a furnace.
Sir Richard and Lady Naylor, not saying anything, did not look at each other, for in the light from the sky they saw too distinctly. (p. 206)

Thus concludes the novel, upon a silence that engulfs the Anglo-Irish.

Bowen is unable to celebrate Irish diction, but damns English gracelessness:

'Oh darling, look at those little teeny black cows. Those are Kerry cows. They farm, you know; they have heaps of cattle.

'I meant to ask you: *are* there Kilkenny cats?'

'Really,' said Mrs. Vermont, annoyed, as her friend yawned again and she felt her own jaw quiver. 'When one thinks these are the people we are defending!' (p. 195)

It is in contrast to these tones, and the vacuity of social life which they bespeak, that Bowen's Irish gentry unfailingly identify themselves, rather than by association with the accents of Michael Connor. The polarisation of the War of Independence leaves them silent.

An objection might be lodged against what I have been assuming here, namely that a certain condescension towards ordinary speech is a *prima facie* disqualification for a place in the literature of the country whose speech it is. For is it not the case that *English* writers, in particular, have systematically condescended towards the speech of *ordinary* people? And is not this simply a reflection of *class* superiority, rather than national distinctiveness – a superiority which provides the obvious explanation of, for instance, the tone of Somerville and Ross? In answer to this it could be suggested that the speech of *ordinary* people in England is precisely not *national* speech, as it is in Ireland: national speech itself is reserved to the English upper classes. One could go on to insist that class differences cannot overcome a presumption of national disqualification in the Irish case, even if there is no such presumption in the English. What distinguishes the cases, I shall argue later, is not just local circumstances, but differences which are of general importance in individuating national literatures.

It would beg the question against Bowen's own claim to an Irish voice in literature to valorise the Connors' accents alone. There are no facts to substantiate her claim, but nor are there any to confute it. What counts as an Irish voice here is determined by what counts as Irish literature rather than by some external test. Its relation to national mores can best be discovered by asking if it is a voice in which to conduct them. But this is a question calling for a decision rather than a question of fact.

PART IV

Sing the peasantry and then
Hard riding country gentlemen,
The holiness of monks and after
Porter-drinkers' rowdy laughter;

So Yeats enjoined Irish poets.[20] It is, I suspect, a particular *subject* matter that strikes O'Faolain as 'so entirely Irish' about *The Last September*. One would expect a certain subject matter – the people and places of the nation – to typify a national literature. But the subject matter must be treated in a certain way, for it cannot be merely a certain kind of content that makes for a national literature, since we could always imagine the same people and places made part of politically conflicting literatures. Indeed, the nineteenth-century literatures of 'the Irish properly so-called' and of the Anglo-Irish may provide examples of this.

It will not be sufficient then, though it will be necessary, to say that the treatment of the subject matter must express an *insider's* view of it. And in speaking of an insider's view we are speaking not just of the content of their knowledge, but of the kind of knowledge that comes from personal involvement. The coolly analytical treatment of Irish character in Iris Murdoch's *The Red and the Green*,[21] disqualifies it, other things being equal, as an example of Irish literature. Of Pat, the Republican fighter, she writes that 'his Ireland was nameless, a pure Ireland of the mind, to be relentlessly served by a naked sense of justice and of naked self assertion. There were in his drama only these two characters, Ireland and himself'. It is no isolated example: Murdoch is not, to use Conor Cruise O'Brien's criterion, 'involved in the Irish situation' or 'mauled by it;.[22]

In Bowen's *The Last September* a similar but sketchier gunman, encountered by chance, is treated quite differently:

> The man's eyes went from one to the other, and remained ironically between them. His face was metal-blue in the dusk and seemed numbed into immobility. 'It is time', he said, 'that yourselves gave up walking. If you have nothing better to do you had better keep in the house while y'have it'. (p. 125)

There is a fascination with a familiar undertone here,[23] however disturbing. Its irony is taken up by Bowen herself in describing the English officer Gerald, who

> would have wished to explain that no one could have a sounder respect than himself and his country, for the whole principle of nationality, and that it was with some awareness of misdirection, even of paradox, that he was out here to hunt and shoot the Irish. (p. 93)

The savagery of that last phrase gives substance to the reactions of the Irish that talk of 'a naked sense of justice' manifestly cannot.

The inside that Bowen is on is, however ambivalently, that of the gunman, not his hunter.

Identifying Bowen's vantage point is easy here. But it depends upon the author's location of herself within an area of political association, not on facts about her text which identify its nationality. Could this kind of identification be made, and how? Two possibilities occur to one – a certain range of imagery articulating the subject matter, and a certain repertoire of tone. As to the first, the stereotypical imagery of Irish literature is, of course, that of a land of saints and scholars, of heroes and high kings, pervasive in a sacralisation and historicisation of landscape.

> The yellow bittern that never broke out
>   In a drinking bout, might as well have drunk;
> His bones are thrown on a naked stone
>   Where he lived alone like a hermit monk . . .
> In a wintering island by Constantine's halls,
>   A bittern calls from a wineless place.
> And tells me that hither he cannot come
>   Till the summer is here and the sunny days . . .

This from an eighteenth-century Gaelic poem[24] is exemplary of a kind of trope that Yeats made canonical. Explicitly, this sort of thing is rare in Bowen's work – though the Danielstown the English visitors see is set in a landscape where 'square cattle moved in the fields like saints, with a mindless certainty. Single trees, on a rath, at the turn of the road, drew up light at their roots' (p. 67). Yet the possibilities of innocence, of understanding, or of achievement in a particular place with a specific history[25] – these, it could be argued, are her prevailing themes.

Yet does Ireland in particular, and its history specifically, stand out as structuring the fictive space? For unless reference to Ireland is an inextricable part of the imaginary world it is hard to see how that world's character can be evidence of Irishness. Two objections to an affirmative answer might be lodged. One would observe that the Ireland of Elizabeth Bowen is, almost invariably, the Ireland of the big house. Unlike the country house in England, this cannot serve as an emblem of Irish national 'heritage' along the same continuum as Gallarus' Oratory and the Rock of Cashel. One might rebut the criticism by observing that the family house, in Bowen's fiction, is no image of confidence and continuity: the house, in its literal or metaphorical sense, is near or at its end, a site of dissolution and dispersion, just like Kilcash in the eighteenth-century Gaelic poem:

> ... My grief and my affliction
> Your gates are taken away
> Your avenue needs attention
> Goats in the garden stray ... [26]

For all their social particularity, Danielstown, Montebello, Mount Morris, Montefort point to an experience central to Irish history and to the problem of Irish national identity. Yet the question of Bowen's relation to this experience is again hardly a factual one. It is rather a question as to whether her fiction provides a vehicle for this shared experience; and that has to do with its reception.

The second objection takes a different tack. It is that Ireland, and specifically the Ireland of the Anglo-Irish past, functions in Bowen as an image of a life of value that is no longer possible in, for example, twentieth-century England; that the Ireland which is important in the fiction is, crucially, a *fictitious* Ireland – not the place to which a real political commitment could be made.[27] Unfair to the work, as I think it is, it is unfairer still to the claim to Irish identity that rests upon it. Different as Bowen's Ireland is from the nationalist stereotype, it is surely the stereotype which is the more open to the objection.

Marcuse claims[28] that bourgeois culture provides an imaginary realm for the celebration of human values for which bourgeois society leaves no room; and that is precisely the criticism of the Irish Literary Revival made by Flann O'Brien:

> ... in this Anglo-Irish literature of ours [i.e. Irish literature in English] which for the most part is neither Anglo, Irish, nor literature, as the man said, nothing in the whole galaxy of fake is comparable with Synge ... and now the curse has come upon us, because I have personally met in the streets of Ireland persons who are clearly out of Synge's plays. They talk and dress like that and damn the drink they'll swally but the mug of porter in the long nights.[29]

Or, developing O'Brien's suggestion that 'we who knew the whole inside outs of it preferred to accept the ignorant valuations of outsiders on things Irish', Anthony Cronin:

> The Irish Literary Revival was an offshoot of British needs. Materialistic, moneyed, torpid late Victorian society wanted an

anti-materialistic land of Heart's Desire . . . Yeats and his friends elected to supply such a never-never land.[30]

It is precisely her lack of centrality in this Irish literary tradition that renders Bowen immune to the criticism that her work contributes to a fantasising stereotype which inhibits political life. Bowen's own inhibitions here are quite general; they stem rather from the ethos of a Bloomsbury that stood opposed both to Victorian materialism and to its idealising counterpart. They scarcely seem to derive from embracing a fantasy, but whether the view they reflect can express an *Irish* involvement is open to debate.

It is in this area that one might appeal to Bowen's repertoire of tone, and, in particular, her use of irony to prevent romantic yearnings from ever finding more than a transitory solace. Elegy is interrupted by bathos in a way characteristic, one might feel, of Irish sensibility (*vide, The Yellow Bittern*) and running counter to detachment – 'the French aesthetic ideal'[31] for which she strove in her prose. Tone, one might go on to suggest, is expressive of authorial character, and authorial character reflective of 'the national character'. Cronin's remarks on the British echo a familiar view of them – or at least of the English part of them – as, in the main conservative and commensensical, but, in some measure, romantic and irrational. It is a combination which has been attributed to the moderation but mistiness of the English climate.[32]

Nonsense of this sort threatens to plunge us from a proposed cultural nationalism straight into racism. It is worth reminding ourselves here of Flann O'Brien's observations of characters 'straight out of Synge's plays'. National character is a good deal more plausibly a *product* of national culture than vice versa. Looking at things like this, prompted by the author's tone; seeing them like this, in response to her imagery – these, we might say, are what is recognised as national character. For, contrary to racist assumptions character is, of course, inculcated, and inculcated through the assimilation of culture in the form of literature and the like. One is left again, without any non-circular factual basis for literary nationality.

PART V

What does this brief discussion of a borderline case tell us about literary nationality? Is it, as the realist would have it, discovered, or is it made? To establish realism we would, I think, need to be able to see certain literary features as indicative of nationality in virtue of some general theory of how kinds of people are distinguished by features of their culture. But what we do see when we look at a particular case is not, on the face of it, at all generalisable. It consists simply in seeing what makes for literary Irishness, say, rather than Englishness, without reference to any general theory of what distinguishes them. When we do come across anything that approximates to a theory – like the racist theory of national character – it is one that makes cultural identity, as might be manifest in literature, a product of national identity otherwise constituted, rather than constitutive of it.

Furthermore, were literary nationality to be attributed on the basis of a theory we would expect the treatment of borderline cases to have a different complexion from the one it wears. We would expect it to involve either the search for further facts which will lead to the determinate classification of these cases on the basis of existing theory, or to the refinement of the theory, since realism abhors vagueness in objects. Consider, for example, how, by these processes the rose Chapeau de Napoleon is relegated, despite appearances, from the Moss to the Provence Rose class, while Maiden's Blush and Queen of Denmark are distinguished from the latter as Albas. No similar processes operate in the literary case: here appearances are all, or nearly all, no theory points us in the direction of undiscovered facts or undeveloped discriminatory devices.

I have been unable to identify any set of intrinsic properties in which a literary nationality – Irishness, say – resides. In contestable cases we run out of literary arguments since there is nothing in the literary facts which calls for one way of organising the data rather than another. In such arguments we cite properties which pull us this way or that in our attributions, but if we ask why they do then we can only appeal to examples which lie within the literature or obviously outside of it. We appeal, in other words, to exemplars of literary nationality, but that they *are* exemplars is not similarly explicable.

Unsurprisingly, it might be objected, the properties relevant to literary nationality turn out to be *extrinsic* ones, and, in particular, the place of the work in a *tradition*, whose character is, of course, to be indicated by examples. What is it, though, for a work to fall within a literary tradition? If there is to be a fact of the matter as to whether it does then, on the one hand, certain similarities to other examples of the tradition are required, but, on the other, a suitable *explanation* of how these similarities come about. Yet it seems doubtful whether a work needs to be part of a tradition in this sense to be part of a national literature. Certainly, some kinds of similarity must be excluded as irrelevant. *Pastiches* of Irish literature, though best done by Irish authors, are not of logical necessity so done. No doubt there are other cases where similarity can be explained in a way that makes it irrelevant to literary nationality, or occurs by chance, its literary nationality being locatable elsewhere. We need to say that the similarities to exemplars of a literary nationality should *not* be explainable in such ways, but no stronger condition for being part of a tradition is required. There *may* be a national tradition, but equally what we *call* a tradition here may have more to do with our preparedness to discover similarities and to project upon the facts an explanation of these similarities – namely that they are due to their all being examples of a national literature. Needless to say, against a background of cultural nationalism such an explanation would be completely vacuous.

If this is the story then constructionism wins out. What is exemplary of a national literature is something chosen to be so, without any grounding in properties that make it so. But this does not imply that, armed with the exemplar, we cannot reliably assign other works to the national literature on the basis of their similarities. After all, we do this sort of thing all the time: we recognise omelettes by reference to exemplars, even though the exemplary omelette is, so to speak, a social construction. It is only when we get to borderline cases, like Spanish omelettes, that we have recourse to the same processes that gave rise to that construction. And so it is with exemplars of national literature. For the most part we are dealing with questions with clear answers, but whose answers depend upon a process of construction which we may wish to endorse or reject.

PART VI

The big question about the construction involved in the formation of national literatures is, surely, who does the constructing. The illustrations I have offered will, I hope, throw light on this. First, one wants to say, it must be done by members of the nation. Recall here Anthony Cronin's suggestion that the Yeatsian Irish Literary Revival was engineered by *British* interests. If that were all there was to it then the examples thereby manufactured could not serve to delineate the culture of an Irish nation, since the members of this nation might reject this characterisation of itself. Flann O'Brien's complaint is that the Irish accepted it. But, if this is so, then it only manifests the familiar 'Black is beautiful' process, whereby a devalued out-group accepts the stereotyped characterisation of itself by the in-group, yet reverses the value set on the stereotype. It is not the origin of the stereotype but its adoption that is important to identify.

My first condition on the formation of national literatures solves no disputes over national literary identity. Yeats was, of course, like Elizabeth Bowen, Anglo-Irish, and his work is proclaimed, like hers, for English literature. Yet, as Donald Davie remarks, 'it would be very strange if an Irish poet, a poet so consciously and deliberately Irish as Yeats was, should have the sort of centrality in the English tradition [claimed for him]'.[33] The same could scarcely be said of Bowen. But she, like the Anglo-Irish in general, was clearly impatient with a monopolisation of judgements as to Irishness which excluded her. Disputes over national literary identity – and this is my second point – may be disputes over who is to do the constructing. It follows that in these cases the construction is a politically contested one, as manifest in conflicts concerning borderline cases.

My own approach in discussing Bowen's claim has been to rely heavily on exemplars canonised by the Irish Literary Revival in order to establish possible parallels in her work. The assumption this approach rests upon is, I must now concede, itself open to question. Why should one not locate her Irishness in a continuation of an Anglo-Irish tradition which has an *equal* claim – and this is now clearly a political point – to contribute to Irish literary identity? More subtly perhaps, one might see her work as a relevant influence on contemporary Irish authors like William Trevor.[34] What counts as a *relevant* influence involves the occurrence of motifs, particularly that of the big house, which are made emblematic of Irishness in the later work. And to make them emblematic is a political, as much as a literary, achievement.

Flann O'Brien's remarks, like *At Swim Two Birds* itself, may be seen as an attack on a certain literary establishment as the arbiter of Irishness. It is an attack in which artistic and political considerations cannot be disentangled. The view of national life their exemplars express is not only 'fake', as insiders know, but it is a fake which restricts personal and communal aspirations. The construction of a national literature is, my third point, not only a literary judgment as to what might exemplify national identity, but a political one as to what national identity consists in.

In fact, it might be better to say that it is not only a political judgement, but a literary one. For the *achievement* lies not in the political act of forging a national identity, but in doing so by literary means – by securing a sense of an identity already given through its literary manifestations. And this requires that a national literature should be made to seem as natural a classification as those embodied in the various genres. Clearly, it is very different: unlike genres, a national literature is not selected by its author; nor, unlike such genres as sentimental ballads or Beat poetry, does it *express* its character; it does not *express* its nationality. The category of national literatures is, in literary terms, a curious category. For, crucially as I have argued, there is no general literary taxonomy of national literatures. Each is inescapably *ad hoc*, as each reflects different political requirements. The achievement in the construction of a national literature lies in none the less accepting the constraints of literary classification so that putative instances can be assigned on purely literary grounds, given a deft choice of exemplars. The literary judgement this involves may or may not be successful, since the construction of a national identity must be usable in two ways. It must be usable by insiders and outsiders alike as a classificatory tool for sorting out the nation's literature from others. And it must be usable by insiders as a vehicle for perceptions of their national life, not just with respect to their observations of its course but with respect to their aspirations as to its direction.

Who those concerned to determine national literary identity are will vary. In some places and at some times they will consist of an elite group producing what Anthony Smith calls a *lateral* ethnie for the nation.[35] Bloomsbury, for example, on the outskirts of which Elizabeth Bowen moved, played this role in inter-war Britain.[36] In other circumstances, perhaps those of Ireland around the time of Independence, people as a whole will generate a *vertical* ethnie which unifies different groups and classes. This provides an answer to the question posed earlier as to why condescension towards ordinary Irish speech is a disqualification for Irish literary identity, though no corresponding requirement exists for English. It is that the construction of exemplars of Irishness is to be performed popularly, rather than by an elite. This requires the possibility of identification with one's own representation that is ruled out by condescension.

It should not be thought, however, that those concerned with national identity can necessarily be identified through any *explicit* political association. Indeed those concerned may be – and in the case of vertical ethnies probably are – indentifiable only through their attachment to a certain culture. Those who construct its exemplars may, for my fourth point, be identifiable only in terms of the exemplars which they collectively valorise. There may be no non-cultural way of identifying their association. It is in this case, and in this case only, that we can properly attribute national identity on the basis of a common culture, but without presupposing the realist theory that underlies cultural nationalism, as ordinarily understood.

This limiting case is exceptional. Yet the possibility of it displays the role of literature as a site of implicit political association. Constructionism regards a national literature as the result of people's choices. But if, implausibly, it is through a shared literature alone that people come together as a nation then, on the voluntarist model, these choices must be those of *all* members of the nation. More plausibly we might suggest that a culture which results from the choices of all its participants could be viewed as associating them together in the way that the voluntarist conception of nationhood requires.[37] Although the nation is identified culturally, it is identified as a voluntary association of its members.

The responses – 'that's how it is for us; that's how we want it to be' – can bind people together in collectivities of many sorts and sizes. The importance of one sort or another can be affirmed or denied by different kinds of work. Ineradicably local literatures shade by degrees through national ones into the deraciné cosmopolitanism – or more properly Europeanism – of the twentieth-century avant-garde. But national literature has a special significance, since it is within the context of the nation-state, and not easily elsewhere, that a view of how things are and of how they might become can have a practical, because a political, application. The agendas of national governments require a high degree of ideological control, which includes control of the national literature. But such control is of necessity fragile, open to subversion by literatures that fail to fit a national stereotype but still lay claim to inclusion because they address a nationally shared expression.

Needless to say, the cultural claim of a former Ascendency, as in Elizabeth Bowen's case, will not be typical of the national borderlines that are in dispute here. Yet it illustrates the possibilities of cultural change – or, as one should rather say, of cultural *revision* – that are unprovided for on the realist model. The principal objection to realist nationalism is that it fails to show why some common property of people should ground the common project required for a political community: the objection to voluntarism is that it fails to establish the conditions required for carrying out the project. A common culture, as articulated in a shared literature, can, it may be argued, do both, by presenting a shareable view of the project as valuable.[38] But it can do so only if the values it promotes are subject to criticism and to change, only, to put the same point differently, if the common project is under the collective control of those actually engaged upon it. The kind of constructivism I have put forward here is, I believe, implied by this. But so is a popular political engagement in literature, and its contemporary media manifestations, which one commonly finds at times of nationalist struggle, but which is as commonly suppressed in established nation-states.

NOTES

1 Anthony Smith, *National Identity*, Harmondsworth, Penguin, 1991, pp. 91–2; emphasis in original.
2 See my 'Criteria of Nationality and the Ethics of Self-determination', *History of European Ideas* 16 (1993) pp. 515–20
3 Discounting, as here I must, the Foucault-inspired objection that the category of fact (– as exemplified in the 'facts' of national history –) is itself a construct. If one thinks it is then my question concerns what *kind* of construction national literature is.
4 Which obviously I do not take to be equivalent to 'literature written in English by Irishmen', *pace* Corkery quoted in A. Warner, *A Guide to Anglo Irish Literature*, Dublin, Gill & Macmillan, 1981, p. 5. The category of Irish literature needs investigation not stipulation: 'such a question as why Goldsmith, Sterne and Sheridan do not belong to Irish literature, while Yeats and Joyce do, needs an answer'; R. Wellek and A. Warren, *Theory of Literature*, Harmondsworth, Penguin, 1973, p. 52.
5 Quoted V. Glendinning, *Elizabeth Bowen: Portrait of a Writer*, Harmondsworth, Penguin, 1977, p. 165.
6 J. Hildebidle, *Five Irish Writers*, Cambridge, MA, Harvard University Press, 1989, p. 8.
7 Warner, op. cit., p. 205–6.
8 As, apparently, does A. N. Jeffares, *Anglo-Irish Literature*, London, Macmillan, 1982, pp. 203, 229–31, 248.
9 Quoted in Glendinning op. cit., p. 120.
10 See Oscar Wilde, 'The Saxon took our lands from us and left them desolate – we took their language and added new beauties to it', quoted in H. M. Hyde, *Oscar Wilde*, London, Methuen, 1976, p. 69.
11 Quoted in D. G. Boyce, *Nationalism in Ireland*, London, Croom Helm, 1982, p. 241.
12 James Joyce, *A Portrait of the Artist as a Young Man* (1914), quoted Jeffares op. cit., p. 222.
13 W. B. Stanford, 'Undertone' in Brendan Kennelly (ed.), *The Penguin Book of Irish Verse*, Harmondsworth, Penguin, 1970.
14 W. B. Yeats, 'A Prayer for My Daughter', *Collected Poems*, London, Macmillan, 1933.
15 Quoted in Warner op. cit., p. 60.
16 E. Somerville and M. Ross, *Some Experiences of an Irish R.M.* (1889),

reproduced in F. O'Connor (ed.), *A Book of Ireland*, London, Collins, 1959, p. 154.

17 J. M. Synge, *The Playboy of the Western World* (1907), reproduced in O'Connor op. cit., p. 247.

18 The phrase is Wolf Tone's, quoted in Boyce op. cit., p. 128.

19 Page references to Penguin edition 1983. *The Last September* and other work of Bowen are discussed in R. F. Foster, 'The Irishness of Elizabeth Bowen' (*Paddy and Mr Punch*, London, Allen Lane, 1993, pp. 102–22) which appeared after this chapter was first written. Foster's treatment invites, it seems to me, the very questions that this chapter sets out to answer.

20 Yeats, 'Under Ben Bulben' (*Collected Poems*), 'but the bourgeoisie of town and country were to be left unnoticed and unsung'; N. Mansergh, *The Irish Question 1840–1921*, London, Allen & Unwin, 1965, p. 255.

21 London, Chatto, 1965, p. 79.

22 Quoted in Warner op. cit., p. 10.

23 See Stanford's poem: '. . . older than harp playing, older than welcomes, an undertone threatens Fomorian danger/when the landfolk of Galway converse with a stranger'.

24 Cathal Buidhe Macelgun, 'The Yellow Bittern' trans. Thomas Macdonagh (the Irish patriot executed after the Easter Rising) in Kennelly op. cit.

25 And not just on the possibility of heroism in modern society, as O'Faolain suggests, quoted H. Lee, *Elizabeth Bowen: An Estimation*, London, Vision, 1981, p. 238.

26 Anon. 'Kilcash' trans. Frank O'Connor, in Kennelly op. cit.

27 *Pace* Hildebidle who views Ireland's role as 'a case of possibly redemptive changelessness' as evidence for Bowen's literary Irishness (op. cit., p. 8).

28 H. Marcuse, 'The Affirmative Character of Cultures' in *Negations*, Harmondsworth, Penguin, 1968.

29 Quoted in Warner op. cit., p. 161. O'Brien lampoons the Revival mercilessly in *At Swim Two Birds*, London, Longmans, 1939.

30 Quoted in Warner op. cit., p. 8.

31 E. Bowen, *English Novelists*, London, Collins, 1945, p. 44.

32 By N. Pevsner, *The Englishness of English Art*, London, Architectural Press, 1956.

33 In W. H. Pritchard (ed.), *W. B. Yeats: A Critical Anthology*, Harmondsworth, Penguin, 1972, p. 303.

34 E.g. in *Fools of Fortune*, London, Bodley Head, 1983 and *The Silence in the Garden*, London, Bodley Head, 1988.

35 Smith op. cit., p. 52–4.

36 To the irritation of F. R. Leavis and others who sought a vertical ethnie for Britain in the wake of the Newbolt Report (see C. Baldick, *The Social Mission of English Criticism 1848–1932*, Oxford, OUP, 1983.

37 Always assuming that the culture is of the right kind to be sustained by the political organisation of a state, and hence to qualify as national.

See my 'Criteria of Nationality and the Ethics of Self-determination' cited above.

38 This conclusion is closely related to that of Margaret Canovan in her chapter in this volume.

10 The anti-imperialism of George Orwell

Stephen Ingle

The focus of this chapter is on George Orwell's attempt to define the nature of a perennial political concern – the proper relationship between the rulers and the ruled – by metaphor, by telling stories. I propose to analyse some of the stories he tells, in order to decipher what I take to be his central themes, and to indicate what Orwell, through imaginative literature, has added to our understanding of the ruler-ruled relationship. But first I should put some cards on the table. Whilst each reading of a work of imaginative literature, bound as it has to be in what Eagleton calls a 'socially structured way of perceiving the world',[1] constitutes what might be termed a deconstruction, texts can nevertheless be said to impose certain restraints on the reader; we are not free agents in this matter. I do not subscribe to the view that 'there are no poets only poems' (which can be interpreted as the reader pleases). This view implies trampling on 'the claim of literary texts in general – to be taken as a social act';[2] that is to say, a communication referring to the world as we know it, with a structure and meaning designed by human intelligence and accessible to human intelligence. I would argue that: 'In every sentence of a novel or poem, if we know how to read it, we feel the speaking voice of the writer',[3] what George Steiner referred to as the writer's real presence. In short, the writer's personality and experience will shape our understanding of a novel. We are not free to read, or deconstruct Orwell or anybody else as we please. Whilst there may be no absolutely right way to read him, there are very clearly wrong ways. We know enough about Orwell's experiences in Burma and about his own attitudes towards those experiences to have a very clear idea of what he felt about his function as an imperial policeman, and why he wrote so dismissively about the imperial mission. There can be little doubt that in his writings on Burma Orwell sought to use these experiences as a kind of metaphor for the whole imperial experience and later to construct from the same metaphor a critical model of relations in capitalist society which reflected the same 'imperial' nexus quite unambiguously.

I wish to pursue two objectives in this chapter. First, to tease out the constituent themes of Orwell's imperialist model from its origins in Burma to its development in the capitalist West and to see whether their interrelationship sheds any light on liberal views of the proper relationship between leaders and led, a relationship which exercises political thinkers as much today[4] as ever it did. Second, and much more briefly, I wish to make some comments upon what it is that Orwell contributes to this debate as an imaginative writer which a political 'scientist', philosopher or historian, for example, would not. First, and more substantively, the model.

Orwell's interest in the British Empire was in the blood. He was, after all, born in Bengal, the son of an administrator in the Indian Civil Service. R. W. Blair had devoted his life to an undistinguished and rather obscure branch of the service, the opium department. It was the task of this department to oversee the production, collection and distribution of Indian opium to China. What Orwell thought of his father's calling is not recorded, but a certain ambivalence might be assumed. With the benefit of historical perspective Michael Shelden refers to the opium trade as 'one of the worst evils of the British Colonial system'[5] and as he grew up in the privileged and sheltered atmosphere of Eton, even Orwell must surely have had some doubts concerning the nature of the specific paternal contribution to the great imperial enterprise. Yet his ambition when leaving Eton was to join the Service. A close friend at Eton spoke of a long-cherished notion of returning to the East. 'He used to talk about the East a great deal, and I always had the impression he was longing to go back there. I mean it was a sort of romantic idea...'[6] No doubt the expectations of both his parents, who regarded a career in the Imperial Civil Service as highly prestigious, would have helped to reinforce the romantic notions of the young Orwell and, following his success in the entry examinations for the Imperial Police, Orwell duly left for Burma in 1922, still only 19 years old.

To put it mildly, Burma and the Police did not live up to his expectations. Within a year, despite a congenial posting (by Imperial Police standards) he appears to have become entirely disenchanted with Burma and with his role as a policeman. He felt himself isolated from fellow expatriates (despite the proximity of his maternal grandmother), from the local Burmese (though he spoke their language) and above all from the values of imperialism. Etonian friend Christopher Hollis met Orwell in Burma whilst on his way to Australia and noted later that Orwell seemed to be a man divided between the conventional Imperial policeman and the radical critic of imperialism. Little doubt, all in all, that well before the end of his first term of duty Orwell heartily disliked Burma and his role in its governance. When he returned home at the end of his first term 'one sniff of English air' persuaded him to resign. He never went back.

Burmese Days,[7] Orwell's first published novel, tells the story of a small outpost in upper Burma, Kyauktada, of a middle-aged timber merchant John Flory, and of his relations with the expatriate community. Flory is an archetypal Orwellian hero, an outsider whose status as such is indicated by a disfiguring birthmark on one side of his face – a physical manifestation of his alienation from society, as one critic called it. His friendship with an Indian doctor in the community earns him not only the contempt of the ex-pats at the local pub but also enmeshes him, unknowingly, in the machinations of a ruthlessly ambitious Burmese magistrate, U Po Kyin. The club at Kyauktada has been advised to give membership to an Asian, as part of government policy, and U Po Kyin has set his sights on being that member. Veraswami, the doctor befriended by Flory, is his only competitor and the magistrate sets about discrediting Veraswami, and in the end Flory, in order to achieve his objective. As a sub-plot, Flory, too, has an objective: to marry Elizabeth, the niece of the Lackersteens, an attractive but small-minded young woman who takes Flory seriously only after the departure from Kyauktada of an arrogantly patrician military policeman who possesses all the social graces and martial virtues that Flory so palpably lacks. Flory's marital prospects are suddenly enhanced by his having proved instrumental in putting down a minor revolt which actually threatened the club and its members. His equally sudden humiliation and disgrace is engineered by U Po Kyin. Elizabeth spurns him and Flory takes his own life. Without the support of his white friend, Veraswami is undermined by the magistrate and U Po Kyin achieves his objective of membership of the club and indeed all his ambitions. This is a story without heroes, a story of mendacity, treachery and hypocrisy, of racial and social repression and hatred.

The story provides the author with the opportunity to expose the imperial elite to ruthless analysis. Amongst the ex-pats is Ellis, an intelligent and able timber executive who felt for all Asians 'a bitter, restless loathing as of something evil and unclean . . . any hint of friendly feeling towards an Oriental seemed to him a horrible perversity'.[8] Ellis's feelings were roused to a fury by the government's policy of encouraging the admittance of non-Europeans to clubs. Orwell makes it clear that Ellis's attitude may be paranoid but it is not without some imperialist rationale: 'Here we are, supposed to be governing a set of damned black swine who've been slaves since the beginning of history, and instead of ruling them in the only way they understand, we go and treat them as equals.'[9]

Only the Lackersteens amongst the expats are as fully drawn as Ellis. Mrs Lackersteen's views on race relations in Burma signal that Orwell was already making connections between overseas and domestic 'imperialism': ' "Really I think the laziness of these servants is getting too shocking", she complained. "We seem to have no authority over the natives nowadays, with all those dreadful reforms and the insolence they learn from the newspapers. In some ways they are getting almost as bad as the lower classes at home." '[10] As for Lackersteen himself, he is shown to be a drunkard and a lecher, part of an empire described by Flory as cemented together by booze (not his aptest metaphor).

Flory declares his own position to be not so much anti-empire as anti-humbug. He, too, wants to make money but not to the extent of participating in the 'slimy white man's burden humbug'. Let's not pretend, he argues, that the white man is in Burma to uplift the Burmese; he is there to rob them. Living the imperial pretence 'corrupts us . . . There's an everlasting sense of being a sneak and a liar that torments us and drives us to justify ourselves night and day'.[11] The whole business of empire, Flory concludes, may be summed up as follows: 'The official holds the Burman down while the businessman goes through his pockets'.[12] This, says Flory, is the Pox Britannica.

Flory deludes himself for at base the humbug he attacks is the lubricant of the imperial machine, allowing both enthusiastic and reluctant imperialists to convince themselves that they are involved in a mighty enterprise for the good of all. As Arthur Koestler pointed out and Orwell himself acknowledged, that humbug constituted the difference between the British Empire in the East and the Japanese. Veraswami too argues that in building up the infrastructure of the subject nations in terms of transport and communications, irrigation, health, education and the legal system, the imperialists had contributed to the well-being of those they governed. But this did nothing to alter the nature of the underlying relationship of exploiter and exploited and indeed could be seen largely as a long-term investment which would facilitate exploitation over a far longer period.

At root Orwell is bitterly critical of a system in which louts fresh from school (where the school song would be something like Flory's own, 'The Scrum of Life'), could kick grey-haired servants, a system in which not only the natives have no liberty but also the masters. Free speech is impossible when every white man is a cog in the wheels of despotism. The only freedoms that existed for the masters were the freedoms to drink and to fornicate. All other actions and thoughts were dictated by the code of the *sahiblog*. Unlike Winston Smith, who finds a revolutionary soul-mate in Airstrip One, Flory discovers that 'in the end the secrecy of your revolt poisons you like a secret disease'.[13] Small wonder that Orwell, whose real-life experiences and perceptions shaped this remorselessly bitter novel, decided to get out of the imperial racket.

'Shooting an Elephant'[14] concerns an elephant on the rampage, an event reported to Orwell, the young Imperial policeman, by the local Burmese, so that this representative of law and order might go and kill the offending animal and minimise the damage it was causing – it had already killed one Indian coolie. Orwell followed the trail of destruction to discover the animal in a paddy field looking no more dangerous than a cow. He knew then that the elephant had not gone wild but had been subject to 'must', an intermittent sexual frenzy, which had since worn off. And he also knew that to shoot the elephant in such circumstances was not only unnecessary but quite immoral. But though master, he was not a free agent; he was part of the imperial system. He was hated by the local Burmese and in return he hated them. But his chief hatred he reserved for his job – 'I hated it more bitterly than I can perhaps make clear'. And here he was, confronting a docile animal, but willed forward by the crowd, willed to kill: he the man with the rifle, with the authority, they the unarmed and apparently powerless group of natives. But in reality, he goes on, 'I was only an absurd puppet pushed to and fro by the will of those yellow faces behind. I perceived in this moment that when the white man turns tyrant it is his own freedom that he destroys.'[15]

'A Hanging'[16] is a less overtly didactic essay which deals with the execution of a prisoner in Burma. We are not told of what the man is guilty, neither is any inference drawn overtly from the events which are described. What Orwell does, however, is to draw the reader up sharp by his reflections on the fact that the condemned man, walking to the gallows, actually steps aside to avoid a puddle.

> It is curious, but till that moment I had never realised what it means to destroy a healthy conscious man. When I saw the prisoner step aside to avoid the puddle I saw the mystery, the unsupportable wrongness, of cutting a life short when it is in full tide ... He and we were a party of men walking together, seeing, hearing, feeling, understanding the same world; and in two minutes, with a sudden snap, one of us would be gone – one mind less, one world less.

For the reader, the important, untold part of the story is that 'justice' is the prerogative of the imperial power, the exploiter, and the recipient of justice is of the exploited nation. Justice is carried out, moreover, by a disillusioned young British officer and a group of Indians unenthusiastic for their task but anxious to win the favours of the British officer. The whole exercise, in short, was a sordid example of the exploiter/exploited relationship that characterised imperialism.

Supporters of imperialism had always acknowledged that the white man's burden was a heavy one, entailing in Kipling's words merely 'the blame of those ye better, the hate of those ye guard'. Yet the assumption had always been that, in the long run, the relationship was of mutual benefit, bringing to the subject races all the advantages of modernisation and Christianity, and to the imperial race not merely clear economic advantages but also the opportunity of serving the great cause of civilisation. Orwell's view may be summarised as accepting the Marxist analysis of the economics of imperialism and as rejecting totally any notion of moral or cultural gains for either side: imperialism debased both sides utterly. Both sides were obliged to adopt policies and attitudes which they privately found distasteful. It is the very condition of the imperialist's role, says Orwell, that 'he shall spend his life in trying to impress the "natives", and so in every case he has got to do what the "natives" expect of him. He wears a mask and his face grows to fit it.'[17] So the nature of the imperialist relationship is an intensely alienating one; both sides are alienated from each other and from their roles (i.e., from themselves).

When Orwell returned to this country he may originally have believed that he was exchanging the tyranny of imperialism for liberty but he apparently did not believe this for long; perhaps he did not entirely believe it even at the beginning. Soon enough he was beginning to use imperialism as a metaphor not merely for the relationship between the classes in Britain but also for any relationship between those with and without power. Every such relationship was based implicitly or explicitly upon exploitation and he devoted the rest of his life to exploring the nature of that relationship, bringing to bear a sharpness of focus and an intimidating directness.

A good example of the use of the imperial metaphor is his account of his school days at St Cyprian's, with the ironic Blakean title 'Such, Such Were the Joys'.[18] Orwell portrays himself – Eric Blair – as the victim of an imperialist system. Although St Cyprian's was a fee-paying boarding school, Eric was on reduced fees (as a potential scholarship boy), a fact of enormous economic and political consequences. If the Head behaved with forbearance to the sons of the wealthy he was almost brutal with the poorer boys. The relationship was purely an economic one, the boys' abilities representing a long-term investment (though in the short term they could be underfed) and its governing principle was not love but fear. From the comfort and security of their families young boys were dropped into a world of power relations, dishonesty and hypocrisy, 'out of a goldfish bowl and into a tank full of pike'. The determining element of the imperialist model was that it was quite impossible, whatever their achievements, for the exploited ever fully to join the exploiters. 'If you climbed to the highest niche that was open to you, you could only be an underling, a hanger-on of the people who really counted.' That, indeed, had been the summit of U Po Kyin's ambition. The decisive factor, says Orwell, is class and the cornerstone of class is inherited wealth. Money, he continues, is synonymous with goodness, with moral virtue. The rich and the strong – the same thing really – always won, and since morality was their agent, they always *deserved* to win.

If the recreation of his school days represented one attempt to apply the imperialist model it was certainly not the chief one: that was to be the nature of class relations in Britain, and it was the one to which, following his return from Burma, Orwell devoted his life and sacrificed his health. It was his visit to the North of England, which bore fruit in the publication of the seminal *Road to Wigan Pier*,[19] that was to transform both his politics and his writing. Orwell understood (or so he thought) the values of the oppressed as he had never been able to do in Burma. By and large, he believed, the stable working class (i.e., those in full-time employment) lived in a 'warm, decent, deeply human atmosphere which is not easy to find elsewhere'.[20] This atmosphere was sustained by a deep sense of equality. Working-class life, he believed, was not dominated by social or financial considerations, was not uprooted by the social and geographical mobility which so often put middle-class family life at risk, rather it was integrated into a community where the values of togetherness – or equality – dominated. In a phrase, he believed he had discovered The Good Life.

This was a new development of the imperialist model. Orwell was now arguing, not merely that the relationship of exploiter and exploited was mutually destructive but that the oppressed actually possessed a moral superiority based primarily upon their espousal of equality. Was this very different to an orthodox definition of socialism? He thought so: the aim of many socialists, after all, to abolish poverty *from above*, actually entailed abolishing the working class. It was precisely because the working class realised that orthodox socialism would destroy its lifestyle and values, said Orwell, that ordinary workmen men showed such scant enthusiasm for it. In fact it was the values of ordinary workers which represented true socialism. Only they held firmly to the 'underlying ideals of social-ism: justice and liberty'[21] and in doing so they rejected the 'socialism' of mechanisation and progress, of thesis, antithesis and synthesis, the 'socialism' of the planner, the sandal-wearing pacifist. The socialist movement, he concluded, should be not 'a league of dialectical materialists but a league of the oppressed against the oppressors'.[22] In the 'imperial' model, orthodox socialists, especially scientific socialists, might well be considered amongst the exploiters and not the exploited.

Orwell's experiences in the North of England were reinforced by those he gained when fighting in the Spanish Civil War. In *Homage to Catalonia*[23] he wrote of Barcelona, which he visited in December 1936, as the first town he had seen where the working class was 'in the saddle', a state of affairs worth fighting for because 'human beings were trying to behave like human beings and not as cogs in the capitalist machine'.[24] Those who define Orwell's socialism as quintessentially English overlook his unambiguous admiration for the Spanish working class whose defining characteristics are identi-fied as decency and a 'real largeness of spirit which I have met with again and again in the most unpromising circumstances.'[25] When he declared that such a state of affairs was worth fighting for, that is exactly what he meant. For Orwell the Spanish Civil War was orig-inally a war between working-class socialism (one might say Orwel-lian socialism) and fascism; that it manifestly became something other than this saddened him greatly. In many respects fascism (especially of the totalitarian variety) represented, for Orwell, the essential ideology of 'imperialism'; he had already identified working-class 'socialism' as its true opponent and Spain confirmed his earlier fears that the centralised, efficient state with which the communists wished to fight fascism, was another version of 'imperialism'.

Until about the middle of the Second World War Orwell appeared to believe that violent revolution was the obvious method by which the working class could end its exploitation; parliamentary methods, the 'rules of the game', were simply part of the mechanics of exploitation. Orwell wished for and expected a popular revolution which would overthrow the British imperial ruling class so that the Axis could be defeated. But the tumbrels of revolution steadfastly refused to rumble and when the government actually armed the potential revolutionaries (in the form of the Home Guard which Orwell himself joined), he must have realised that imminent revolution was beyond the bounds of credulity. Towards the end of the world war Orwell, reflecting on events in Spain and the USSR, came to the view that the betrayal of the working class would be an almost inevitable consequence of revolution. *Animal Farm*[26] was certainly written as a critique of the Soviet revolution and its consequences but it can also be read as a work which exposes the inevitable dominance, in the turmoil of revolution, of an intellectual class whose aim would be to capture and retain power. That power would not be used to further the causes of the revolution but to bolster the capacity of the intellectual class to exploit the workers. The model of revolutionary power, then, corresponds not to an egalitarian power model but to the imperialist one.

Much has been made of Orwell's patriotic writing during the war[27] by those who seek to emphasise his essential Englishness, and thus, by extension, his limitation as a thinker. Paradoxically in situating his final work, *Nineteen Eighty-Four*,[28] in the United Kingdom, Orwell gives the lie to any change of parochialism for he clearly intends it to be understood that any society, even the allegedly liberal and tolerant British, has a potential to develop into what he came to recognise as the most extreme model of imperialism/fascism, namely, totalitarianism. Moreover, Orwell identifies totalitarianism (and thus 'imperialism') not merely as a particularly pernicious ideology but as a personality trait. In *Nineteen Eighty-Four* power is measured by the capacity to inflict pain; this is the 'imperial' model finally stripped to its essentials, the strong triumphing over the weak, the exploiters over the exploited. A suitable logo for the 'imperial' relationship is to be found in an image taken from a book which Orwell quotes: that of the hero stamping on somebody's face and then grinding his heel round and round. The model recognises no value beyond the equation of might with right. As Gollo Mann summarised, Orwell's argument is that the 'totalitarian danger lies within ourselves and in all the political systems of our time'.[29] Yet Orwell goes further than this and associates this desire for power as he defined it *specifically* with socialist intellectuals in whom the 'imperialistic' concepts of the worship of success, totalitarianism and sadism interconnect. Intellectuals were 'imperialists', and socialist intellectuals such as Shaw and Wells were amongst the worst. No wonder Bellow's young 1960s' radical in *Mr Sammler's Planet* describes Orwell as a 'sick counter-revolutionary fink'. Even as perceptive a critic as Raymond Williams was unable to forgive Orwell for attacking totalitarianism (imperialism) through the example of socialism.[30] Orwell's ruling elite in Oceania represents a perversion of Platonism for the sole reward for leadership was not virtue but power. This constitutes a theory of power as psychosis: those who seek power do so principally to inflict suffering on others in as direct a way as possible. George Kateb, amongst others, feels that Orwell's linking of power to sadism is unsound and diminishes the strength of his message.[31] Orwell is surely on firmer ground, however, when he links power to ideology and, like Popper, sees the latter as an instrument of power and not vice versa.

The alleged moral superiority of the poor is, in direct contrast, associated with their powerlessness. In an essay analysing the success of Charlie Chaplin, Orwell ascribed it to Chaplin's infallible ability to characterise 'the ineradicable belief in decency that exists in the hearts of ordinary people'.[32] He explored this decency in greater depth in another essay, 'The Art of Donald McGill'.[33] McGill's holiday postcards, like the antics of Chaplin, depict the world and the values of the oppressed, to whom those with incomes much above or below £5 per week were ridiculous. It was a world in which people actually wanted to be good – 'but not too good and not quite all the time'. It was a world which, though staunchly patriotic, guyed patriotism and mocked all pretensions pitilessly. Orwell declared that he could never hear solemn proclamations by Great Men without also hearing, in the background, 'a chorus of raspberries from all the millions of common men'. All over Britain '. . . there are men by scores of thousands whose attitude to life, if only they could express it . . . would change the whole consciousness of our race'.[34]

To summarise the argument, I have suggested that Orwell's political perspective was shaped by his Burmese experiences which provided him with a framework of analysis of contemporary capitalist society. It must be borne in mind that he had gone to Burma with two conflicting sets of values concerning imperialism. The first was the product of his upbringing. It esteemed the traditional imperialist virtues as a modern adaptation of the classical concept of *virtu*. The second was the product of his intellectual nourishment at Eton and was iconoclastic, dismissive, Shavian. As we have seen, those who met him in Burma, such as old Etonian Christopher Hollis, described him as torn between these two visions of the imperial project. If he was intellectually able to will the *ends* of imperialism (or some of them), his experiences rendered him increasingly incapable of willing the *means*. Imperialism might or might not be justified as a concept; but it involved so much inhumanity as to be unjustifiable in reality. Like Arthur Koestler he was unimpressed by the 'necessity of breaking eggs to make an omelette' argument: he said that those who justify their actions in these terms never finish with an omelette.[35] Indeed, Orwell's position on this issue shows him to have been primarily concerned not so much with political thought as moral thought and to have focused on and made judgements about human conduct rather than political conflict. It was his intention to reduce political problems to their fundamentals and imperialism was reduced to the exploiter/exploited nexus. He was not concerned to unravel the ambiguities and complexities of imperialist political relationships so much as to lay bare what he took to be its essential moral constituents. The resulting 'imperialist' model needed to be simple; it had to expose actions as either morally right or wrong. His was a bipolar monochrome world: black and white but no greys. Grey was the casuist's colour. In *Homage to Catalonia* Orwell had claimed that if ever he saw working men struggling with their 'natural enemies', the police, he knew instinctively which side he was on.[36] The analogy shows precisely the nature of his 'imperialist' model. One was either exploiter or exploited and as he said, in the 'imperialist' power model the exploited were always right and the exploiters always wrong.

Orwell's basic concern, then, was not so much with politics as with human nature. If his human was clearly the part-man and part-beast of traditional dualism, s/he was nevertheless transformed by the nature of the social relationship. Imperialist, and indeed all capitalist social relations, were founded on power and for Orwell it was immaterial whether those who held power believed themselves (erroneously of course) to be motivated by a desire to improve the lot of their fellows or by a naked, cynical desire for gratification; the effect was the same. To attempt to place self-denying ordinances on the powerful, as Confucius and Plato and many later had done, was simple illusion. Power itself had to be defused and 'imperialism' as the base of social relationships replaced by equality. He added to this analysis a transformative insight by which he recognised in the lives of the oppressed a set of values (referred to in shorthand as 'decency') which could form the basis of a democratic, egalitarian society. So much for Orwell's model.

The question is: 'Does the "imperialism" model contribute anything at all to the development of political theories of the ruler–ruled relationship?' There would be general agreement that at first sight the model seems demonstrably simplistic, as consequently, does Orwell's analysis of power relations. The motives which impelled so many to participate in the imperial enterprise could not realistically be written off as invariably exploitative; the intentions of socialist intellectuals and ideologues to improve the lot of the poor (their 'imperial' enterprise) could not plausibly be represented as simply an attempt to exercise power for its own sake. Contrary to the assumptions of the model, the oppressors are *not* always wrong. Nor does the evidence (even Orwell's evidence) lend much substance to the claim that the oppressed are always right. Moreover, do the oppressed actually possess the qualities Orwell perceives? Violence as well as decency has always played a large part in working-class life; so has gross gender inequality and so, for that matter, has paternal authoritarianism (consider, for example, *Sons and Lovers* by D. H. Lawrence, himself the son of a miner). Do the opposition in Burma today believe that their government is less 'imperialist' than were the British former masters? Have not some of the oppressed become oppressors? And if it *were* true that, all in all, the exploited possessed this quality of 'decency', hasn't Orwell himself portrayed this as a consequence of exploitation? Remove the exigencies through greater disposable income, better welfare provision, housing and so on, and decency will surely atrophy.

There is another, perhaps deeper line of criticism of Orwell's alternative power model. When he speaks of the value of working-class life he is in effect retreating from the public to the private realm. Nowhere does he write about power structures within working-class political movements such as the trade unions. Whereas even Machiavelli recognised the value to the polity of private virtue, he thought it had little place in statecraft.

Is it conceivable that as astute and careful an observer as Orwell was unaware of these criticisms? I believe not. I believe that he thought that working-class values, warts and all, offered the only bastion against 'imperialism'. What Orwell passionately cared about was the better treatment by men of their fellows. As Rorty has suggested, Orwell wrote against those who exercised cruelty even through the rhetoric of human equality.[37] The values of the non-ideological, non-imperialistic socialism that he fought for were, in fact, fundamentally the same as those of non-doctrinaire Christianity. That he selected, simplified and exaggerated in attributing these qualities to the working class in greater measure than any other is surely forgivable; after all, fundamentally he agreed with Huxley's Illidge, in *Point Counter Point*, who declares; 'If you live on less than £5 a week you've damned well got to be a Christian'.[38]

Are the values of the exploited of any political significance if they cannot be articulated? After all, O'Brien insists during his interrogation of Winston Smith that the proles would never revolt, not in a thousand years, not in a million. Winston retained a residual faith in the proles only because their values had survived. Their instinctive loyalty was not to any ideology nor to the state but to each other. There was a moral and political force in their gestures of love, compassion and understanding: in their code of decency. So long as decency survived, so did hope.

When Orwell argued for the penetration of power relations by that private value system which he called decency, he was arguing against Machiavelli's widely-held case for a separate moral category for politics. Machiavelli's injunction to the 'good man', in *The Prince*, is that to become a successful ruler he must learn how not to be good. As Hampshire writes, 'a fastidiousness about the means employed, appropriate in personal relations, is a moral dereliction in a politician'.[39] Following the Vietnam War this injunction became contentiously relevant to the debate upon the American conduct of the war, the so-called 'dirty hands' debate. This phrase had been highlighted earlier by Jean-Paul Sartre's appropriately titled play *Les Mains sales*,[40] in which the communist leader declared that his hands were dirty right up to the elbow, having been plunged in filth and blood. 'Do you think you can govern innocently?', he asks metaphorically. The debate concerns the relationship between politics and morality, more specifically between public and private morality. Machiavelli's (and Sartre's) contention is that politics is a distinctive activity. Walzer[41] sees three justifications for this view: the politician acts on our behalf, speaks in our name, 'lies and intrigues for us'; the politician rules over us, directs our affairs in a comprehensive fashion; and finally, the politician uses or threatens violence both for us and perhaps against us – he may kill in our name. No-one succeeds in politics without getting his hands dirty and traditional Christian theology made allowances for this. St Augustine's melancholy soldier knew that war could be both just and horrific. Basil the Great, as Walzer reminds us, advised that all who killed even in a just war should abstain from communion for three years because their hands were unclean.[42] There is a general acceptance amongst 'dirty-hands' theorists that, as Machiavelli suggests, 'when the act accuses, the result excuses',[43] but their general project is somehow to constrain leaders morally; dirty their hands may be, but not free.

Few of these theorists actually believe that politics forms an entirely separate category of human activity. After all, we can get our hands dirty in private life, says Walzer, and we can keep our hands clear in warfare. (Orwell's famous account in *Homage to Catalonia* of his refusal at the front to shoot a fascist because he had his trousers down is an excellent example of Nagel's dictum: 'our conflict is with the soldier not with his existence as a human being'.[44]) Hampshire, too, agrees that there can be no 'distinct and clear dividing line' between the public and private realm. Would not the bosses of multinational companies, or indeed the leaders of any large organisation (say, a headteacher of a large secondary school) wish to claim much the same immunity? Some feminist writers have argued that even family life is dominated by structures of power which are public rather than private. So Orwell's argument for the penetration of public life by private values should not be dismissed out of hand. The thrust of his argument is that *no* political system could develop beyond 'imperialism' if it was not founded on a sense of right and wrong and that the most likely source of that moral dimension was to be found in the lives of ordinary people.

'Dirty-hands' issues, entwined as they are within important and complex categories of absolute and utilitarian moral reason, nevertheless confront Orwell's thought only tangentially. These theorists are concerned to understand the paradox of a leader who is directed in his private actions by a moral system which prevents him from injuring others but who, as a political leader, feels compelled sometimes to act immorally on behalf of those he represents. Like Koestler's Spartacus he who alone can understand, acts on behalf of those who cannot. For Orwell, though, as we have seen, those who attain political power do so for self-gratification. If that was not their original motive (but it probably was), it soon becomes their motive. Power is an end not a means and they are not tortured moral souls. Whilst Nagel at least is aware of the 'pleasure of power' and regards it as one of the most primitive of human feelings,[45] even he does not pursue this line of thought. For Orwell the central issue is one which the 'dirty-hands' theorists only touch on; the structure of power itself. The leaders whom these theorists discuss are modern versions of Machiavelli's prince. They may indeed allude to the representative character of a modern democracy but the profundity of the difference such structures make upon the exercise of power is by no means made explicit. What Orwell argues for, of course, is the substitution of traditional ('imperialist') structures of power by not merely representative but truly egalitarian ones, with such consequences as we shall now go on to explore.

Orwell was by no means the first to extol the virtues of the oppressed; Dickens and Tolstoy, among others, could have been said to have done so far more comprehensively. More recently, Vaclav Havel, in an influential essay written in 1978 entitled *The Power of the Powerless*,[46] spoke of a force which stood against Czechoslovakia's totalitarian despotism, openness to truth. The power of truth, he argued, is only a potential power and does not participate directly in any struggle for power, making its presence felt in the arena of being itself. Yet if it can oblige a small, obscure boy to call out that the emperor has no clothes then an entire political edifice may crash to the ground as a consequence: so private values may indeed penetrate power relations. Like Orwell,[47] Havel believes in the overriding political importance of a popular moral system, for he believes that a more just political and economical system can only come from a widely held moral code (and not vice versa *à la* Marx). Havel is clearly working from the same tradition as Orwell but he adds a prescriptive dimension to that tradition. 'There can and must be structures that are open, dynamic and small ... Any accumulation of power whatsoever ... should be profoundly alien ... They would be structures not in the sense of organisations or institutions, but like a community.'[48] This is how Havel perceives that 'decency' might transform 'imperialism'.

It is interesting to note that even modern capitalism has found a version of the Orwellian and Havelian model attractive. John Naisbitt, for example, speaks of the 'radical downsizing' of some major companies. 'Big companies ... are deconstructing themselves and creating new structures, many as networks of autonomous units. Deconstruction is now in fashion, because it is the best way to search for survival.'[49] As one manager of GE explained: 'What we are trying to do is to get that small company soul . . . inside our big company body'.[50] A power structure resembling a community; an egalitarian not an imperial power model. What Orwell might have made of this partial conversion of the enemy (for all the wrong reasons?) is an interesting topic for speculation.

Orwell recognised that politics frequently involves choosing the lesser of two evils but believed that the more ordinary people were involved in such decisions the less often morally unacceptable decisions would be taken. To accept the challenge of such involvement would require a genuine commitment to making the policy processes open to ordinary people. For a start, it would mean a political discourse less dominated by jargon. As long as politics remains a specialised activity conducted centrally by intellectuals claiming a special expertise, ordinary people will be effectively disempowered. So long as there exists, within structures of power, a ready potential for one group to dominate and exploit another, it will do so, says Orwell. Conversely, the more power is diffused, the more power structures are disaggregated, the more difficult 'imperialism' becomes. If Orwell is right, it is only by dispersing and demystifying power that society can rid itself of the menace of Big Brother and the threat of 'imperialism', be it fascist, socialist or managerial, for it is only by dispersing and demystifying power that politics may be made accessible to the oppressed. This is what follows from Orwell's 'imperialism' model. Its particular intellectual force lies precisely in depicting the relationship between ruler and ruled in so uncompromising a way and with such a clear message.

The quality of Orwell's contribution to political thought is shaped very largely by its quality as literature, and it is to this theme that I shall now turn. Eagleton and others might wish to argue the absurdity of such a proposition. 'Literature,' says Eagleton, 'in the sense of a set of works of assured and unalterable value, distinguished by certain shared inherent properties, does not exist.'[51] If this were true then perhaps we might need to invent literature, rather like Voltaire's God. Kenneth Quinn clearly thinks it is not true. He argues that literary texts can be distinguished from other texts rather as cars can be distinguished from trucks. They occupy different places in our lives and we use them in different ways. 'We expect poets or novelists to be particular about the words they use. The more particular they are the better the novel or poem is likely to be. But there's more to it than that. A bad novel is still a novel of sorts . . . all such texts have something in common: *they work in a particular way . . .*'[52]

In earlier times literature clearly encompassed every serious discipline, its concern being the whole of knowledge. By the nineteenth century, however, knowledge had fractured and intellectual activity quickly became differentiated. There emerged kinds of writing that quite clearly were consciously instrumental and consciously non-literary. But there was also writing that intended to influence 'by characteristically non-objective techniques, our perception of the world and our moral understanding'.[53] Creative or imaginative writing – literature – is first and foremost an artistic enterprise. It has a structure, a field of significance and it adopts a position to which one can react. In short, 'literature is experience reorganised as a structure of words that can be perceived both as artistic creations and as a representation of life that is essentially true'.[54] Although it may very well be argued that literary boundaries are not as easily demarcated – or for that matter, trucks and cars as easily distinguishable as Quinn suggests (indeed truck-like cars these days enjoy a certain chic), he is surely right to want to distinguish between the aims of creative or imaginative writing and those of other forms of writing. Orwell's imaginative writing – his fiction – for example, is not readily separable from his journalism and neither did he wish it to be. *Down and Out, Clergyman's Daughter*, and *Homage* straddle both, and accounts of Orwell's northern experiences in *Wigan Pier* differ from his diary account. It would be unhelpful, then, to try to draw a distinction between his fiction and journalism: Orwell himself drew no such distinction. This difficulty does not detract from Quinn's central point: recognising a text as literature means recognising that reading it offers the prospect of a literary experience. We read it *differently* to, say, an ESRC document on social science research. Quinn goes on to argue that a literary text has no immediate, easily understood purpose, yet it *does* possess a quality that other kinds of text do not. He encapsulates that quality by suggesting that literature is not primarily concerned with the transmission of information but the sharing of experience.

It is precisely in these senses that Orwell's analysis of imperialism should be viewed. The author attempts to share his experiences of 'imperialism' with us. He has, quite literally, reorganised these experiences so as to represent to us a view of life that many will perceive to be essentially 'true'. This idea of sharing an experience is of fundamental importance to Orwell's project; it is probably the only method open to him to expose us to 'the truth' of imperialism.

Were he to have employed the more orthodox philosophical, economic or ideological form of analysis which his critics have called for, then, so far as he was concerned, he would have been sucked into an 'imperialistic' relationship; he would himself have become an 'intellectual' and so an exploiter. Orwell usually used the word intellectual synonymously with ideologue. His intellectual was a spokesman for a system of thought the exclusive nature of which could be penetrated only by other intellectuals; only they would have the key. As an imaginative writer sharing his experiences rather than an intellectual guarding the integrity of a system of thought, Orwell was committed not so much to giving anyone who wanted a duplicate key as to leaving the door open. *That* is the nature of imaginative literature and it represents a medium of communication ideally suited to the moralist who wishes us to realise that political issues are moral issues and that to assign a special moral category to politics is the first decisive step in engendering 'imperialism'.

Orwell attempted to provide us with a metaphor depicting how human relationships should *not* be structured. What Rorty writes à propos of *Animal Farm*, suitably modified, provides a fitting testimony to Orwell's metaphorical analysis of imperialism: Orwell, he writes, 'attacks the incredibly complex and sophisticated character of leftist political discussion ... by retelling the political history of this century entirely in terms suitable for children'.[55] Sartre, who argued that Picasso's great anti-fascist, anti-war painting *Guernica* won not a single convert to the Republican cause, would no doubt think Orwell's project was doomed to failure, yet such evidence as exists[56] suggests that if anything the metaphor is as powerful a means as any of giving, in Calvi's words, 'a voice to whoever is without a voice'.[57]

NOTES

1 Terry Eagleton, 'The Rise of English', in Dennis Walder (ed.), *Literature in the Modern World*, Oxford, Oxford University Press, 1990, p. 25.
2 Kenneth Quinn, *How Literature Works*, London, Macmillan, 1992, p. 18.
3 Quinn, *How Literature Works*, p. 20.
4 See, for example, the debate generated in the pages of *Political Studies* 41 (1993) and 42 (1994) by David Beetham's *The Legitimation of Power*.
5 Michael Shelden, *Orwell: The Authorised Biography*, London, Heinemann, 1991, pp. 13–15.
6 Stephen Wadhams, *Remembering Orwell*, Harmondsworth, Penguin, 1984, p. 21.
7 *Burmese Days*, London, Gollanz, 1935, Penguin edition, 1969 (subsequent page numbers refer to the Penguin edition).

8 *Burmese Days*, p. 24.
9 *Burmese Days*, p. 24.
10 *Burmese Days*, p. 28.
11 *Burmese Days*, p. 29.
12 *Burmese Days*, p. 37.
13 *Burmese Days*, p. 66.
14 'Shooting an Elephant', 1936, *Collected Essays, Journalism and Letters of George Orwell* (hereafter referred to as *CEJL*), 1, London, Secker & Warburg, 1968, pp 235–42.
15 'Shooting an Elephant', p. 239.
16 'A Hanging', 1931, *CEJL*, 1, pp. 44–8; quoted at p. 46.
17 'Shooting an Elephant', p. 239.
18 'Such, Such Were the Joys', *CEJL*, 4, pp. 330–69.
19 *Road to Wigan Pier*, London, Gollancz, 1936, Penguin edition, 1963 (subsequent page numbers refer to the Penguin edition).
20 *Wigan Pier*, p. 104.
21 *Wigan Pier*, p. 189.
22 *Wigan Pier*, p. 195.
23 *Homage to Catalonia*, London, Gollancz, 1938, Penguin edition, 1962 (subsequent page numbers refer to the Penguin edition).
24 *Catalonia*, pp. 8–9.
25 *Catalonia*, p. 15.
26 *Animal Farm*, London, Secker & Warburg, 1945, Penguin edition, 1958.
27 Such as 'The Lion and the Unicorn', *CEJL*, 2, pp 56–109 and 'England Your England', *Inside the Whale and Other Essays*, Harmondsworth, Penguin, 1960, pp. 63–90.
28 *Nineteen Eighty-Four*, London, Secker & Warburg, 1948, Penguin edition, 1960.
29 Gollo Mann, *Frankfurter Rundschau*, 5 November 1949, Jeffrey Meyers (ed.) *George Orwell: The Critical Heritage*, London and Boston, MA, Routledge & Kegan Paul, 1975 p. 277–81.
30 Raymond Williams, *Orwell*, London, Fontana, 1971.
31 George Kateb, 'The Road to Nineteen Eighty-Four', *Political Science Quarterly*, 4, 1966, pp. 565–81.
32 See 'The English People', *CEJL*, 3, pp. 1–37.
33 'The Art of Donald McGill', *CEJL*, pp. 155–64.
34 Review of *Caliban Shrieks* by Jack Hilton, *CEJL*, 1, pp. 148–50.
35 See Orwell's essay 'Arthur Koestler', *CEJL*, pp. 234–44.
36 *Catalonia*, p. 119.
37 Richard Rorty, *Contingency, Irony and Solidarity*, Cambridge, Cambridge University Press, 1989.
38 Aldous Huxley, *Point Counter Point*, Harmondsworth, Penguin, 1971 edition, p. 59.
39 Stuart Hampshire, *Public and Private Morality*, London, Cambridge University Press, 1978, p. 50.
40 J.-P. Sartre, *Les Mains Sales*, Paris, Gallimard, 1948. The key relationship between private and public morality to which Sartre's work alludes is also dealt with by Anthony Arblaster and Maureen Whitebrook in their respective chapters.
41 Michael Walzer, 'Political Action: The Problem of Dirty Hands', in

Marshall Cohen *et al.* (ed.), *War and Moral Responsibility*, Princeton, Princeton University Press, 1974, pp. 64–6.
42 Walzer, 'Political Action', p. 69, Note 9.
43 Machiavelli, *Discourses*, bk 1, Chapter IX, p. 139.
44 Thomas Nagel, 'War and Massacre', in Marshall Cohen *et al.*, *Moral Responsibility*, p. 21.
45 Thomas Nagel, 'Ruthlessness in Public Life', in Hampshire, *Public and Private Morality*, p. 77.
46 Vaclav Havel, 'The Power of the Powerless', in J. Vladislav, *Vaclav Havel or Living from Truth*, London, Faber & Faber, 1987, pp. 36–122.
47 What distinguishes Havel from Orwell is that the former allows a role in the process of penetration to intellectuals: Havel's intellectuals did not constitute a pampered and feted cosmopolitan group but dissidents whose stand threatened their liberty and even their lives.
48 Havel, 'The Power of the Powerless', p. 118.
49 John Naisbitt, *Global Paradox*, London, NB Publishing, 1994, p. 13.
50 Naisbitt, *Global Paradox*, p. 14.
51 Eagleton, 'The Rise of English', in Quinn, *How Literature Works*, p. 22.
52 Quinn, *How Literature Works*, p. 9; emphasis in original.
53 Quinn, *How Literature Works*, p. 43.
54 Quinn, *How Literature Works*, p. 55.
55 Rorty, *Contingency*, p. 174.
56 See, for example, Stephen Ingle, 'Socialism and Literature: The Contribution of Imaginative Writers to the Development of the British Labour Party', *Political Studies*, 2, June 1975, pp. 158–67.
57 Italo Calvi, *The Uses of Literature*, New York, Harcourt, Brace, Jovanovic, 1986, p. 101.

11 Contemporary feminist Utopianism
Practising Utopia on Utopia

Lucy Sargisson

INTRODUCTION

Utopia is paradoxical.[1] It is always easier to destroy than to create, and Utopia does both. Born out of discontent, Utopia, traditionally understood, desires an end to the political present and depicts an alternative way of being. Even the word itself is etymologically contrary: outopia is no place, eutopia is a good place. Implied in the etymological pun is a tension between the fields of what is possible and what is desirable. In terms of genre or discipline, Utopia presents a further problem as it crosses and combines disciplines and schools. Utopian studies then could incorporate research into medicine, architecture, music and visual arts,[2] as well as the perhaps more commonly associated fields of literature and political theory. This chapter is confined to consideration of feminist textual Utopianism and its focus is on redefining Utopia.

In the first instance I propose to argue that Utopia needs to be redefined, and much of this chapter represents a critique of standard definitions of Utopia. Discussion begins with a reading of standard approaches to Utopia which is informed by contemporary debates within postmodern and poststructuralist theory. I then propose an alternative vision of what Utopianism might be seen to represent. It is in this sense that I have described this chapter as 'practising Utopia on Utopia'.

Briefly, standard approaches to Utopia rely upon the following criteria for definition:

1 Utopia is assumed to be of an inherently political nature;
2 Utopia provides a blueprint for the future that is static and finite;
3 Utopia is critical of the political present, this critique being achieved through the Utopian conventions of estrangement and subversion;

4 Utopia is an imaginative genre, often expressed in fictional forms.

To this are added to further dimensions by socialist and feminist Utopian commentary:

5 Utopia is connected to social movements, thus addressing questions of agency;
6 the introduction of a dialectical or dualistic conception of the function of Utopia.

A central argument of this chapter is that a shift can be identified within contemporary feminist Utopianism away from the universalist tendencies traditionally associated with Utopia. These texts move towards a new, open-ended, and multiple approach towards the present and the future. A new conception of Utopian opposition is developed: one that adequately reflects the diversity of contemporary feminisms and escapes restrictive universalisms.

A sub-theme of my discussion is a consideration of the state of feminist theory, and in particular of the relations between feminist and postmodernist theory. I suggest that postmodernism represents perpetual critique, the result of which is immobility, as the postmodernist theorist talks his/herself literally into silence. For social movements such as contemporary feminisms, critique must be accompanied by construction. Postmodernism, therefore is empowering to women only up to a point. A non-modernist, or postmodernist, non-logocentric conception of Utopia can, I propose to argue, serve as a potential (and perhaps temporary) bridge between the empowerment and disempowerment that postmodernism represents to feminism(s).

This chapter begins by examining standard definitions and approaches to the genre of Utopia. A new conception of Utopia is then proposed. Utopia bridges art, politics and literature, thus opening these otherwise closed systems to the scrutiny of the others. It is both paradoxical and transgressive and this, I suggest, is the strength of Utopia.

DEFINING UTOPIA: STANDARD DEFINITIONS

Standard definitions of Utopia tend to focus upon the fact that Utopia blueprints the future. For J. C. Davis, for example, Utopia is distinguishable from other forms of ideal society in that it creates systems which will justly cope with the deficiencies of man (sic) and nature. These systems are, according to Davis, recognisable as pertaining to the modern state: 'Such systems are inevitably bureaucratic, institutional, legal and educational, artificial and organisational.'³ Utopia, says Davis, idealises organisation. It is, moreover, inherently political:

> If politics is about the distribution of opportunities, rewards and satisfactions, the setting of human behaviour and policing the abnormal, then ideal societies are, in a sense, all about the end of politics. . . . Utopia, by contrast, accepts the distributional problems posed by the deficiency of resources and the moral disabilities of men. Unlike the others, therefore, it accepts the bases of the problem from which politics arise. Out of the minds and wills of human beings must come organisational forms and practices which will guarantee the just distribution of finite resources and contain the anti-social proclivities of men and women.⁴

The definition of politics from which Davis works is, from both a political-theoretical and a feminist perspective, inadequate and superficial. Politics is about power, be it power structures in a society that may affect the distribution of wealth and resources, or power relations between and within different groups and classes or between states. Whilst agreeing therefore with Davis that Utopia can be characterised partly by their political nature, I would begin by deepening his concept of the political. Some feminist Utopian work contains elements of concern with the superficial power structures about which Davis is concerned. Shulamith Firestone's *The Dialectic of Sex*,⁵ for instance, proposes institutional arrangements to protect the freedom and autonomy of children and women, and Marge Piercy's *Woman on the Edge of Time*⁶ has a kind of communal council through which disputes are settled. In both of these cases, however, these structures play a secondary and perhaps supportive role to the redressing of the balance of sexual power.

All feminist Utopias are, almost by definition, political in the sense that I outline above. All are concerned to some extent with power relations, all with sexual power, some also with the exploitative relations between patriarchy and nature. Their concerns are with diverse manifestations of sexual power relations. Psychoanalytic Utopians, for instance, are concerned in part with the gendered power relations which are perceived to be embodied in language, whereas others focus on social and reproductive relations.

Staying with Davis for a moment we can find in his work a common conception amongst standard commentators: that Utopia is finite. The depiction of Utopia, he says, is a once-for-all political act; a set of decisions against which there is no appeal. . . . Once the utopian has solved the political problem by organisational means, there is no longer need for politics in Utopia . . . When politics stops, so does change. Perfection is not relative. The dynamic utopia is a myth.[7]

This view of Utopia as finite and static occurs in most of the existing literature on Utopias. Barbara Goodwin, for instance, includes this as a characterising feature in her work on Utopia. She also connects Utopian perfectibility with its finality:

> Furthermore, 'perfect' connotes a superlative state which must be considered beyond the reach or necessity of change, since there is no progressing beyond the perfect. This syntactical dictate, literally obeyed, gives many utopian states a static, unreal quality, which detracts from their credibility.[8]

The static and indeed stagnant quality of Utopia thus defined is, in most cases, absent in contemporary feminist Utopian works. The depiction of multiple worlds is in actuality a defining characteristic of many modern feminist Utopias. I return to this theme of the static and universal Utopia later in some detail. For the sake of the present discussion, however, it is sufficient to note that feminist Utopias do not 'fit' into a definition which relies on finality of end. The Utopia that Goodwin and others outline needs to be reconceived. Progress, movement and the perpetuation of struggle take the place of finality in many feminist Utopian texts.

The issue of Utopia as the perfection (or death) of politics/society is of some interest: not all feminist Utopian writing presents such a model and those that do rarely present it as a didactic device. It is more common to find in contemporary feminist literature and theory of this kind several worlds, often contrasting, none perfect. These worlds play speculative, meditative or critical roles rather than instructing as to the creation of a perfect world. Examples of this multiplicity can be found for instance in Doris Lessing's *Marriage Between Zones Three, Four and Five*[9] in which the central characters, Al*ith and Ben Ata move between them in and out of the book's four zones. Angela Carter's *Heroes and Villains*[10] presents two modes of existence in the one world, those of the Professors and the Barbarians, self-contained and with no contact between the two apart from the occasional Barbarian raiding party on a Professor village. Each of these societies considers itself better than the other, both are exposed to criticism by Carter. Rather, the book can be read as representing a satire of the concept of perfection: at one level, the concept of Utopia is satirised, as the 'worlds' of the Professors and the Barbarians can be taken to represent the traditional Utopias of the Noble Savage and the Rational Society. And at the level of symbolism, images of stagnancy and decay permeate the text. The clocks in the dry and static world of the Professors, for example, have stopped ticking, one of which is symbolically buried by the character Marrianne. Carter's other eu/dystopian novel, *The Passion of a New Eve*,[11] is also fiercely satirical of the eutopian project.

One further example of the fluidity of contemporary feminist Utopianism is perhaps permissible.[12] Marge Piercy's *Woman on the Edge of Time* is perhaps the most widely read of these texts. It combines realism with Utopianism, but does not blueprint the future. Rather, a number of alternatives are sketched to the present, which is in itself a possible future. All of the alternatives are experienced by Connie, the central character, in the present tense. All are equally possible and none are distanced temporally from her own present. The eutopia of Mattapoissett, and the dystopias of war and macho-technology could all exist as a result of her own time, since neither the future nor the present are fixed in this text. Luce Irigaray[13] has evoked an understanding of time and the relation between the present and the future which speaks to this, she calls it the 'conditional presence', conditional, that is on our actions and perceptions in the here and now. Piercy and Irigaray both provoke radical and transgressive attitudes towards what might be called 'the possible', their work is quite profoundly Utopian, but neither invokes or desires the ideal polity.

There is, then a discernible shift within contemporary feminist Utopian literature away from the practice of rigid blueprinting. Similar moves can be observed within recent works of feminist political and ethical theory. Much contemporary feminist theory exhibits suspicion and/or caution regarding universalist or totalising theory *per se*. Common themes of such works include a concern regarding universal conceptions of human nature and related debates about essentialism.[14] One way in which concern regarding universalism is manifested is in the growing self-consciousness of contemporary feminist theory of the multifaceted nature of feminism itself. At the most basic level, factors such as religion, class, ethnicity and sexuality are argued to play at least equal roles in the construction of identity as does gender. Stances such as that taken by Shulamith Firestone in the 1970s regarding monolithic sex classes are generally rejected today as oversimplifying the complexities of contemporary political, cultural and social life. Firestone's *The Dialectic of Sex* is a piece of Utopian political theory that is appropriate both to the feminism of its time and to standard definitions of the genre. It builds a detailed picture of the perfect world and is shamelessly universalist. Recognition that the universalist approach is not appropriate to feminist theory has been forced largely by Black feminist writers such as bell hooks[15] and Patricia Hill Collins.[16] Cherrie Morgan and Gloria Anduzula's *This Bridge Called My Back*[17] is an example of a text which explores explicit and implicit racism within the mainstream feminist movements which, in assuming the authority to represent all women stands accused of cultural imperialism and exclusively.

Connected to suspicions regarding universalist theories is a discernible tendency within these areas of theory and philosophy towards the interrogation of Western systems of binary oppositional thought. Utopianism, traditionally understood, for instance, posits a binary choice between the imperfect present and the (supposedly) perfect future. Briefly, I suggest that there can be found a rejection of the position of either/or and a demand for *more*.[18]

Utopia then, according to standard definitions, blueprints the future and is (literally) representative of perfection, of the end of change. There are, I am suggesting, discernible currents in feminist theory away from such universalism and certainty. I intend in the following section to draw these strands together in an application of the work of the controversial but influential theorist, Jacques Derrida.

Analysis of the thought of Derrida requires time and caution beyond that which I have space for here. The discussion that follows therefore has a primary function of extrapolation and appropriation of certain themes within his work. For present purposes I will briefly contextualise his work but will focus primarily on his notion of the Drive of the Proper, analysis of which is particularly appropriate to discussions of Utopia.

According to contemporary theories of binary oppositional thought our understanding of the world is constructed by language in which meaning is referential rather than inherent. Nothing, in other words, has meaning in itself, but rather by reference to other words, concepts and ideas. Good, for instance, is good only in reference to bad. Similarly, the universal stands in an oppositional and referential relation to the particular, the objective to the subjective and reason to desire. The relationship between binary oppositional pairs is hierarchical, one term being subordinate to the other. This subordination, in the Derridian critique, is not simple because the first (dominant) term relies on the second (subordinate) for its meaning.

Derrida plays a deconstructive textual game. The term deconstruction has come to be thought of as synonymous with the name Derrida and is widely used and misused in discussions of his work. Deconstruction is most accessibly described as consisting of two 'parts' or elements[19]. The first involves inversion or reversal of the binary oppositions through which meaning is constructed in Western thought. The second involves the forging of new or different meanings. An effect of deconstruction is to uncover, expose and hold up for examination the phallologocentic system of language within which we function.[20]

Derrida plays with the word 'proper', from which the concepts of 'property' and 'appropriate' derive. The Concise Oxford Dictionary lays out the following meanings:

> *Proper*: 1. own. 2. (astron) -*motion*, that part of the apparent motion of fixed star supposed to be due to its actual movement in space. 3. Belonging, relating, exclusively or distinctively (to). 4. (gram) -*noun* or *name*, name used to designate an individual person, animal, town, ship, etc. 5. Accurate, correct. 6. strictly so called, real, genuine. 7. Thorough, complete. 8. Handsome. 9. Fit, suitable, right. 10. In conformity with demands of society, decent, respectable.
>
> *Property*: 1. owning, being owned; thing owned, possessions(s). 2. (theatr.) Article of costume, furniture. 3. Attribute, quality; (Logic) quality common to a class but not necessary to distinguish it from others.
>
> *Appropriate*: 1. Belonging, peculiar (to); suitable, proper. 2. Take possession of; take to oneself; devote to special purposes.

All meanings invoked by the words proper, property and appropriate are conflated and condensed in Derrida's reading. They constitute the 'Drive of the Proper', the function of which is profoundly repressive of difference. The possibility of conceptuality is, according to this critique, a profound expression of the possibility of naming, which is claiming, which is enclosing and restricting.

There is no objectivity or neutrality possible in the Derridean text(ual game of deconstructive reading). All texts are locked into language which silently speaks (in) its own doctrinal system. The implications of this for a universalist model of Utopia are that, thus contextualised, the Drive of the Proper can be observed to propel the desire to blueprint a perfect future. Utopia, as understood by standard commentators, encloses both the future, and our perceptions of the possible/desirable. The *desire* which propels Utopianism (traditionally understood) is a desire to restrict and to appropriate. Utopian thought, then, which at first glance appears radical, is, according to the logic of deconstruction, quite profoundly conservative and repressive of difference and change: not only does it not transform the system of language which Derrida identifies as restrictive, but it also embodies the 'worst' features of that system.

Naming, for Derrida, is *claiming*. Naming, asking and deciding 'What is it?' is central to philosophical discourses and relies upon the possibility of attaining the truth. It assumes the (possible) presence of truth, hence logocentrism. This project for Derrida is corrupt: it is not a neutral quest of enquiry, but rather an imposition of an order which is normative and repressive. Utopia, traditionally understood, can be seen to name and claim the future in the form of the blueprint.

The view that naming is claiming can be further illustrated by reference to what Derrida calls the corrupt gift: 'In giving his name, a name of his choice, in giving all names, the father [God] would be at the origin of language, and that power would belong by right to God the father.'[21]

'In the beginning was the word and the word was God.' As the root of all names God the omni-absent ultimate presence owns the power of naming. Derrida can be read as preoccupied with the (im)possibility of giving – his concern can be read as follows: if giving (a name) is taking (possession) in logocentric discourse, can there be a 'true' gift? This question can, I believe, be seen to underlie, or overlie, (in the background and in the foreground) much of his work.

He asks in Pysche whether he can make an incorrupt gift (in this case to the work of Emanuel Levinas):

> I would like to do it faultlessly [*san faute*], with a 'faultlessness' [*sans faute*] that no longer belongs to the time or logic of the rendezvous. Beyond any possible restitution, there would be need for my gesture to operate without any debt, in absolute ingratitude.[22]

Giving, he finds, belongs to a cultural economy, the character of which can be understood in terms of the Proper, the drive for appropriation. Giving has an economic return which is normally manifested as debt or gratitude. Derrida's 'faultless' gift does not escape this economic exchange as giving thus can only be paying homage. Homage is given in an act for which the script is written, homage is an act which *requires* ingratitude. Ingratitude, in this economy, is the return of the gift. Hence, says Derrida, 'The gift is *not.*'[23] It is not a gift, there is no such thing as a gift, gift being euphemistic for investment.

On the one hand, the application of Derridian techniques to the universalist concept of Utopia can, I believe, be enabling to a feminist critique. Deconstruction, from this perspective, strips the construct of Utopia of its pretensions towards neutrality and universalism. Thus deprived, Utopia can be seen to be uncompromisingly exclusive. A single Utopian vision, for instance, cannot reflect the multifaceted reality of feminism today. Nor should it attempt to. If the project of feminism is to represent the desires and aspirations of women, then it must resist the closure that Utopia (traditionally understood) represents. In this sense, postmodernism, with its persistent critique of universalist concepts, is a useful and empowering field to enter. Likewise, poststructuralist approaches to language can be seen to speak to debates with which contemporary feminism is preoccupied.

A further consequence of the exercise, however, is one of profound disablement. If the Drive of the Proper motivates and (in)forms conceptualisation, and if, as suggested, Utopia is the ultimate in conceptualisation, then Utopia cannot be reconceived. This way leads to silence and impotence.

Postmodernism, or poststructuralism, would appear to take away with one hand what it offers with the other. For social movements, such as those represented by the various feminisms, such an approach empowers and disempowers simultaneously. Should it perhaps be rejected? Rather than accept this as a dilemma in which a choice between one of two alternatives is necessary, I propose that we exceed the binary position of either/or and say both, neither and more. We can, I suggest, both accept and reject, thus creating a new space beyond binary opposition in which something else (the unforeseeable) can be foreseen. Thus, we neither (fully) accept nor (fully) reject, and either/or is no longer a meaningful position.[24] This further allows for *more*, a more which, in the discussion that follows I characterise as 'feminine'. This new space, this new position, is profoundly Utopian.

This Utopian situation is one in which *binary* opposition has been surpassed. My position is informed by the work of theorists such as

Hélène Cixous, who draws inspiration from Derrida. It can be said to be grounded in difference. The same/other relation in a what Cixous calls a 'masculine' economy of social exchange takes sameness as its root.[25] The other is marked by difference: the other is the stranger, the alien.[26] Hostility, distrust and fear mark the relation to the other in the (masculine) present.

This can, I believe, be connected to an extension of Hélène Cixous' conception of a (libidinally) feminine economy that can be characterised by a certain letting go (of the notion(s) of property and possession). This letting go, if applied to the same/other relation, opens a space in which difference can potentially be loved rather than feared. Sameness, let go, leaves difference intact. The repressive, oppressive and exclusionary functions of difference in an economy which privileges sameness, however, no longer apply. The relation between the self and the other (whether same or different (other)) can, therefore, be one of reciprocal sharing of different knowledges. This, as suggested above, speaks quite profoundly to contemporary feminisms.

TOWARDS A NEW MODEL OF UTOPIA

I stated above that standard definitions of Utopia relied upon certain criteria for definition. The discussion above has focused primarily on the political nature of Utopia and on the issue of Utopia as representation of perfection, as the blueprint of the ideal polity. The following section focuses briefly on the remaining criteria: Utopian critique, estrangement and the use of the imagination.

A primary function of feminist Utopian thought is to critique existing society, a characteristic of all Utopian writing that is, I suggest, related to its political nature. For Barbara Goodwin, this function is central to the value of Utopianism to political theory:

> If a culture is to be criticised radically, by reference to alternative values outside its own ideology, a utopian model is a valuable device. When the theorist wishes to refashion society wholesale, utopia offers to him a useful space, devoid of preconceived features, within which to work.[27]

Two points are being made here, the first concerns the critical function of Utopia, the second asserts that Utopia presents a perfect space for radical criticism.

The mirror metaphor is often employed when illustrating these points: Utopian writing places in front of the society it critiques a construct (theoretical or literary) which reflects back to that society the writers perception of it. Like the queen's mirror in Snow White, this mirror is not compliant but tells the viewer/reader that the fairest of them all is actually elsewhere – perhaps even nowhere. Thus, the reader is often shocked out of his/her cultural narcissism. Luce Irigaray's tactic of textual mimesis reflects a similarly exaggerated vision of the current situation as does the presentation of an actual Utopian ideal of dystopian mirror. Mimesis, for Irigaray, allows critique to occur concurrently with debate. She assumes exaggeratedly 'feminine' writing tactics, flirting with the philosophers with whose texts she is involved. Thus, she highlights the artificial position of femininity which they dictate whilst engaging in scholarly debate with the texts.

This critical function is present in all forms of Utopian writing. Utopia has, because of this, historically been perceived as a subversive genre. Krishan Kumar puts it thus:

> Utopia challenges by supplying alternatives, certainly. It shows what could be. But its most persistent function, the real source of its subversiveness, is as a critical commentary on the arrangements of society.[28]

Feminism too has radically subversive potential, it is the transgressive or critical character of contemporary feminisms that make the genre of Utopia a particularly comfortable position from which to work and theorise. Utopia moreover allows distance from the present world. As has already been pointed out, the etymology of the word contains a double pun – outopia is a nowhere, eutopia a good place – the spoken word condensing and compressing the pun. From the Utopian genre has come the eutopia, the dystopia and the anti-Utopia. Writing from or towards a good place that is no place, glancing over her shoulder at the place whence she came, the Utopian feminist escapes the restrictions of patriarchal scholarship. New and inventive languages can best be imagined and employed in a new world as can different social, sexual and symbolic relations. The new Utopianism about which I write stresses the 'ou' of Utopia, and is free of restrictions of time and space, existing rather in the present, the (albeit conditional) here-and-now. The link with (perceived) reality is of central import for the creation of Utopian thought.

The imagination plays an important role in the expression of Utopian thought. Northrop Frye, whose work has been influential amongst standard debates of Utopianism, describes this role in the article 'Varieties of Literary Utopias':

> Utopian thought is imaginative, with its roots in literature, and the literary imagination is less concerned with achieving ends than with visualizing possibilities. . . . The word 'imaginative' refers to hypothetical constructions, like those of literature or mathematics. The word 'imaginary' refers to something that does not exist.[29]

Because it is explicitly imaginative, Utopian theory and literature has been devalued in the schools of political theory and philosophy as escapist, fanciful, and above all, unscientific in disciplines which favour rational debate, logical argument and serious scholarship. It is, perhaps, ironic that within this undervalued genre the contribution of women writers should be in turn denied voice as, for the main part, women writers of earlier centuries are rendered invisible by concentration on their male counterparts. It is also, perhaps, ironic that the words used to depreciate Utopianism are those which Western binary thought designates 'feminine' as opposed to the rationality of masculine 'scientific' debate. Its imaginative nature, its literary rather than explicitly theoretical form, contribute to Utopia's cultural and social femininity.

Linked to the literary connection is the supposition that Utopia is fiction, common in standard discussions of the genre and consistent in contemporary feminist works.

> All utopias are, by definition fictions; unlike say historical writing, they deal with possible, not actual, worlds. To this extent they are like all forms of imaginative literature. They go further than conventional fiction in their extension of the bounds of the possible to include what to many may seem impossible or at the very least improbable.[30]

The dictionary defines the word 'fiction' as follows:

> Feigning, invention; thing feigned or imagined; invented statement or narrative; literature consisting of such narrative; conventionally accepted falsehood (esp. legal, polite, ~).' For 'fictitious' the dictionary gives the following explanation: 'counterfeit, not genuine; (of name or character) assumed; imaginary, unreal; of, in, novels; regarded as what it is called by legal or conventional fiction. (*Concise Oxford*)

These definitions appear particularly appropriate to the feminist Utopian text and pull together many of the points discussed above.

The imaginative nature and literary form of feminist Utopias earn them the title 'fictitious'. The inclusion in the definitions of the word 'feigned' is provocative. To feign is to invent but does not have particularly positive or favourable implications. To feign is to pretend, simulate, from its etymological root, the French 'feindre', also comes the word 'feint'.

Implied then, in the statement that 'utopias are by definition fictions' is that Utopias are shams, pretences, falsehoods. This, I suggest, can grant to Utopias a potentially powerful weapon of illusion. Angela Carter's work provides perhaps the clearest examples of sham Utopianism. Illusion and allusion, densely punning language, multiple metaphors, seep through her texts so that nothing is as it first appears. These texts are quite profoundly estranged from the political and material present.

Vincent Geoghegan makes an interesting point regarding Utopian estrangement and otherness. He refers, in the following statement, to the classical Utopian form but I find his point relevant to modern works:

> The classical utopia anticipates and criticizes. Its alternative fundamentally interrogates the present, piercing through existing societies' defensive mechanism – common sense, realism, positivism and scientism. Its unabashed and flagrant otherness gives it a power which is lacking in other analytical devices. By playing fast and loose with time and space, logic and morality and by thinking the unthinkable, a utopia asks the most awkward, the most embarrassing questions.[31]

Utopianism, by virtue of its otherness, estranged nature, or profound distance from the present, exits 'outside'. One receives a different perspective when looking in than from being in. This Tom Moylan expresses in terms of 'a dialogue between the world as we know it and the better world that is not yet', which, he claims, constitutes a manifesto of otherness.[32]

> This manifesto of otherness, with its particular systems that mark the uniqueness of each utopian text and carry out the ideological contest in diverse forms, is the commonly accepted *raison d'être* of the utopian narrative.[33]

Women, feminist political and social theorists state, subsist on the exterior of patriarchal structures of power and status, be they economic, political, or socio-cultural. Woman, psychoanalytic theorists say, is other, perpetually and by necessity the outsider, despite and because of her position inside the systems by which the masculine self is constructed.

Utopia then in its radical otherness, has power and strength. It explores and challenges the assumed boundaries and limits to that which is possible. An open-ended approach to the future further allows an openness or receptivity to other perspectives.

With regards to language, this can be worked toward by moving away from the naming process outlined above towards an open language, one in which the opacity of words, for example, is apparent; their potential multiplicity exploited. Naming, or conceptualising, in such a way, does not claim to impose a unitary truth. In Joan Slonczewski's *A Door Into Ocean*, for example language is reconceived to the extent that each word, each name, is understood to invoke all possible meanings, including its inverse. It is of particular interest to a discussion focusing on universal truths that for the inhabitants of Shora, a Utopian and strange community, the concept of perfection is equated with death and ultimate immobility:

> What is the name of perfect good? Is it freedom? Perfect freedom is death. Is it peace? Perfect peace is death. Is it love? Perfect love is to chose to love death, that others may live.[34]

There has been, within contemporary feminist Utopianism, a move away from the traditional Utopian form which blueprints the future and which is universally applicable. These texts, I suggest, let go of the notion of a singular truth, thus truth is defetishised. Utopian texts which I would describe as 'feminine' are marked by the absence of the 'gift' of the blueprint. They transgress the rules and boundaries which constitute the present, constantly moving away from the axis of binarity and dialectical opposition. Their move towards multiplicity is open-ended and unrestrictive. It allows avoidance of the imperialistic imposition of a singular truth in the guise of a model society.

CONCLUSION

Those elements of Utopia in standard definitions which, historically, have contributed to its devaluation as a 'feminine' genre persist in the new open-ended text. Utopia's 'otherworldliness', for instance, its imaginative nature and fictional status that keep it off the reading lists in many academic departments, linger. It is, none the less, profoundly political.

Imaginary inventiveness is a mark of feminist Utopianism and is frequently directed at language. Above all, feminist Utopianism tends to embrace the excess and extremity that are associated with libidinal femininity. In some works, such as those of Angela Carter, this is manifested in the setting: unbelievably lush landscapes and huge overripe fruits fill her landscapes. Excess in the texts of Luce Irigarary takes the form of mimesis, of, for instance, hysteria.

These themes of excess are of relevance to the point at which the new Utopianism diverges most sharply from the course of the old. The refusal to depict a perfect state is, however, of paramount importance. Its significance cannot be overstressed. It is at this point that Utopia moves towards what Cixous calls 'libidinal femininity'. The characters of feminist Utopias move between and within worlds, conveying a sense of continuing progression. This is a Utopianism of *process* rather than of perfection. The stress is on challenging and transgressing perceptions of the possible in the political present rather than alluding to a spatially and temporally different future.

I have attempted, in this chapter to draw into conversation a number of apparently unrelated discourses. Due to confines of space and time my discussion has been almost painfully dense. Standard definitions of Utopia have been rejected for their logocenrism. Utopia, it has been argued can and should not attempt to bring the 'truth' of perfection into being. A universalist Utopian text names and therefore claims the future for its author and the (usually dominant) social and cultural group which s/he represents. Rather an alternative understanding of Utopia has been argued, one that I have suggested can be characterised as 'feminine'.

A Utopia of process is political, critical, imaginative and fictitious. It represents multiple expressions of otherness. It is transgressive of the boundaries of dominant definitions. In this sense it is close to what Tom Moylan calls the 'critical utopia' which transforms, destroys and revives. Attention is focused on the present, the reader is encouraged to engage actively with the text. Utopianism, thus understood, is a process of perpetual challenge and critique; one of constant movement. On a conceptual level, Utopianism, thus understood, attempts to 'foresee the unforeseeable', to scrutinise (pre)conceptions of the moment and to allow the creation of new and different conceptual space.[35] In this sense, as illustrated above, Derridian tactics of deconstruction are particularly appropriate to this mode of thought and expression.

What I have called the new Utopianism of process is also profoundly transgressive of the concept of binary opposition. This chapter has worked from the premise that a binary oppositional (hierarchial) framework lies at the base of language thus constructing our perceptions of the world. It follows postmodernist and poststructuralist critiques of logocentrism, arguing that language can and does not reflect reality but rather shapes it. Any transgression of binarity, therefore, is of quite profound political and intellectual import. This chapter has deconstructed the concept of opposition, showing that binarity or dialectical opposition is being exceeded, made multiple. Feminist Utopianism *is* oppositional: it opposes patriarchal society. The concept of opposition, however, is reconceived: the position of either/or is thus transcended.

Through such a move a new space is created, this new space is Utopia and Utopian, transgressive of the very foundations of language and culture. In this space, the concept of domination is destroyed, rendered impotent. In developing a new conceptual space for Utopia I have, in this chapter, practised a Utopia on Utopia. From this space new understandings of the world can, perhaps, grow.

NOTES

1 A Utopia is a specific form or manifestation of Utopian thought. Utopian thought is sometimes expressed in forms other than the Utopia. This much said, it must be noted that the boundaries are sometimes hazy. For the sake of convenience and clarity, 'a Utopia' will be described as such, whilst the word 'Utopia' is used without the indefinite article to refer to Utopian thought and to the manifestation of Utopian thought, i.e., to depict the genre. Likewise 'Utopianism' is used in this broader sense.

2 E. Block, *The Principle of Hope*, trans. N. Plaice, S. Plaice and P. Knight, Oxford, Blackwell, 1986.

3 J. C. Davis, 'The History of Utopia: The Chronology of Nowhere', in Alexander and P. Gill (eds), *Utopias*, London. Duckworth, 1984, p. 9.

4 R. Davis, 'The History of Utopia' pp. 9–10.

5 S. Firestone, *The Dialectic of Sex*, London, Paladin, 1972.

6 M. Piercy *Woman on the Edge of Time*, London, The Women's Press, 1979.

7 Davis, 'The History of Utopia' p. 10.

8 B. Goodwin *Social Science and Utopia*, Sussex. Harvester, 1978, p. 5.

9 D. Lessing, *The Marriage of Zones Three, Four and Five*, London, Cape, 1980.

10 A. Carter, *Heroes and Villains*, Harmondsworth, Penguin, 1986.

11 A. Carter, *The Passion of a New Eve*, London, Virago, 1982.

12 Time and space prevent full exploration of this point, which is developed more fully in my PhD thesis (Routledge, forthcoming).

13 L. Irigaray *The Sex Which is Not One*, trans. C. Porter, Ithaca, NY,

Cornell University Press, 1985, and *Speculum of the Other Woman*, trans, G. Gill, Ithaca, NY, Cornell University Press, 1985.

14 See, for instance, L. Nicholson, *Feminism/Postmodernism*, London, Routledge, 1990.

15 bell hooks, *Feminist Theory – from Margin to Center*, Boston, MA, South End Press, 1984.

16 P. H. Collins, *Black Feminist Thought*, Boston, MA, Unwin Hyman, 1990.

17 C. Morgan and G. Anduzula, *This Bridge Called My Back*, Wattertown, MA, Persephone Press, 1981.

18 I return to this point later in the chapter.

19 Although 'best' described as consisting of two parts, the deconstructive process is not one of sequential movement from the first to the second. Rather, the two are simultaneous.

20 Derrida adopts an understanding of how the visual penis is confused with the phallus which is similar to Lacan's. For Derrida, however, the phallus is not neutral as neutrality is impossible and pretensions to it serve to cover this fact. The phallus, as the signifier of presence, is indissociable from the logos, the word.

21 Derrida, 'Des Tours de Babel', in P. Kamuf, *A Derrida Reader: Between the Blinds*, Hemel Hempstead, Harvester, 1985, p. 246.

22 Derrida, 'Geschlect: Sexual Difference, Ontological Difference' in P. Kamuf, *A Derrida Reader: Between the Blinds*, p. 408.

23 Derrida, 'Geschlect' p. 410.

24 Literally, for if the binary opposition has henceforth created meaning, to surpass the position of either/or is to pass beyond opposition towards a new multiplicity.

25 For Cixous, this economy is the context within which the symbolic ordering of language occurs. See, for example, H. Cixous, 'The Laugh of the Medusa', in E. Marks and E. de Courtivron (eds), *New French Feminisms*, Brighton, Harvester, 1981.

26 A dictionary definition of the word alien runs thus: '1) Not one's own: foreign, under foreign allegiance; differing in nature (from); repugnant (to).'

27 Goodwin, *Social Science and Utopia*, p. 3.

28 K. Kumar, *Utopianism*, Buckinghamshire, Open University Press, 1991, pp. 87–8.

29 N. Frye, 'Varieties of Literary Utopias' in F. Manuel (ed.), *Utopias and Utopian Thought* London, Souvenir Press, 1966, p. 32.

30 Kumar, *Utopianism*, p. 60.

31 V. Geoghegan, *Utopianism and Marxism*, London, Methuen, 1987, pp. 1–2.

32 T. Moylan, *Demand the Impossible: Science Fiction and the Utopian Imagination*, London: Methuen, 1986, p. 37.

33 Moylan, *Demand the Impossible*, p. 37.

34 J. Slonczewski, *A Door Into Ocean* London, The Women's Press, 1986, p. 151.

35 '. . . what I have to say has at least two sides and two aims: to break up

and destroy; and to foresee the unforeseeable, to project' (Cixous, 'Sorties', in Cixous and Clement, *The Newly Born Woman*, trans. B. Wing, Manchester, Manchester University Press, 1986).

Index